T0301465

Getting Women on to Corporate Boards

Getting Women on to Corporate Boards

A Snowball Starting in Norway

Edited by

Silke Machold

University of Wolverhampton, UK

Morten Huse

*University of Witten/Herdecke, Germany and
BI Norwegian Business School, Norway*

Katrin Hansen

Westfälische Hochschule, Germany

Marina Brogi

Sapienza University of Rome, Italy

Edward Elgar

Cheltenham, UK • Northampton, MA, USA

Published by
Edward Elgar Publishing Limited
The Lypiatts
15 Lansdown Road
Cheltenham
Glos GL50 2JA
UK

Edward Elgar Publishing, Inc.
William Pratt House
9 Dewey Court
Northampton
Massachusetts 01060
USA

A catalogue record for this book
is available from the British Library

Library of Congress Control Number: 2013942241

This book is available electronically in the ElgarOnline.com Business Subject Collection, E-ISBN 978 1 78254 794 5

ISBN 978 1 78254 792 1 (cased)

Typeset by Columns Design XML Ltd, Reading
Printed and bound in Great Britain by T.J. International Ltd, Padstow

Contents

List of contributors   viii
Acknowledgements   xv

Introduction   1
Morten Huse and Marina Brogi

PART I   THE NORWEGIAN POLITICAL BACKGROUND

1. The political process behind the gender balance law   9
    Morten Huse
2. Women on board   17
    Laila Dåvøy
3. Women mean business: why and how Norway legislated gender
    balance on the boards of listed companies   21
    Kirsti Bergstø
4. Concluding remarks to Part I   24
    Morten Huse

PART II   NORWEGIAN AND INTERNATIONAL ADVOCACY

5. Institutionalizing women's representation on boards:
    an introduction to the advocacy movement   27
    Silke Machold
6. Competence at board level: the Norwegian case   37
    Elbjørg Gui Standal
7. Professionalizing boards: the work of the Professional
    Boards Forum   40
    Elin Hurvenes
8. The Swiss case of women on boards of directors   46
    Christine Wetli
9. Boards and role models for supporting the climb upwards:
    Italy and Women Corporate Directors (WCD)   52
    Cristina Finocchi Mahne

10. Research and considerations regarding women on boards   60
    Heather Foust-Cummings
11. Concluding remarks to Part II   64
    Silke Machold

PART III   NORWEGIAN BOARD MEMBERS: STORIES
           FROM THE FIELD

12. Characteristics and background of the Norwegian women
    directors   69
    Morten Huse
13. Stories from four Norwegian multi-board women   78
    Nini Høegh Nergaard, Merete Lütken, Thorhild Widvey,
    Ingvild Ragna Myhre and Morten Huse
14. Concluding remarks to Part III   94
    Morten Huse

PART IV   LESSONS FROM RESEARCH ON GENDER ON
          BOARDS

15. Women on boards: what we know, what we do not yet know and
    how we should further advance knowledge   101
    Katrin Hansen
16. Women on boards: the United States in a global comparison   113
    Dorothy Perrin Moore
17. Consequences of the Norwegian gender quota regulation for
    public limited company boards   119
    Vibeke Heidenreich
18. Women directors and corporate innovation: a critical mass
    perspective   126
    Mariateresa Torchia
19. Gender-balanced corporate boards   136
    Agnes Bolsø, Hilde Bjørkhaug and Siri Øyslebø Sørensen
20. Gender quotas on corporate boards in Norway, necessary
    but not ideal   138
    Cathrine Seierstad
21. Legitimacy, inclusion and influence: investigating women
    directors' board experiences   147
    Gro Ladegård
22. Lessons from previous research on women on boards for
    future research   155
    Andrea D. Bührmann

23. Concluding remarks to Part IV   161
    Katrin Hansen

PART V   POLICY IMPLICATIONS AT THE INTERNATIONAL
          LEVEL

24. Policy approaches to gender diversity on boards: an introduction
    to characteristics and determinants   167
    Silke Machold and Katrin Hansen
25. Women on boards: lessons learnt from Norway   179
    Monika Schulz-Strelow
26. Professionalization on the supervisory board, diversity and
    women   184
    Daniela Weber-Rey
27. Italy's lessons learnt from Norway   187
    Marina Brogi
28. Women on boards in the UK: accelerating the pace of change?   191
    Ruth Sealy and Susan Vinnicombe
29. Winning the board game: Europe's economy needs more
    women in business   201
    Viviane Reding
30. Concluding remarks to Part V   210
    Katrin Hansen and Silke Machold

Conclusions   215
Katrin Hansen and Silke Machold

Index   225

Contributors

Kirsti Bergstø is a Norwegian politician for the Socialist Left Party. She is the former leader of the Socialist Youth, the youth wing of the Socialist Left Party, and held this position between 2006 and 2008. Coming from Nesseby, she served as a deputy representative to the Parliament of Norway from Finnmark during the term 2005–2009. She was a deputy member of Finnmark county council from 1999 to 2003. From 2010 to 2012 she was a State Secretary in the Ministry of Children, Equality and Social Inclusion.

Hilde Bjørkhaug has been a researcher at the Center for Rural Research in Norway since 1997. She has a PhD in Sociology and throughout her career has been involved in research on different aspects of agricultural restructuring. More recently, she has conducted research on power relations in the food chains in Norway and internationally. Gender perspectives have been employed in most projects, and many also had a specific gender focus. She has followed the Norwegian legislation on gender balance in the boardroom through research projects and the public debate. She has published widely on this topic.

Agnes Bolsø, Associate Professor, is head of Gender Studies and Deputy of Department of Interdisciplinary Studies of Culture, Norwegian University of Science and Technology, former editor of the *Norwegian Journal for Gender Studies*, currently managing 'Mirror, mirror on the wall, who's most powerful of them all? Gender as a symbolic and social structure in organizations', a research project funded by the Research Council of Norway. The project involves 14 scholars from Norway, Sweden, the UK and the USA.

Marina Brogi is Full Professor of Capital Markets as of 2007 and Deputy Dean as of 2011 at the Faculty of Economics of Università di Roma 'La Sapienza', and she has over 20 years of experience in research and training in banking and finance at both university and executive level. She is the author of numerous publications on banking, corporate governance and capital markets. She participated as Commissioner in the Examinations for CONSOB (Italy's Securities Markets Authority) and worked as a consultant to the Italian Ministry of Interior. She serves on the supervisory board and board of directors of several Italian listed and non-listed companies.

Andrea D. Bührmann is a Professor at the University of Goettingen, Germany. Her main research fields are entrepreneurship studies, diversity and gender studies, and sociological methodologies and methods. Recent publications are: Unternehmertum jenseits des Normalunternehmertums: Für eine praxistheoretisch inspirierte Erforschung unternehmerischer Aktivitäten, *Berliner Journal für Soziologie*, 2012, 1: 129–156; and with K. Hansen, Broadening the view: diverse types of entrepreneurs, *Rivista di Politica Economista*, 2012, April: 53–72.

Laila Dåvøy is a Norwegian politician for the Christian Democratic Party. She has been a member of the Norwegian parliament since 2005. She was leader of the Norwegian Nurses Association, 1992–1998. From 1989 to 1990, during the Syse cabinet, Dåvøy was appointed State Secretary in the Ministry of Culture and Church Affairs. In 1999–2000 she was appointed Norwegian Minister of Labour and Administration in the first Bondevik cabinet. In the second Bondevik cabinet, Dåvøy was Norwegian Minister of Children and Family Affairs 2001–2005.

Cristina Finocchi Mahne is an economist, an expert on corporate governance, and Professor of Advanced Business Administration at Rome University La Sapienza, Faculty of Economics, Italy. She is a board member of listed companies; Co-Chair Italy of WCD (Women Corporate Directors), international association of board members. Previously, she was a member of the Management Committee, as Director of Investor Relations and Group Strategic Communication, of two main financial blue-chip companies, both with a market capitalization over €5 billion. She has been a keynote speaker at national and international conferences.

Heather Foust-Cummings, PhD, leads Catalyst's research on corporate governance, with a focus on understanding relationships between diversity, corporate governance, and board and firm performance. Prior to joining Catalyst, Dr Foust-Cummings taught at Columbia University and conducted brand analyses at Young & Rubicam. Dr Foust-Cummings received her PhD and MA from Emory University, USA; she received her BS from the University of Tennessee at Chattanooga, USA.

Katrin Hansen is a Professor at Westfälische Hochschule in Germany, Ruhr Area. Currently she holds the position as Vice-President Planning, Finances, and International Relations. Her teaching field is management and human resources development. She has research interests in the fields of organizational development, women leaders and women on boards, women entrepreneurs, diversity management and intercultural management, recently integrating these streams into the field of entrepreneurial diversity.

Vibeke Heidenreich is a PhD student in sociology at the University of Oslo, Norway. She is studying the effects of gender quota on recruitment to Norwegian company boards. Heidenreich is a sociologist (cand.polit) and a historian (cand.philol).

Elin Hurvenes was a key player when Norway implemented bold, world-leading legislation requiring Oslo Stock Exchange-listed companies to have 40 per cent women on their boards. Through a series of pioneering events she generated an arena for chairmen and chief executive officers to expand their network to women board candidates whilst tackling complex financial and strategic issues in a board-like situation. The Forum now operates in the UK, www.boardsforum.co.uk; and the Netherlands, www.boardsforum.nl; and will open in Switzerland and Hong Kong in 2014. Elin has a BA from Oxford Brookes University and an MBA from London Business School, UK.

Morten Huse is Reinhard-Mohn-Chair of Management and Governance at the University of Witten/Herdecke, Germany, and Professor of Organisation and Management at BI Norwegian Business School. His research focus is on value-creating boards and the human side of corporate governance. He has published extensively about women on boards, and has been a speaker at executive and academic events in many countries, including presentations at the Italian and British parliaments and on TV channels in several countries.

Gro Ladegård is Associate Professor in Leadership and Organization Science at UMB School of Economics and Business, Norway, and has several years of experience as a business consultant on human capital development. She has a PhD in Business Administration from the Norwegian School of Economics. Her main research areas are human capital of corporate boards, leadership and leadership development.

Merete Lütken has 20 years' top management experience in Norwegian business and 12 years' experience as non-executive board member in companies within technology, health, education, media and industry. Currently she is working as a management consultant, board member, speaker and writer. She is Vice-President of the Norwegian board network Styrelederen, and a member of the expert panel at lederkilden.no. Her work is published in the scientific magazine *Magma*, and she is the author of the financial thriller *Supergirl*. The novel is on the syllabus list at BI Norwegian Business School.

Silke Machold, PhD, is Professor of Corporate Governance at the University of Wolverhampton Business School, UK, where she also serves as Co-Director of the Management Research Centre. She is the founding co-editor of the *International Journal of Business Governance and Ethics*, and current chair of the Strategic Interest Group on Corporate Governance at the European Academy of Management. Her research interests are in board processes and behaviours, and feminist perspectives on corporate governance. She teaches and consults on these topics in the UK and overseas.

Dorothy Perrin Moore, PhD, is an Emeritus Professor of Business Administration at The Citadel. Her most recent book, *Womenpreneurs: 21st Century Success Strategies*, is a nominee for the 2013 Axiom Book Award. She is also the author of *Careerpreneurs: Lessons from Leading Women Entrepreneurs on Building a Career Without Boundaries*, a Foreword Magazine Gold Award winner in business. Her co-authored book, *Island in the Storm, Sullivan's Island and Hurricane Hugo*, a bronze award winner, is now available as an e-book.

Ingvild Ragna Myhre gained a degree in 1982 as a civil engineer, and shortly thereafter she became a sought-after board member. During the past 20 years she has been a board member and also board chair of many of Norway's most important and largest enterprises. She is now working as a partner in the consultancy LOS, and her main activity is as a board member.

Nini Høegh Nergaard was born in 1972 in Oslo, Norway. In 1998 she graduated from the University of Oslo with a law degree. She then went on to work in the Investment Banking division of Svenska Handels-banken. When leaving the banking world in 2005 she devoted herself to motherhood and board work. Currently she holds three board positions. Nini lives just outside Oslo with her husband and two sons.

Viviane Reding is Vice-President of the European Commission, in charge of Justice, Fundamental Rights and Citizenship policies. She began her third five-year term in February 2010 and is currently the Commission's longest-serving member. In 1999, she was named Education, Culture, Media and Sports Commissioner. Mrs Reding was re-appointed in 2004 and served as Telecoms and Media Commissioner. She was responsible for reforming EU telecommunications rules and cutting the price of mobile telephone roaming charges. Her career in European politics began in 1989 when she was elected a Member of the European Parliament, where she served two consecutive terms.

Monika Schulz-Strelow is President of FidAR – Frauen in die Aufsichtsräte e.V. In 2006 Monika Schulz-Strelow founded FidAR – Frauen in die Aufsichtsräte e.V. (Women to the Boards) which is a non-partisan, Germany-wide, well-known initiative, campaigning for an increase of female board members in Germany. She studied political sciences and has worked in international business. Through Monika's long-standing affiliation with the BAO BERLIN International GmbH, where she spent nine years on the board, she is very experienced with supervisory boards and is a member of the board of the Deutsche Klassenlotterie Berlin. With her company b.international group, she advises international investment agencies.

Ruth Sealy has global expertise on women on corporate boards, and has led the research for the UK's annual Female FTSE Women on Boards report since 2007. Ruth's research interests cover many aspects of women in leadership. She speaks regularly at academic and practitioner conferences, lectures on postgraduate courses, and has written a number of book chapters and journal articles. Prior to becoming an academic, Ruth was the Managing Director of a specialist holiday company. She then worked as a management psychologist, before joining Cranfield in 2004.

Cathrine Seierstad is a Lecturer in Human Resource Management at Brunel Business School, Brunel University London, UK. Her research and publications focus upon aspects of gender, equality, diversity, leadership, corporate governance and the use of affirmative action strategies. She has published in *Work, Employment and Society* and the *Scandinavian Journal of Management* and has also contributed to various books and edited editions.

Siri Øyslebø Sørensen gained her PhD in 2013 from the Norwegian University of Science and Technology (NTNU) in Trondheim, Norway. The title of her PhD is 'Genderless equality? A study of how gender quotas on corporate boards were assembled as a policy reform'. The PhD thesis explores the cultural meanings of gender equality in Norwegian policy-making, analyzing the process of introducing gender quotas to corporate boards. She has been a visiting scholar at Stanford University, USA, and her publications have received awards. She is now a researcher at Department of Interdisciplinary Studies of Culture at NTNU.

Elbjørg Gui Standal worked at BI the Norwegian Business School, Norway. In 1995 she founded the consultancy company Elinora Consulting Ltd, doing business with a number of Norwegian companies. Before she joined BI she held a number of senior positions in Norwegian companies. From 1968 she worked with board questions, and initiated the research work and teaching within this field at BI. She was responsible for all the courses that BI teaches in Board Competence – from Bachelors to Masters programmes. She held a number of board positions in Norwegian companies. She published several books including *Diversity in the Board Room* and *Handbook for Board Members*. Elbjørg Gui Standal died in February 2013.

Mariateresa Torchia, PhD, is Post-Doctoral Researcher at Witten/ Herdecke University, Germany. Her main research interests are in the area of boards of directors, with a specific focus on the topic of women directors and board diversity. She is the author of several publications on the topic and she is involved in the European Academy of Management where she co-chairs a track on women directors on corporate boards.

Susan Vinnicombe OBE, MA, PhD, MCIM, FRSA is Director of the Cranfield International Centre for Women Leaders, Cranfield School of Management, UK. Her particular research interests are gender diversity on corporate boards, women's leadership styles, and the issues involved in women developing their managerial careers. Her research centre is unique in the UK with its focus on women leaders, and the annual Female FTSE 100 Index is regarded as the UK's premier research resource on women directors. Susan has written ten books and over 100 articles, reports and conference papers. Susan was awarded an OBE for Services to Diversity in the Queen's New Year's Honours List in 2005.

Daniela Weber-Rey is Partner at Clifford Chance, Frankfurt, Germany, and has been a member of the Partnership Council since 2010. In 2008, she became a member of the German Government's Corporate Governance Code Commission, and was nominated to membership of EIOPA (Re-insurance Stakeholder Group). She has over 25 years' legal experience in company law, corporate governance and mergers and acquisitions. Since 2012, she has been a member of the European Corporate Governance Institute (ECGI, Brussels) and an Advisory Board member of the International Centre for Insurance Regulation (ICIR, Frankfurt).

Christine Wetli (MA HSG) is currently a Doctoral student at the University of St Gallen, Switzerland. Her research focuses on the contribution of women on boards of directors in publicly listed companies.

Thorhild Widvey was a member of the Norwegian Parliament 1989–
1997. She represented the Moderate Party (Høyre), and during 2004–
2005 she was the Norwegian Minister of Oil and Energy. She also has
experience as Political Secretary in other ministries. Since she ended her
tenure as Minister of Oil and Energy she has been a very popular
candidate for many boards in Norway as well as in other countries.

Acknowledgements

There are many people who contributed generously with their ideas and time to this project. We would especially like to thank the following people and organizations for their invaluable advice, contributions and support: all participants of the Women on Board workshop in Oslo 2011 for their insightful contributions and challenging discussions; Innovation Norway, the main sponsor of the project; Luise Wille for her invaluable help in translating the German contributions to English; and Mariateresa Torchia for her patient assistance with the compilation of contributors' details.

Introduction

Morten Huse and Marina Brogi

THE WORLD IS LOOKING TO NORWAY

The world is looking to Norway (FAZ, 2011; *La Repubblica*, 2011). In February 2002 Ansgar Gabrielsen, the Norwegian Minister of Trade and Industry, announced that a law should come into force regulating gender balance on corporate boards. Ambitions about achieving gender balance in the upper echelons of Norwegian companies had existed for a long time, as had efforts to attain these ambitions. However, any advances in increasing the number of women on corporate boards had little visible effects. In 1992, only 4 percent of the members of boards in corporations listed on the Oslo Stock Exchange were women, and in 2002 this figure had increased to only 6 percent despite a multitude of voluntary efforts. This was the background for the Norwegian law on gender balance in corporate boards, and in 2008 about 40 percent of the board members in Norwegian publicly traded companies were women.

The Norwegian story is about how legal requirements succeeded in achieving gender balance and increasing the number of women on boards. And the world is looking to Norway. Can and should similar means be used in other countries? The Norwegian snowball has started rolling, and the effects seem to be dynamic and accelerating. Some will even compare the developments to an avalanche. One country after another is following the Norwegian example. The discussion on this topic is spreading fast, and there are indications from a number of countries that the trend is in the direction of favoring legal regulations.

THE STORY OF A THINK TANK

The book is written as a follow-up of a Think Tank organized in Oslo in March 2011 and summarized in *Repubblica* (2011, p. 37). The purpose of the Think Tank was to provide evidence-based reflections on gender balance in the boardroom coming from policy-makers, board members and scholars at national and international levels. There are various reasons for the current international efforts under way to achieve gender balance. There are societal reasons related to democracy, values and equality; there are objectives related to women's career progression and the need to shatter the 'glass ceiling'; and there are reasons related to boards, corporate effectiveness and organizational value creation. Norway has become a benchmark for other countries in achieving gender balance, and throughout the book we will reflect on the experiences of Norway. Can we now reach conclusions about whether the Norwegian law on gender balance in the boardroom has been positive for society, for women and corporations? What more do we need to know before conclusions about the law's efficacy are made? And what are the implications for other countries that seek to attain gender balance in upper echelons?

Similar workshops for thought leaders are being held in various countries. This Think Tank meeting focused on the lessons from Norway, and we therefore organized it in Norway. Lessons about policy issues, insights from the experience of women serving on boards, and results and findings from research were highlighted. In this workshop we aimed at moving beyond the metrics, body counting and general assumptions, and instead explored actual contributions and consequences.

WOMEN AND GENDER BALANCE ON CORPORATE BOARDS AND HOW TO ACHIEVE IT

A key purpose of the book is to contribute to the discussion currently taking place in different countries about how to achieve gender balance on corporate boards. Should the example from Norway be followed? We examine how the snowball starting in Norway is increasing in size and in speed. We chart the progress of countries on the legislative front, as well as regulatory efforts and voluntary initiatives (Catalyst, 2012). We also discuss why there is an escalating degree of attention by other countries to the Norwegian law on gender balance in corporate boards, and analyze whether and how the Norwegian success story may be a blueprint for other countries.

This book builds on, integrates and extends previous presentations and research on boards of directors, women in business and management, and diversity quotas, for example Bilimoria and Piderit (2007), Gröschl and Takagi (2012), Huse (2007) and Vinnicombe et al. (2008). However, the presentation and discussion of the Norwegian case and its implications is unique. The book takes as its starting point the experiences in

Europe and in countries with civil law systems, but the implications go well beyond the borders of these countries, and interest in the Norwegian success story is fast becoming a global phenomenon. The Norwegian law builds on a European one-tier board system. This implies that the boards generally are considered to be supervisory boards. However, Anglo-American one-tier system types (as for example in Australia, New Zealand, the UK and the USA) and European two-tier board system types (as in Germany and in the Netherlands) have, with modifications, similar challenges.

In this book we present various arguments for increasing the number of women on boards. The societal case has typically been the starting point for much of the attention to this question, and it is also commonly the reason behind some of the most far-reaching initiatives to increase the number of women on boards. The individual case arguments are often related to the debate on the glass ceiling that women continue to face. The business case relates to questions of why and how women on corporate boards will improve corporate performance. The Norwegian law had a background in societal concerns and individual case arguments, but the formal rationale used by the Norwegian Minister of Trade and Industry who announced the law related to the business case. Many of the contributions in this book are related to the business case, but we will not draw a distinctive line between the societal, individual and business arguments as this is not done in practice either.

The book leans on institutional perspectives, which means that we explore the importance of variations in systems, traditions and cultures in various countries (Aguilera and Jackson, 2003; Grosvold and Brammer, 2011). It is precisely because of this focus that it is important to understand the Norwegian background, culture and institutions when deriving recommendations for other countries. Variations in gender egalitarianism are therefore an important dimension to be considered in any debate about women on boards. Gender egalitarianism is defined as the degree to which a collective minimizes gender inequality (House et al., 2004, p. 30). Recent studies have indicated that Norway leads on gender egalitarian scores (4.03), compared with other countries such as the UK (3.67), France (3.64) and Spain (3.01) (ibid.). In our discussions, we also relate to Billing and Alvesson's (1989) work about women's opportunities and contributions in top management positions.

LESSONS TO BE LEARNT FROM NORWAY

The snowball starting in Norway is growing, and rolling ever faster. Almost all over the world debates are developing about the Norwegian experiment with legal requirements to get women on corporate boards. There are many lessons to be learnt from Norway. First and foremost, notwithstanding Norway's considerable gender-balance attention, it was necessary to introduce a law in order to make significant increases in the number of women on boards. Striking similarities emerge when comparing the evolution of the Norwegian law with the developments in other countries. The pattern starts with a very small number of women on boards, followed by increasing public and policy attention to the societal, individual and business case for gender equality, but no concomitant substantive change in the number and proportions of female board members. This brings about an increasing awareness that some form of affirmative action is necessary, followed by a decision to propose a law. An intense debate then accompanies proposals for legislative interventions, which typically centers around two aspects: (1) the need for a law and the likelihood of its unintended consequences; and (2) the 'problem' of there being only 'a limited number of capable women available' and 'women who have the right qualifications make it to boards in any case'. When the law comes into force, numbers start to change and even companies which are not subject to the law introduce more women on their boards. The book provides valuable and unique insights on the obstacles which had to be overcome in Norway, which are uncannily echoed in the experience of follower countries. By bringing together and sharing experiences of politicians, business people, advocacy groups and scholars, we can start to understand the lessons that we can learn from Norway that can ultimately inform whether and how similar laws are implemented in other countries.

In addition to providing unique and valuable insight for policy-makers and activists, the book tells the story from the perspective of the practitioners: Norway's women directors, their sponsors and mentors. Combined with the contributions from research, the book shows how women can make a concrete difference once they are appointed in boards. There is a set of contributors who by means of presenting their stories on being directors provide guidance to future generations of female board members on the challenges that they will be facing. Lastly, the book illustrates how the law is meeting the expectations which led to its introduction.

OUTLINE OF THE BOOK

The book is organized in five main parts and a conclusion. In Part I we present 'The Norwegian Political Background'. This part is edited by Morten Huse and captures the stories of how the law developed. It charts the law's evolution from its initial ideas rooted in Norwegian gender equality, the political process of getting it approved including the successes and failures along the way, to when it was finally implemented. This part includes chapters from Laila Dåvøy and Kirsti Bergstø. They present the stories of the parents of the law and the political debate in Norway that surrounded the law.

Part II deals with 'Norwegian and International Advocacy' for women on boards and is edited by Silke Machold. This part captures stories of the advocacy movement, that is, the range of initiatives originating from Norway and internationally that sought to promote the business and social case behind the law. The part includes chapters by Elbjørg Gui Standal and Elin Hurvenes. They are representative of those Norwegians who created the networks, educational opportunities and awareness in boards to facilitate the law's implementation and ultimately turn aspirations into reality. Reflections from other countries on how to develop the necessary institutions are presented by Christine Wetli (University of St Gallen, Switzerland), Cristina Finocchi Mahne (La Sapienza University, Italy) and Heather Foust Cummings (Catalyst International).

Part III, 'Norwegian Board Members: Stories from the Field', is edited by Morten Huse. This part tells the story of women on boards from the perspective of the female directors themselves, with emphasis on their individual and collective contributions, motivations and challenges. The part contains reflections from Nini Høegh Nergaard, Merethe Lütken, Thorhild Widvey, Ingvild Ragna Myhre written up by Morten Huse. They are representative of the different types of women who are now active on Norwegian corporate boards.

Part IV, 'Lessons from Research on Gender on Boards', is edited by Katrin Hansen. This part contains a series of short chapters detailing some of the important research findings in relation to quota laws. There are chapters from Andrea Bührmann (Germany), Mariateresa Torchia (Italy), Dorothy Perrin Moore (USA), Cathrine Seierstad, Vibeke Heidenreich, Gro Ladegård and Agnes Bolsø and colleagues (all Norway).

'Policy Implications at the International Level' are presented in Part V. The part is edited by Silke Machold and Katrin Hansen and presents the experiences from other countries in promoting quota laws, that is, the most recent developments. Whereas Part II on advocacy focuses on practical initiatives to get women into boardrooms, Part V discusses the policy approaches to gender equality in different national contexts. This part also investigates policy implications at the international level, that is, moving away from national considerations to supra-national ones. In this part we include chapters by Monika Schulz-Strelow and Daniela Weber-Rey (both Germany), Marina Brogi (Italy), Ruth Sealy and Susan Vinnicombe (UK) and EU Commissioner Viviane Reding.

Finally, the book concludes with a summary of the lessons learnt and future challenges in promoting gender equality in boards, by Katrin Hansen and Silke Machold.

REFERENCES

Aguilera, R.V. and Jackson, G. (2003) The cross-national diversity of corporate governance: Dimensions and determinants, *Academy of Management Review*, 28(3): 447–465.

Bilimoria, D. and Piderit, S.K. (eds) (2007) *Handbook on Women in Business and Management*, Cheltenham, UK and Northampton, MA, USA: Edward Elgar.

Billing, Y.D. and Alvesson, M. (1989) Four ways of looking at women and leadership, *Scandinavian Journal of Management*, 5(1): 63–80.

Catalyst (2012) Increasing gender diversity on boards: Current index of formal approaches, available at http://www.catalyst.org/publication/514/increasing-gender-diversity-on-boards-current-index-of-formal-approaches (accessed June 2012).

FAZ (Frankfurter Allgemeine Zeitung) (2011) Goldröcke und Großmütter an der Macht, 15 February, p. 18.

Gröschl, S. and Takagi, J. (eds) (2012) *Diversity Quotas, Diverse Perspectives: The Case of Gender*, Farnham, UK: Gower Publishers.

Grosvold, J. and Brammer, S. (2011) National institutional systems as antecedents of female board representation: An empirical study, *Corporate Governance: An International Review*, 19(2): 116–135.

House, R.J., Hanges, P.M., Javidan, M., Dorfman, P. and Gupta, V. (eds) (2004) *Culture, Leadership and Organizations: The GLOBE Study of 62 Societies*, Thousand Oaks, CA: Sage.

Huse, M. (2007) *Boards, Governance and Value Creation*, Cambridge, UK: Cambridge University Press.

La Repubblica (2011) Nel paradise della parità dove comandano le manager, 8 March, p. 49.

Vinnicombe, S., Singh, V., Burke, R.J., Bilimoria, D. and Huse, M. (eds) (2008) *Women on Corporate Boards of Directors*, Cheltenham, UK and Northampton, MA, USA: Edward Elgar.

PART I

The Norwegian political background

1. The political process behind the gender balance law

Morten Huse

The story of how Norway developed and implemented the law on gender equality on boards is presented throughout the book. In this chapter we focus on those individuals and groups who were instrumental in the conception and development of the law, that is, the Norwegian politicians who initiated the formulation of the law, promoted its passage through the political and legal system, and ultimately facilitated its implementation.

We reflect in Part I on the debate surrounding the law's conception in Norway, and on the political processes that shaped its passage. We bring to light the struggles behind the scenes through interviews with some of the core political actors, including the Think Tank participants Laila Dåvøy and Kirsti Bergstø. Laila Dåvøy was the Norwegian Minister of Equality in 2002 at the time that the law proposal was introduced, while Kirsti Bergstø was State Secretary in the Ministry of Equality in 2012. We commence in this chapter with reflections from Ansgar Gabrielsen and past Prime Minister Kjell Magne Bondevik on the announcement of the law. Gabrielsen was the Minister of Trade and Industry who received much of the credit for the law. He has been considered as the father of the law, and has internationally received substantial attention not only for what he did, but also for how it did it. He proposed the law in the press without informing anybody – not the Prime Minister, not the Minister of Equality, nor the leaders of his own political party.

Norway is considered one of the most progressive countries with regards to increasing the number of women on boards, thanks to it being an early adopter of legislation to force companies to recruit women to the boardroom. For many feminists, the decision to legislate for gender equality on boards was the boldest move anywhere to breach one of the most durable barriers to gender equality. In 2003, amendments to the Public Limited Companies Act in Norway included a requirement for a certain minimum proportion of directors from each gender. This has led to a dramatic increase in the number of women on the boards of Norwegian companies. Other countries that are considering the adoption of an enforced quota scheme are looking at the results from Norway and planning accordingly.

The role of women in society is changing. This is not only in the public and private spheres, but also in the business world. These changes are found in many countries, but the speed and focus may vary. There are various arguments to develop ways to increase the number of women on corporate boards of directors. Corporate boards of directors have traditionally been seen as meeting places for societal and business elites. The boards have been considered as arenas where the interests of the 'old boys' networks' are promoted, and it has been argued that an invisible glass ceiling is preventing women from getting into board and top management positions. Several initiatives for breaking through this glass ceiling have been researched and discussed (Vinnicombe et al., 2008).

Lessons can be learned from Norway about ways to increase the number of women on corporate boards. We will reflect on the results achieved after a law reform was introduced with the objective to have 40 percent of the board members coming from the least-represented gender. In practice, the law forced the largest Norwegian corporations to have at least 40 percent women among the board members. The reflections will consider the effectiveness of various programs or means to increase the number of women on corporate boards, as well as the consequences for businesses and the individual women becoming board members.

BOARDS AND CORPORATE GOVERNANCE IN NORWAY[1]

When describing the Norwegian corporate governance arena it is important to understand the Norwegian history and the main actors. Norway is a small country with only a few large corporations, there are not many people with a long history of being wealthy, and the state and public authorities are important actors. In practice that means that there are few traditional family companies, but that even small companies have had active boards of directors, public policy initiatives have been of major importance, and recent movements of investor activism have received considerable attention.

The Norwegian authorities are clearly key actors in the corporate governance arena. The authorities act as both lawmakers and owners. However, there are also various other actors that define and shape the corporate governance arena. Norway has a civil law system, and there exist various forms of incorporation.

There are certain particular features that characterize the Norwegian corporate governance system. These include Norwegian traditions and particular corporate governance events, the division between ASA (publicly tradable) and AS (private limited) companies, the concentrated ownership of the Oslo Stock Exchange, the importance of governmental and municipal ownership, the compulsory delegation of executive tasks (a two-tier system), and corporate co-determination. In 2008 there were 414 ASA companies and 224 of them were listed on the Oslo Stock Exchange. The number of ASA companies is about 0.1 percent of all registered companies in Norway (Rasmussen and Huse, 2010).

Employee-elected board members are part of the industrial relations system in Norway. This dates back to 1935 when the Basic Agreement was concluded between the main employee federation (LO) and the main employers' federation (NAF/NHO). This agreement laid down collaboration rules, specifically the rights to collective agreement in the workplace, the right to strike and the labor peace guarantee, and the right to elect shop stewards (Hagen and Huse, 2007, p. 162). This collective (basic) agreement has been considered as 'the constitution of Norwegian working life'. The notion of what corporations are in reality, and that employee participation and co-determination are important tools in business development, may be traced back to the first collective (basic) agreement.

THE CONTROVERSIAL ANNOUNCEMENT OF THE LAW

It is 22 February 2002 and the Norwegian Minister of Trade and Industry Ansgar Gabrielsen sits in his office in the government quarter. His heart probably beats faster this afternoon than usually. He picks up the phone and dials a number. At the other end is a journalist, who is currently unaware that he will soon get the hottest story of the year. 'Hey,' says Gabrielsen. 'I have a great case for you. I can't say it on the phone, but if you come here to my office then I think that we have something that really will get attention.'

About ten years later, the former Minister is proud when recalling this moment from memory. When it happened, there was no one who was able to stop him. Not even the Prime Minister. 'It was a very unusual way to contact the media for a politician, and I knew it. But I had acted very nicely throughout my political career. Until then, I had been minister for three months, and had decided to leave politics when I turned fifty. At this time there were four years again. But before I left, I wanted to do something big. Something that would last throughout my term. I saw the opportunity, and I found out how I was going to do it.'

Ansgar Gabrielsen did not ask his party leader. He did not even consult with his party colleagues, nor the Prime Minister Kjell Magne Bondevik. And the topic was controversial.

'At six o'clock the next morning the top Secretary at Prime Minister's Office called', Gabrielsen says about the event in 2002. 'She asked, "Have you seen the newspaper?" And I said, "No. Is there anything in particular?" "Well," she answered, "I'll read it to you now." She read out the passage and asked, "Are you properly quoted?" "Yes. I did quote check yesterday, so this is one hundred percent correct." "And you mean it?" she asked. "Yeah, I mean it." I said. "I mean it and I stand for it – to my absolute last day in Government!"' (Source: Dysthe, 2010.)

ABOUT TEN YEARS LATER

We are in Ex-Prime Minster Kjell Magne Bondevik's office. How did he experience it when one of his ministers in 2002 contacted the journalists and acted this way?

'It was a kind of coup', he concedes. 'And I haven't yet quite figured out why Ansgar made it that way. But what he has said to me is that in order to get something you have to occasionally resort to unorthodox methods. I think probably the primary reason was that he knew he would face opposition in his own party. The usual procedure when one draws up new legislative proposals, is that of designing a Government memo which goes out for consultation before it reaches the Government conference. But Ansgar would then have been meeting opposition from the ministries governed by his colleagues from the conservative party. He chose instead to coup them, which caused considerable irritation within his own party.'

'It was reported in the media that you rebuked him?'

'Yes, I had to do that. There were several that responded and asked if I had cleared his statements. Normally you would think that if a minister goes out in the media in that way, that the Prime Minister had cleared it beforehand. But I had not. And this is neither a common nor a good practice. So I had to rebuke him, not least because of pressure from other Cabinet Ministers. I said, "Ansgar, you know that I share your view on this question, so that is not the problem, but how you proceeded". The reason why I had to do this was that it too easily could have created a precedent. If a Minister starts to use such a procedure and does not get any reactions to it, then others will start following the same procedures to achieve fast progress in achieving their objectives. And the Government could not live with such procedures. So I rebuked Gabrielsen to set an example.' (Source: Dysthe, 2010.)

THE NORWEGIAN AFFIRMATIVE ACTION TRADITION

The history of the Norwegian law on affirmative action to ensure gender balance in boards goes back a long way. In Norway, equality between the genders is an integral part of employment policy and the social dialogue between the government and various parties in the employment sphere, including employer associations and trade unions, and there are many rules about reporting on gender balance. In 1981 Norway made it a requirement, stipulated in and enforced through the Equality Act, that public sector boards, councils, working groups and delegations must comprise 40 percent of the least represented gender, be that male or female. In 1993, parental leave was extended to 42 weeks. Four of these weeks were earmarked for fathers, and they could not be transferred to mothers. In 2009, there was an increase from four to ten weeks for fathers' parental leave.

Societal reasons have been the starting point for much of the attention paid to this subject, and it is these reasons that lie behind the most radical initiatives to get more women onto the boards. The societal reasons have been about justice in society, democracy, participation, equality between the genders, human rights and compliance with various conventions of the United Nations and the European Economic Area. The individual-level and career-based arguments have largely been related to the 'glass ceiling' discussions. Business is about the reasons why and how women on corporate boards will contribute to improving companies' performance. These arguments are especially used in contexts where social reasons are not accepted. The most common business case argument relates to the benefits of increased diversity, and that women contribute differently than men.

Although the Norwegian law had its origins in social concerns about gender equality, the subsequent debates in public and behind the scenes also surfaced justifications based on attendant commercial benefits and the individual rights of women. Yet, when it comes to the evaluation of a political initiative, it must be judged against the attainment of its original purpose. If the original rationale is associated with gender balance in society, then the initiative should not first and foremost be evaluated on the basis of corporate profitability, or based on the career development of individual women. Of course attendant effects, both positive and negative, should not be neglected, but the most important evaluation criterion must be the societal.

VARIOUS NORWEGIAN INITIATIVES TO INCREASE THE NUMBER OF WOMEN ON BOARDS

Discussions have also taken place internationally for over 30 years on reasons for and how to get women into controlling positions in enterprises. Many different initiatives and programs have been reviewed, and these include:

- political debates;
- development of women's networks;
- funding of research and dissemination of research results;
- courses and seminars to educate and prepare women to work on boards;
- mentorship and sponsorship programs;
- databases and other instruments to find board-qualified women;
- law proposal hearings and soft law recommendations or requirements;
- hard laws and legislation.

The Confederation of Norwegian Enterprise (NHO) established in the mid-1990s a program called 'Women to the Top' in cooperation with the Norwegian Confederation of Sports. In this initiative NHO ran seminars for women who were to establish themselves at the top, and also included seminars to prepare women for board positions. The Norwegian Director of Equality, Ingunn Yssen, ran a number of programs to increase the number of women in boards. Among other things, she established in 1999 along with then Labor and Administration Minister Laila Dåvøy, and Children and Equality Minister Valgerd Svarstad Haugland, registers of women who wished to undertake directorships. Several thousand women signed up and entered their curriculum vitaes (CVs) in the female board database. Previous Equality Ministers Valgerd Svarstad Haugland (1997–2000) and Karita Bekkemellom (2000–2001) explored options for affirmative action for getting women on boards. Hearings were sent out on law proposals for consultation that, from Haugland, entailed a 25 percent share of women in all public companies; while Karita Bekkemellom sent out a hearing for the proposal of 40 percent of ASA company boards. From 2001, Equality Minister Laila Dåvøy (2001–2005), together with the Minister of Trade and Industry, Ansgar Gabrielsen, continued efforts to promote a law proposal for gender balance in boards. The various initiatives have had different purposes. Some have been geared towards training and preparing women, some have been aimed at motivating those who choose board members, and some have had the aim to simplify the recruitment process. The effects of these initiatives vary depending on the context and the central actors who are involved.

The ratio of women on corporate boards in publicly listed companies did not change between 1990 and 2002. During this period it averaged around 4 to 7 percent, with the only increase in 1994 caused by the introduction of new types of companies on the Oslo Stock Exchange. The real change started to take place after Ansgar Gabrielsen's meeting in 2002 with the press. The law was then introduced in 2003, but it was introduced as a 'sunset law'. That means that the law would not come into effect if the goals of gender balance were achieved in the course of two years. The work of Children and Equality Minister Karita Bekkemellom (2005–2007) ensured the implementation of the law, and in 2008 all ASA companies had to have a gender-balanced board of directors, that is, a minimum of about 40 percent of the least-represented sex. ASA companies which did not follow the law had to be dissolved or had to find another form of incorporation. The goal of gender balance in ASA boards was achieved.

In the remainder of Part I we present two contributions from the Think Tank in March 2011. They are from Laila Dåvøy and Kirsti Bergstø. While Ansgar Gabrielsen is often viewed as the father of the Norwegian gender balance law, many consider Laila Dåvøy to be the mother of the law. Kirsti Bergstø was State Secretary in the Ministry of Equality in 2011, and she represented the then Norwegian Minister of Equality Audun Lysbakken.

NOTE

1. The paragraphs in this section are from Rasmussen and Huse (2010).

REFERENCES

Dysthe, Pernille (2010) Da kvoteringsloven kom til verden: En politisk styrtfød-sel, Intervju med Ansgar Gabrielsen og Kjell Magne Bondevik, *Magma*, 7: 15–19.

Hagen, I.M. and Huse, M. (2007) Do employee representatives make a difference on corporate boards? Examples from Norway, in Jürgens, U., Sadowski, D., Schuppert, G.F. and Weiss, M. (eds), *Perspektiven der Corporate Governance*, Baden-Baden: Nomos, pp. 156–181.

Rasmussen, J.L. and Huse, M. (2011) Corporate governance in Norway: Women and employee-elected board members, in Mallin, C. (ed.), *International Corporate Governance*, Cheltenham, UK and Northampton, MA, USA: Edward Elgar, pp. 121–146.

Vinnicombe, S., Singh, V., Burke, R., Bilimoria, D. and Huse, M. (eds) (2008) *Women on Corporate Boards of Directors: International Research and Practice*, Cheltenham, UK and Northampton, MA, USA: Edward Elgar.

2. Women on board

Laila Dåvøy

I am proud to be the Minister of Children and Family Affairs who proposed the law on gender balance in the boardrooms to Parliament. But I was not the minister who started this initiative. Rather, this was a lengthy process that took about eight years of discussions and two hearings before the proposal finally ended up in the Parliament.

My former party leader and former Equality Minister Valgerd Svarstad Haugland was the first minister to take the initiative. This was in Prime Minister's Kjell Magne Bondevik's first Cabinet. Valgerd Svarstad Haugland organized a hearing and the debate was intense. The protests raised by some of the owners and leaders of companies represented at the hearing made it seem as though this law would sound the death knell of stock exchange-listed companies, those who would be affected by the new law.

In Prime Minister's Kjell Magne Bondevik's second Cabinet, the question of women in boardrooms was raised again. This cabinet consisted of three parties: the Conservative Party, the Liberal Party and the Christian Democratic Party, which was the party I belonged to. I would lie if I said that it was easy to pass this proposal through the Cabinet. Different ministers were for and against it. The two main issues of contention were the law in itself, and the discussion about sanctions if companies did not abide by the law once it was implemented.

Hard work in the form of administrative, professional and political overtime was the key to ultimate success. Arni Hole, as the Director General, was responsible in the Ministry of Children and Family Affairs. She did a wonderful job, not least towards and together with the Ministry of Trade and Industry, and the Ministry of Justice. An intergovernmental group consisting of representatives from these three ministries was working hard. It was of vital importance that these three ministries stood unanimously behind the law. But I remember that Arni sometimes felt that the work was proceeding too slowly, and that she was always several steps ahead of others. A possible explanation could be that it was our Ministry that in some sense had 'ownership' of this law. The Minister of

17

Trade and Industry Ansgar Gabrielsen became dedicated, and his support was essential, not least because he was from the Conservative Party, which was the biggest one in the Cabinet.

Not long ago, I met Ansgar Gabrielsen when he visited Parliament. We were talking about the law. He suddenly said: 'Well Laila, you are the mother and I am the father of the law.' Later, I have been thinking that: yes, what he said is a good analogy. But as usual, when it comes to pregnancy, it is the woman who has to bear the heaviest burden, to take care of the unborn life and to fight for its survival before birth.

Why was this law so important politically, in my view? Few women were appointed as board members. The same men were sitting on different boards and there was even one example where a businessman had been appointed to sit on 80 boards. Women took up only 6 percent of board positions in 2002, and in April 2003 it had risen to a meager 7.3 percent.

It was also a matter of diversity and democracy. Being the Minister of Equality, I was convinced that responsibility, influence and benefits in society should be shared equally between men and women. Real equality is about more than peoples' rights not to be discriminated against. It is also about how to organize work and society, not least in a family-friendly way. The equality debate in Norway at that time was also about how men could take more responsibility in the family.

And then there was also the matter of power. A lot of men would have to leave the boards. The new law would bring about better sharing and a more equal distribution of power. It would give women more influence in society.

And it was a matter of competence. Almost 60 percent of the students who graduated from universities and high schools were women. So this was not about using a quota to bring unqualified women into board-rooms; rather, the issue was to use that potential and provide opportunities to 50 percent of the adult population in Norway: women. It was of pivotal importance to use the resources that women's competences were representing.

In addition, every step that we could take to decrease the segregated working system in our country should be welcomed. And of course, women really are important consumers. Who decides what to buy in a family? Purchases such as furniture, equipment, clothes, cars, holidays – the list of purchasing decisions made by women goes on. So why should they not be on boards?

Finally, women on boards would make an important contribution to companies' value creation, especially when it comes to creativity and human resources. It would strengthen management and competitive ability in the business sector. All of the above was in my mind and the Ministries' thinking behind the new Law.

International Women's Day, 8 March 2002, was the day when our government was ready to declare that we wanted 40 percent women, or more accurately at least 40 percent of each gender, on the boards of public limited companies quoted on the stock exchange, of which there were about 590. This was a day that marked a real breakthrough for equality in Norway. We could now declare that the Ministry of Children and Family Affairs would present a proposition to Parliament. After a long hearing, the law was finally passed in November 2003 by majority vote in Parliament. It came into force on 1 January 2004, and in the first instance applied to three types of publicly owned companies, the most important of these being wholly state-owned companies (of which there were 69). These companies already had on average 45.7 percent representation by women on their boards, and it was important for us that they should act as an example for public limited companies to follow.

The law was mainly intended for public limited companies. But they needed time, as they started off with having less than 8 percent women on their boards. If the companies achieved the goal of 40 percent women representation voluntarily during the course of 2005, the law would not come into force. But if they did not reach that goal, the law would come into effect. And as we know today, the companies did not succeed in increasing women's representation. After the election in September 2005, the new government, Stoltenberg 1, followed this up when they took over the Cabinet at the end of 2005. And from 1 January 2006, the law became a reality. The companies had to start their process of reaching 40 percent of each gender represented on the board by 2008. So they were given another two years to fulfill this, and they did.

Looking back on the events now leads me to some reflections. I often felt that many company owners and leaders were thinking that this law would never be implemented at all. This was because of the nature of the sanctions that would be applied if they did not fulfill the 40 percent quota. The sanctions were that they would have to close down their company. It would be illegal to continue operations. And that this could happen was unbelievable and inconceivable for some, and so they were quite relaxed about it. But there was no turning back.

And the debate in public was intense. I had to debate in different media. That was challenging but also fun. I met a company owner once who declared that this law meant that pure incompetence would now walk into the boardrooms. Another one said that I personally could never have seen a boardroom, and that I had no competence at all when it came to making decisions about companies. Well, he hadn't read my curriculum vitae, that is for sure.

To stimulate the process, the government entered into partnership with the private sector and its main representative organizations, and we engaged in projects and research. Benchmarking research was conducted by researchers, amongst them Marit Hoel. 'Female Future' was important in creating networks and awareness. To provide courses in how to become a good board member was also important. Other measures included the compilation of databases for women (Female Future, Women@Base, Innovasjon Norge). Here, the companies could search for and find well-qualified women when looking for candidates for board or top management positions.

In every debate I joined, when the arguments surfaced that there are not enough competent women and that they have no experience, I always referred to these databases where companies could choose amongst well-educated and experienced women. And of course I said that I would very much like to help them find the right ones. Rhetorically, I asked: 'When did a man ever have to take courses or education to become a board member, or even to prove their competence?'

I will conclude with the words of a French politician, Francoise Giroud, who said: 'Full equality will not be a reality until incompetent women are in top positions.'

3. Women mean business: why and how Norway legislated gender balance on the boards of listed companies

Kirsti Bergstø

No country can afford not to focus on gender equality as a key to economic stability, innovation and growth. We have strong indications to support this, and I think no one would disagree. Human capital is a vital part of our economy and represents close to 80 percent of our national wealth. Oil only accounts for 7 percent. Therefore, it is important how we make use of our hands and heads.

Traditional patterns die hard, and sometimes it takes legal and radical affirmative actions such as quotas to produce results. There are two major reasons for why we need affirmative actions such as quotas. First, fundamentally, it is a moral issue. Equal opportunity for all is about democracy and representation. Quotas may be necessary to ensure equal outputs. Second, it is sound economics! Our human capital is vital. A modern, competitive economy needs all talents, and the best brains regardless of gender.

Let me give you a brief picture of the quotas we have introduced by law, in some areas in Norway. We have a history, spanning several Cabinets, of combining traditional efforts for equal opportunities with radical affirmative actions. The use of so-called 'quotas' started in the 1970s with voluntary gender balance in all the political parties but one. Today we have gender parity in the Cabinet, 40 percent women in Parliament, and 38 percent women in the elected municipal councils. Further, in 1988 the Gender Equality Act introduced a demand for 40 percent of either gender to be represented on all governmental committees, councils and delegations.

In 1993, the father's quota (by law) within the Parental Leave Scheme was introduced. That law mandates that parental leave time is reserved for the father and is not transferable to the mother. From July 2011, the father's quota has been 12 weeks of parental leave out of a total period of 47/57 weeks (of 57 weeks in total, a maximum of 47 can be taken by one person). This legal quota for father's parental leave has contributed to a mental change in the business community and among the fathers and mothers. Taking care of your children is the normal and expected thing to do.

In 2003 we introduced a requirement for 40 percent of either gender to be represented on the companies' elected board of directors. Four different company laws were amended. We did this because in 2002 women were almost totally absent in the boardrooms of public limited companies. Then, only 7 percent of elected members were women; today the score is 40.2 percent.

We had invested billions in educating our daughters and our sons. An equal number of women graduated from universities and colleges around 2000; and they graduated in law and increasingly in economics. Their ongoing exclusion from corporate boards and top management in the private sector – so important to society – just did not make economic sense. It was neither democratic nor moral.

The legal proposals in 2003 created a lot of heated discussions in the media and general public debate. Several top Norwegian business leaders say today that they were opposed in principle to quotas, but believe the law has been effective and are happy with the results. The quota is simply a tool to display women's competence, not a goal in itself.

Norway still has a way to go regarding gender balance in top management. We hope to see more of a positive spillover effect from the increased number of women on boards, to real gender balance in corporate management jobs. Being a board member is a stamp of approval.

I can highly recommend the use of quotas if you combine equality policies with modern, gender-neutral family laws; parental leave and fathers' quotas; full coverage of early childcare places at an affordable price; and flexibility in work life for parents with sick children. Quotas are not a quick fix to achieve gender equality in business life. Quotas are only effective if such welfare measures are in place.

We still face important challenges, including a gender-segregated labor market and lower average pay per hour for women. Men do not prioritize education and jobs in the health and care sectors. Their traditional educational choices represent a challenge for the equality between the genders. We need more hands, including men's, in the future care sector.

There has been huge international interest in the Norwegian experience. Our initiatives and results have inspired other countries to follow suit. I think diversity is good for the strategic capacities of boards. France has just adopted a similar law to Norway. I have learned that the demand for women on company boards applies to all kind of companies with a certain level of annual sales and a certain number of employees. In Norway the quota applies to all state-owned and municipally owned enterprises, and of course most famously to public limited companies listed on the stock exchange. We have not used quotas, so far, for elections to the boardrooms of the 160 000 privately owned companies. Some of these are quite large. I have noticed with interest that the French initiative is connected to annual sales and number of employees, instead of how a company is incorporated.

Let me conclude by saying that we would never have seen such a rapid increase in the number of women on company boards without the use of quotas. Profound political will is necessary to set a target, and to introduce adequate measures to reach the target. To increase the level of gender equality in all sectors of society, women have to be visible in the labor market, be evident as a pool of competence. And men and fathers have to 'come home'. This is about redistribution of power.

I would like to wrap up my reflections by underscoring my previous point on diversity and board capacities. I do firmly believe that there is a lot of competence to be found among educated persons from our minorities and persons with disabilities, and that this can be used for board work purposes.

4. Concluding remarks to Part I

Morten Huse

A snowball started to roll in 2002 in Norway. The conditions were conducive to the formation of the snowball; nevertheless many co-incidences were behind the snowball effect. Activists and feminists in politics played their part together with a Conservative minister. The feminists had prepared the landscape and made the snowball, but it was pushed by the Minister of Trade and Industry who had private reasons to do so. The snowball is now rolling with increasing speed and size to the rest of the world, and many countries have followed Norway's example.

In Part I we have through interviews heard and read the stories from Minister Ansgar Gabrielsen and Prime Minister Kjell Magne Bondevik. They may be considered as the father and the grandfather of the law. However, the mother and the grandmother of the law are the previous Ministers of Equality, Laila Dåvøy and Valgerd Svarstad Haugland. Together they worked to develop the Norwegian law on gender balance in the boardrooms, and it was not an easy birth.

Ten years later the main actors from 2002 offer in Part I their reflections on the process. They are proud of what they helped to start. The process and the effects have far exceeded their expectations, and nowadays the world looks to Norway. Voluntary action did not succeed in increasing the number of women on corporate board, but formal regulation through a quota law worked. There is now a gender balance in the boards of Norwegian publicly traded companies.

PART II

Norwegian and international advocacy

5. Institutionalizing women's representation on boards: an introduction to the advocacy movement

Silke Machold

In Part I, we described how the Norwegian gender quota law emerged, its passage through the political system, and finally its implementation and results. The focus then was on the actors in the political sphere, and especially the political 'parents' of the law. In Part II we turn to the story of other actors that were and are involved in shaping at various levels gender diversity on boards, both in Norway and internationally. Further, Part II focuses on the processes and mechanisms by which women representation on boards may become accepted business practice. A common theme throughout this book is that action is needed to address the low levels of women representation in the upper echelons of business. Yet, outrage, disbelief and opposition have been almost universal reactions of the business community, some businesswomen included, to the mooting of quota laws (see, for example, Chapter 2 by Dåvøy, Chapter 7 by Hurvenes and Chapter 27 by Brogi, in this book). Gay Charles, a senior consultant at the international recruitment company Odgers Berndtson, described at the Oslo Think Tank how senior Dutch business figures lambasted the corporate governance recommendations on gender diversity in boards as 'absurd' because boards would not be able to find suitable women candidates. In the face of such adversity, is it possible that women representation on boards will ever be taken for granted?

Sociologists have long been interested in understanding how and why organizational structures and practices become institutionalized (or not); that is, how and why some practices become habitualized and enduring (Scott, 1987). DiMaggio and Powell (1983) identified three processes by which organizational practices become prevalent across sectors and countries, referred to as coercive, normative and mimetic isomorphism.

Coercive isomorphic processes are those that compel or force organizations to adapt a practice, usually by means of governmental intervention and the legal system. Quota laws, or other forms of formal approaches to gender diversity such as corporate governance codes, are examples of coercive mechanisms that can bring about gender parity on boards as organizations conform to their requirements. Mimetic isomorphism is related to the spread of practice through imitation. Simply put, organizations copy each other's practices, especially under environmental conditions of uncertainty (DiMaggio and Powell, 1983). In relation to gender on boards, such mimetic processes are evident at two levels: (1) at national policy level, countries are looking towards Norway and the outcomes achieved to discuss and model their own policy responses (see Part I and Part V of this book); and (2) companies look at each other's practices regarding board composition and recruitment of women to boards, and imitate those that are perceived to be leaders in the field (see Chapter 28 by Sealy and Vinnicombe in this book). Thus, having high-profile companies and corporate leaders supporting and advocating gender balance on boards, as described by Hurvenes in Chapter 7, facilitates the dissemination and acceptance of women on boards beyond the coercive means of the law. Finally, normative isomorphism is associated with the legitimization of practices via their endorsement and promulgation by educational institutions, professional associations and networks (DiMaggio and Powell, 1983). Here, the efforts by national and international advocacy institutions to stimulate public discussion on gender imbalance on boards and facilitate female board member selection are important in the spreading of these norms.

These three isomorphic processes are strongly intertwined and often work in tandem. Part I and Part V of this book deal especially with the formal approaches that are more aligned with coercive mechanisms, by discussing the Norwegian quota law and other countries' soft and hard law approaches respectively. In Part II, the focus is primarily on the normative and, to a lesser degree, on the mimetic mechanisms. Before introducing the chapter contributions from representatives of national and international advocacy groups, I examine four institutional dimensions that serve to promulgate greater gender equality on boards, namely professional education, the role of networks and networking, research and information, and the importance of role models.

EDUCATION

A frequent argument in support of the case for women on boards is the need to make full use of the talent pool. If half of graduates from universities are female (see for example Chapter 29 by Viviane Reding in this book), then companies are missing out competitively if they fail to consider this pool of talent. But what knowledge, skills and experience are needed at board level? There is general agreement that to perform effectively, boards need to have the right mix of knowledge, skills and experience, which should include functional as well as firm- and industry-specific knowledge (Forbes and Milliken, 1999; Huse, 2005). Corporate governance codes reflect that general requirement, yet have been found to lack detail on the specific competences required (Zattoni and Cuomo, 2010). The exception tends to be recommendations for subcommittees where most frequently financial literacy and accounting and financial qualifications are specified for audit committee members (Zattoni and Cuomo, 2010). Equally, conversations with chief executive officers (CEOs) and chairpersons of boards highlight that the qualifications sought typically include a good first degree and preferably an MBA (Hurvenes, Chapter 7 in this book). Although MBAs have historically attracted more male than female graduates, efforts by business schools for more flexible delivery patterns and changing images of career paths following an MBA have led to an increase in the number of women completing MBA programs, with some leading business schools having achieved gender balance on their MBA programs (Finn, 2012).

Formal qualifications are, however, only one side of the story. Experience in senior management and leadership, and prior board positions are seen as just as important, if not more, than qualifications per se (Hurvenes, Chapter 7), and such requirements may well be the more intransigent barrier. Given the figures on women's representation on boards presented in this book and elsewhere, of course the pool of women with board experience is limited. Furthermore, research has shown that women are also under-represented in senior management (Finocchi Mahne, Chapter 9 in this book), and that the pipeline for CEO positions remains woefully male-biased (Helfat et al., 2006).

Business schools and other educational and training providers play an important role in breaking through these barriers. First, as indicated above, business schools' efforts in making MBA programs accessible to women are not only good business but also provide professional certification of management skills and experiences. In other words, MBAs contribute to human capital formation (Terjesen et al., 2009), and they also act as important signalling devices of the quality of education received. Here, initiatives supported by leading international business schools such the European Union's 'Global Board Ready Women' (EU, 2012) serve to inform about and legitimize the competences of women board directors. Second, business schools are important providers of specific training in board competences (see Chapter 6 by Standal and Chapter 8 by Wetli in this book). Not only do these programs develop board-relevant knowledge and skills, but they also provide formal certification of competences and, most importantly, serve as a meeting place for both male and female directors or board candidates. In sum, educational opportunities offered by business schools and other providers are an important vehicle in facilitating human capital formation, signalling competences of female board members and thus normatively influencing how women on boards are perceived.

NETWORKS AND NETWORKING

The importance of networks and networking for developing individuals' social capital, their influence in organizations' promotional paths, and the access they provide for recruitment to board and top management positions has been extensively documented (Brass, 1985; Burt, 1997). These studies also show that there remain gender differences in terms of network characteristics, the practice and behavior of networking, and consequently the outcomes. For example, Forret and Dougherty (2004) showed that networking behaviors had stronger effects for men than women in securing promotions and the level of compensation, but there was a stronger effect of networking behaviors for the perceived career success of females. There are two explanations for these findings. First, other individual, organizational or societal-level determinants have a greater explanatory power for the (lack of) career progression of females, thus masking the effects of networks and networking behaviors. The second explanation that has been advanced is that women may not have access to networks that matter (Forret and Dougherty, 2004); that is, the networks that women are involved in are not highly visible, nor are they comprised of powerful and influential individuals (Kanter, 1977).

These findings are important for women on boards since we know the importance of networks and networking in attaining board positions, board reappointments and the ability to exert influence in the boardroom (Van der Walt and Ingley, 2003; Westphal and Milton, 2000). Networks for women directors exist in many shapes and sizes. There are global networks (e.g. Women Corporate Directors, WCD, see Chapter 9 by

Finocchi Mahne) and national or regional ones (e.g. Talent Tuning in Norway or FidAR in Germany); there are women-only networks (e.g. Female Board Pool in Switzerland, see Chapter 8 by Wetli) and networks that deliberately set out to connect women with chairmen, CEOs and investors. An example of the latter is the Professional Boards Forum whose founder Elin Hurvenes shares her experiences in Chapter 7. Several factors account for the success of this initiative in Norway and more recently in the international arena: (1) connections to powerful players from industry and politics; (2) high-profile media coverage; and (3) women's attitudes and networking behaviors. In particular, Hurvenes reports that a proactive approach to raising their own visibility has served participating women well in attaining board appointments, a finding that echoes extant research into gendered characteristics of networking behaviors (Forret and Dougherty, 2004).

These networks are created by a range of organizations (for-profit and not-for-profit), serve different purposes and create impacts at several levels. In the first instance, there are the reported benefits to women candidates securing board positions, an outcome that is congruent with the stated aims of many advocacy organizations. Second, for boards these networks present another avenue for recruiting talent. The challenge here is to grow and expand the networks to mitigate the potential for 'glass network' effects (Hawarden and Marsland, 2011) whereby a salient elite of women dominates the recruitment pool. Finally, networks serve as a source of normative isomorphism (DiMaggio and Powell, 1983), as they disseminate and diffuse practices and thus further legitimize the status of women on boards. The Global Board Ready Women initiative (EU, 2012) is a good example of how networks and the high-status actors within the network authenticate women's credentials for board appointments.

RESEARCH AND INFORMATION

The increased interest in the phenomenon on women on boards is perhaps most evident in the proliferation of research and information on the topic. A Google search in 2012 on 'women on boards' returned approximately 117 million results, most of which are published from 2000 onwards. A similar pattern is evident in research databases: for example ABI/ INFORM Global has approximately 3600 publications on 'women on boards' in the 1980s, 26 300 in the 1990s and 51 300 in the 2000s. One of the pioneers in bringing information on women on boards into the public domain is Catalyst, a member-based organization set up in 1962 to promote equality for women in the workplace. Early in the

1970s, Catalyst focused attention on women in the upper echelons by providing consultancy services to companies, raising awareness at annual gala events, and gathering and publicizing information on women representation on boards and in top management teams (www.catalyst.org). On the back of these pioneering awareness-raising campaigns, Catalyst then proceeded to conduct regular and ad hoc surveys and other research to chart progress and assess the impact of women on boards (see Chapter 10 by Foust-Cummings in this book).

Advocacy organizations such as Catalyst blazed a trail in bringing information about women on boards into the public domain. Since then, the topic has been taken up by a range of other organizations and companies, most notably in recent years by international consultancy firms. Prominent amongst these has been McKinsey & Co. which publishes the regular and widely cited 'Women Matter' reports (http://www.mckinsey.com/features/women_matter), alongside a number of ad hoc reports on women on boards, and in leadership and management. Other well-known publications on the topic include the 'Women in the boardroom: global perspectives' (Deloitte, 2011), 'Getting on board' (Ernst & Young, 2012), or the Boston Consulting Group Perspective's 'Shattering the glass ceiling' (Dyrchs and Strack, 2012). In addition, consulting firms such as PwC and Accenture have sponsored academic and practitioner conferences on the topic. Finally, in the wake of the development of ESG (environment, social, governance) investments, companies such as Bloomberg and GMI now routinely compile data on women on boards as part of their ESG investment metrics (see, for example, http://www. gmiratings.com/pri.aspx).

The effects of such activities are manifold. Not only is the topic of women on boards more widely publicized and discussed, but it is also brought to the attention of actors that matter in boardroom appointments: chairs, investors, and members of board nomination committees. Governance metrics are clear and tangible targets that companies are compared against and upon which investment decisions are based. Finally, global consultancy companies are important trend- and principle-setters and as such play an important role in mainstreaming the topic and in normatively influencing companies' practices.

ROLE MODELS

As noted above, a powerful mechanism for institutionalizing practices is mimetic isomorphism, or the spread of practices through copying what others are doing (DiMaggio and Powell, 1983; Scott, 1987). Perceptions of what is 'best practice' in a field, or observations of role models, are examples of sources of such mimetic isomorphism. When it comes to women on boards, there are two challenges in particular. The first is that historically there have been very few role models. As Finocchi Mahne in Chapter 9 discusses, not only is there a relative dearth of female role models in high-profile public and corporate settings, but surveys also show that the lack of role models impacts career progression of women at various levels in organizational hierarchies. The second challenge lies in how female role models are socially constructed and perceived. At an anecdotal level, female leaders are frequently tagged with derogatory labels: Margaret Thatcher was best known as the 'Iron Lady' but was also nicknamed 'Attila the Hen', Angela Merkel has been referred to as 'Mutti' (Mum or Mummy), and Nancy Pelosi was dubbed the 'Grandmother in Pearls' by the *Washington Post*. Eagly and Karau (2002) examine the construction of prejudices towards female leaders through the lens of social role theory, and conclude that role incongruity generates unfavorable attitudes towards and evaluations of women leaders, and associated with this are greater difficulties for women achieving and maintaining leadership roles.

These barriers are not easy to dismantle, not least because role prejudices and stereotypes can be self-reinforcing (Eagly and Karau, 2002). However, activities by both sexes to challenge gender stereotypes in leadership positions and to promote diversity of role models at different organizational levels are all important in deconstructing and reconstructing social reality. Advocacy organizations play an important role in showcasing female role models (www.catalyst.org), creating meeting places for male and female leaders, board members and candidates (Chapter 7 by Hurvenes and Chapter 6 by Standal), and challenging derogatory labels for female board members that may undermine their perceived and actual board contributions (see Bolsø et al., Chapter 19 in this book).

Much of the discussion of the Norwegian success story has centered around its quota law, but perhaps less obvious is that Norway has had adjunct initiatives, institutions and processes that helped institutionalize women on boards. Similar and new initiatives are also under way in other countries. In Part II we commence with the Norwegian advocacy movement and Elbjørg Gui Standal, who was one of the early pioneers in developing accredited and non-accredited higher education programs on leadership from a female perspective. In Chapter 6, she discusses how this early work fed into later programs on building competences for board work. Importantly, these board programs were delivered by male and female tutors with research and practitioner experiences, and delivered to men and women board members and board candidates. A similar approach to breaking down gender divides and thus challenging stereotypes was taken by Elin Hurvenes. In Chapter 7, she talks about why and how she developed the work of the Professional Boards Forum, an initiative that is still growing in international prominence and impact. Both Standal and Hurvenes stress professionalization of boards as a key factor in the conception and delivery of these initiatives, which is congruent with the development of norms about gender and boards.

Christine Wetli and Cristina Finocchi Mahne present initiatives from Switzerland and Italy respectively. Both countries have historically had low women's representation on corporate boards, but Italy has opted for quota legislation whereas Switzerland has not done so despite several attempts. Wetli in Chapter 8 describes the work of the IFMP Center for Corporate Governance at the University of St Gallen, where the Female Board Pool initiative has been launched by Professor Martin Hilb. Closely aligned with the work of the IFMP center, this initiative provides training and networking opportunities for experienced and aspiring board members, as well as influencing policy on women on boards through good governance guidelines. This is followed by Chapter 9 by Cristina Finocchi Mahne, who was one of the first 'board-ready women' listed in the EU database developed by Viviane Reding. She commences her discussion wearing the hat of the scholar and she examines the roots of stereotypes and public depictions of women leaders. She finishes wearing the hat of the successful board member and activist in the global Women Corporate Director (WCD) initiative by outlining the successes of WCD in Italy and beyond. Chapter 10 is by Heather Foust-Cummings who also has an impressively diverse background and high-profile career. As the Vice President for Research at Catalyst, she discusses the different ways in which gender diversity on boards can be achieved, and especially how and why it is important to involve men in such endeavors.

REFERENCES

Brass, D.J. (1985) Men's and women's networks: A study of interaction patterns and influence in an organization, *Academy of Management Journal*, 28: 327–343.
Burt, R.S. (1997) A note on social capital and network content, *Social Networks*, 19(4): 355–373.

Deloitte (2011) Women in the boardroom: Global perspectives, available from http://www.deloitte.com/view/en_GX/global/press/global-press-releases-en/3c b4d5721baad210VgnVCM3000001c56f00aRCRD.htm (accessed December 2012).

DiMaggio, P.J. and Powell, W.W. (1983) The iron cage revisited: Institutional isomorphism and collective rationality in organizational fields, *American Sociological Review*, 48(2): 147–160.

Dyrchs, S. and Strack, R. (2012) Shattering the glass ceiling: An analytical approach to advancing women into leadership positions, BCG Perspectives, available from https://www.bcgperspectives.com/content/articles/leadership_ change_management_shattering_the_glass_ceiling/ (accessed December 2012).

Eagly, A.H. and Karau, S.J. (2002) Role congruity theory of prejudice towards female leaders, *Psychological Review*, 109(3): 573–598.

Ernst & Young (2012) Getting on board, available from http://www.ey.com/ Publication/vwLUAssets/Getting_on_board/$FILE/Getting_on_board.pdf (accessed December 2012).

European Union (2012) Shattering myths and glass ceilings: Launch of database of 'Global Board Ready Women', available from http://europa.eu/rapid/press-release_IP-12-1358_en.htm (accessed December 2012).

Finn, W. (2012) MBA women: Breaking down barriers at business schools, *Telegraph*, 22 November.

Forbes, D. and Milliken, F. (1999) Cognition and corporate governance: Understanding boards of directors as strategic decision-making groups, *Academy of Management Review*, 24(3): 489–505.

Forret, M.L. and Dougherty, T.W. (2004) Networking behaviors and career outcomes: Differences for men and women?, *Journal of Organizational Behavior*, 25: 419–437.

Helfat, C.E., Harris, D. and Wolfson, P.J. (2006) The pipeline to the top: Women and men in the top executive ranks of US corporations, *Academy of Management Perspectives*, 20(4): 42–64.

Huse, M. (2005) Accountability and creating accountability: A framework for exploring behavioural perspectives of corporate governance, *British Journal of Management*, 16(s1): s65–s79.

Kanter, R.M. (1977) *Men and Women of the Corporation*, New York: Basic Books.

Scott, W.R. (1987) The adolescence of institutional theory, *Administrative Science Quarterly*, 32(4): 493–511.

Terjesen, S., Sealy, R. and Singh, V. (2009) Women directors on corporate boards: A review and research agenda, *Corporate Governance: An International Review*, 17(3): 320–337.

Van der Walt, N. and Ingley, C. (2003) Professional background, gender and ethnic diversity of directors, *Corporate Governance: An International Review*, 11(3): 218–234.

Westphal, J.D. and Milton, L.P. (2000) How experience and network ties affect the influence of demographic minorities on corporate boards, *Administrative Science Quarterly*, 45(2): 366–398.

Zattoni, A. and Cuomo, F. (2010) How independent, competent and incentivized should non-executive directors be? An empirical investigation of good governance codes, *British Journal of Management*, 21(1): 63–79.

6. Competence at board level: the Norwegian case

Elbjørg Gui Standal

Approximately 22 years ago in 1989, I was one of a group of women who developed a program called Leadership from a Female Perspective. The leader of the group was Bitten Schei. We received funding to run the program from Likestillingsrådet, and the program took place at the Industrial University at Notodden, in Sortland and at the Women's University at Løten. We were very proud of our efforts to highlight female leadership, and to encourage women to be leaders and managers.

In 1997, the group was re-established, again under the leadership of Bitten Schei. We gave ourselves the name 'Women in Business'. I had been teaching organizational management, and was wondering: Why do the authors of the books that we recommend to our students neglect to say anything about the board of directors? Is it because the subject matter is not important, or is it obvious to everyone how the work of a board member should be carried out? The group Women in Business became an advisory group for Mrs Aud Sanner at SND, which is now Innovation Norway. She was head of a program called 'Women in Focus'. We decided to concentrate on board work, and since we should stimulate female activities within business we focused on board work for women.

In 1998 I started working as an industrial professor at BI, the Norwegian Business School, and in my new role I developed the course 'Board Competence'. This formed part of the above-mentioned program run by Aud Sanner, and students earned six credits on completion. At the outset, the course was meant to be for women only, but we very soon realized that this was not a good idea. We asked ourselves: 'Who knows how to work as board members?' And the answer was 'Men'. We needed men in the classroom, because they had the knowledge about boards, and that was of course very important. We had to tap their brains, because at the time, little was written in Norwegian about working as a board member. As course literature, however, we had a book written by Professor Morten Huse, a book we still use as required reading today.

In the very beginning we therefore opened up the courses for both men and women, and we wanted the course cohorts to be roughly 50 percent of each gender. This proved to be successful, because we stimulated valuable discussions, and developed common knowledge about how to work in the boardroom. Many men also had to admit that they had not known how many competent women were interested in working as board members.

The first course on 'Board Competence' was followed up by 'Board Competence II', as many participants sought to continue to increase their competence as board directors. The courses have been run since 1999 with approximately 3500 students participating from all over Norway. In recent years Anne Marie Kittelsen of Innovation Norway has been our contact. Innovation Norway has developed a database of candidates from the courses. The participants are offered an exam, and when the exam is passed, they may register in the database.

My husband Kjell Standal is lecturing with me on the courses, along with Anne Breiby who works as a professional board member. We certainly have an academic approach, but in addition all of us have real-life experience, having been board members in numerous companies. We also focus on using the latest research results on boards of directors. We have to combine the best of the academic and the practitioner worlds. Some years ago 'Board Competence I' was offered as part of the Female Future Programme, run by the Confederation of Norwegian Enterprises (NHO), and nowadays the course is also part of the Global Future Programme. We also run open programs for people interested in the topic.

What are the results? We have seen that the participants of our courses have been more aware of the importance of doing a good job within the boardroom, and we also think that this has contributed to the increased interest for board work that we see these days. We have not been directly part of the work on gender quotas, but we would like to think that we have encouraged the interest and need for more diversity in the board room. So much for the 'Board Competence' courses that we teach.

In 2000, we started a big research program on boards, and we named the program 'The Value Creating Board'. Morten Huse is the professor in charge of the program, and he uses the results as background for his books and many articles. We also started 'The Value Creating Board' as a Master of Management program, where Professor Tore Bråthen shares responsibility for the academic content with me. Morten Huse is also a very important contributor to the program. As mentioned above, the interest in boards of directors has increased over the years, and at the Norwegian Business School we have also developed non-credit-bearing programs. These are shorter programs compared with the ones that give the students credits.

I am very proud of being part of this very important work concerning boards of directors. I strongly believe in education, including in this extremely complex field. It is necessary to do research on the topic, it is necessary to develop educational programs and it is necessary to teach and learn. There are too many people who think they can act as board members without any formal training. Of course this is possible, but learning more about the board of directors' focus and work will contribute to increased value creation in the companies. And that is what working as board members is all about.

7. Professionalizing boards: the work of the Professional Boards Forum

Elin Hurvenes

In Norway in 1993, there were only 3 percent women on our corporate boards. By 2002 this had risen to 6 percent. At that rate of growth, experts estimated it would take about 100 years to reach some resemblance of gender parity in Norwegian boardrooms.

If you were not in Norway when the women on boards quota legislation was first introduced you would be forgiven for assuming that the legislation received a warm welcome, that we in our egalitarian society simply embraced the concept of 40 percent women on our corporate boards as the natural next step. The truth is that there was a public outcry. The media reported strong objections to the law. Women came forward claiming they feared becoming second-class board members and maintained that they wanted to be appointed to boards on merit and not via quotas. This was despite the fact that boards up until that date had shown little, if any, interest in their merits.

Chairmen and investors, in fact most of the Norwegian business community, came forward opposing the quota law as a bad idea that would be impossible to implement, mainly due to a lack of qualified women candidates. One chairman explained to me: 'Women are not interested in board work. If they were interested, there would be more than six percent of them on our boards'. Others argued that 'women don't have relevant experience' and 'we don't know where to find them'.

It was the latter argument that directly led me to founding the Professional Boards Forum in 2003, Styrefaglig Møteplass. At the time, Norwegian board members were recruited from the circles of business associates and friends of chairmen, chief executive officers (CEOs), nomination committees and investors, and I realized that these key people all lacked networks with senior women. Men had networks with other men, women had networks with other women, and there was simply not enough overlap between these. Without really applying myself I was able to produce quite a good list of women who I thought would be an asset to almost any board. This led me to believe there were many more out there that I did not already know of. When I started looking seriously, I found there were many women in senior leadership roles who had been delivering excellent results for years. These women were not beating their own drums or drawing much attention to their achievements. Nor did they network with people who influenced board appointments, as there was no natural arena for them to meet. This is what I set out to generate: a forum where outstanding board-ready women could meet and get to know the people who were in charge of board appointments in Norway.

I spoke with a number of chairmen and investors who hitherto had no women on their boards in order to find out what they would be looking for should they ever consider appointing a woman. In general they narrowed it down to four items:

- a good first degree, preferably also an MBA;
- solid work experience or leadership experience of 20 years or more;
- CEO experience;
- board experience.

I knew women could easily deliver on the first two items but the last two prerequisites would effectively take them out of the race. It was puzzling to me how anyone, male or female, would ever make their first non-executive director appointment if past board experience were a prerequisite. Giving the number of men on Norwegian boards, I assumed that this was only a prerequisite for women. When I looked at the issue of CEO experience, I discovered that practically none of the Oslo Stock Exchange companies had boards where all board members had CEO experience. On the contrary, one chairman expressed horror at the thought, saying he would run a mile if asked to chair a board with seven CEOs: 'We'd never get anything done!'

It seemed to me that the lack of networks was holding women back, and that board appointments were a question not only of what you know but also who you know. A board appointment is about skills and experience, but also a matter of confidence and trust. The former chairman of DnBNOR Bank, incidentally one of the first companies to meet the quota, Mr Olav Hytta explained it to me beautifully: 'We look to appoint someone we know we can work with.'

To establish the Forum I was able to enlist support from the Ministry of Trade and Industry, Innovation Norway, venture capital firm Four Seasons Venture (now Verdane Capital), and several public listed companies including Eiendomspar ASA, Telenor ASA, Hydro ASA, Hafslund

ASA and Visma ASA. Having seen their attitude expressed in the media, I was very pleased to find quite a number of chairmen, CEOs and investors with a genuine interest and an open approach to the idea of the Professional Boards Forum.

The first Forum was hosted in Oslo in September 2004. Fifty carefully selected senior women participated. They were all leaders in their fields and represented a diverse range of backgrounds and experiences. I tried to avoid the 'usual suspects', that is, the women who were already on boards and well known. This was about raising the profiles and visibility of clever and experienced women who were not already in the public eye.

Right from the start I had wanted to give the Professional Boards Forum events a structure designed to give the women a chance to excel and to give the chairmen an instant insight into the skills and abilities these women might bring to a board. This proved a successful formula. In my experience, women are not very good at self-promotion, but put a task in front of them and you will see them excel and comfortably demonstrate their skills and insights. Twenty-five chairmen, CEOs, investors and nomination committee members participated and the event came off fantastically with one of the sponsors describing the atmosphere as 'euphoric'. One of the national networks sent a TV reporter and crew to interview chairmen and candidates, and we made the national evening news and also got write-ups in all the major papers. To my delight, one of the candidates was offered a board position following this high-profile exposure.

The feedback was excellent from chairmen, women and sponsors alike, with several chairmen claiming surprise at the abundance of talented women, saying they had had no idea they existed. This comment has been a regular one at most events, and even though it is sad that women in this day and age are still invisible, I am always pleased to help raise their profiles.

Based on the good feedback and huge interest I went on to host 14 forum events in Norway, mainly in Oslo but also in Bergen, Stavanger, Trondheim and Moss. They always received the kind support of the Norwegian business community. After the first two events, I traced the board progress of the women candidates and found that 50 percent of them got new board roles within 18 months of attending the forum.

After my careful vetting of all candidates I was keen to learn why some were successful and others were not, considering that they all shared good credentials and experience. From conversations with the candidates a very clear picture emerged: women with no new board roles had 'defocused' from the boardroom quest and gave the following reasons:

- a new and time-consuming job;
- new executive appointment or promotion;
- employer did not permit them to accept board roles;
- new baby;
- illness, divorce or house move;
- elderly parents.

It also transpired that whereas men, in the past, had simply informed their employer that they were taking on a non-executive role, women asked for permission. Employers, given this option, often refused permission on the grounds of conflict of interest or by saying that the workload of being a non-executive director was not compatible with the women's day job.

The women who had successfully got onto boards also had several things in common. They had all:

- been vocal about their aspirations to become a non-executive director;
- used their networks and expanded these extensively at every opportunity;
- enlisted help from mentors;
- participated in arenas where they would meet investors and chairmen;
- been proactive and spent a considerable amount of time positioning themselves for a non-executive director's role;
- been very determined that a board role was the next step and been prepared to work hard to achieve this.

My experience in the UK, where there is no quota legislation, echoes the Norwegian experience, and has led me to conclude that women wishing to secure board roles must be proactive and do most of the work themselves.

In the months leading up to the 1 January 2008 deadline, the world media turned its attention to Norway and the firms that were not yet in compliance with the 40 percent quota. However, as expected, they all met the quota; there were no closures or delistings from the Oslo Stock Exchange. In fact, I am very impressed by the Norwegian business community; this was a law few welcomed, and the opposition was fierce. However, Norwegian companies were able to absorb and adjust to the new regime in a very short period of time. They took on the challenge of finding competent women for their boards, and succeeded.

Today it is business as usual in Norway and the merits of a gender-balanced board are no longer a big issue. To illustrate this I instigated and hosted the international conference 'Board Impact – Leveraging Diversity' in October 2010. The conference was in cooperation with the Norwegian Ministry for Trade and Industry, the Ministry for Children, Gender and Social Inclusion, the Ministry for Foreign Affairs, the Grieg Group, McKinsey & Co., DLA Piper and PwC. We brought together leading chairmen, CEOs, politicians and investors as well as male and female board members who all shared their experiences following the quota legislation. The website is still running and all the material from the conference as well as media reports can be viewed on www.board impact.com.

One of the main conclusions from chairmen and investors was that whereas they still opposed the idea of gender quotas, they were highly content with the results and happy with the contributions made by the women board members. They also agreed that gender parity in the boardroom:

- increased the level of pre-meeting preparation from all board members;
- added to the width and the quality of the boardroom discussions even though discussions could be more time-consuming;
- created a more open and less competitive atmosphere;
- led to more informed decision-making processes, hence reducing risk.

I often refer to this conclusion when speaking on this issue abroad and offer what I call 'the Norwegian Acid Test': would we, if the legislation were abolished today, revert back to 6 percent women on Norwegian corporate boards? I think we know the answer is no.

As Norway met the 40 percent target in 2008, I assumed my home market was saturated and with my MBA colleague from London Business School, Jane Scott, I set up the Forum in the UK. With no quota legislation to support the progress of women onto UK boards, several board experts warned that there would be no interest in the UK for this type of activity. Despite these warnings we were able to secure involvement and commitment to the Forum from leading UK chairmen such as Sir Philip Hampton (Royal Bank of Scotland), Sir Roger Carr (Centrica), Sir Rob Margetts (former chair of Legal & General) and Sir John Bond (former chair of Vodafone), and this sparked the interest of other chairmen. In May 2009, we were in a position to welcome

25 FTSE 100/250 chairmen to the inaugural event where they met, worked and networked with 50 outstanding women executives.

Since the start of the work in the UK, we have hosted six forums with the support of leading corporations such as Vodafone plc, RBS Group plc, Accenture, PwC, Anglo-American plc, Pearson plc, Deutsche Bank, Hogan Lovells, BoardEx and Cmi. So far, more than 35 non-executive director roles have been awarded to the Forum alumni. Of all the 2010 appointments to the FTSE 100 boards, 18 percent were Forum alumni, which I think is a great result. However, the main credit is due to the women who are actively pursuing board careers, putting themselves forward for non-executive director roles, and doing all the groundbreaking work. A list of their achievements can be found on www. boardsforum.co.uk under 'New Appointments'. In 2012 the Professional Boards Forum expanded to the Netherlands, where the first event was held in November 2012.

Further developments are also taking place in Norway where the Forum, in cooperation with the Leadership Foundation and Lisa Cooper, will host a special Professional Boards Forum event for foreign nationals living and working in Norway. Many of them have valuable international leadership experience yet their skills and backgrounds have not been utilized by Norwegian boards. Many of them find themselves in the same position as Norwegian women prior to the quota legislation; they lack networks to people who influence board appointments and knowledge of how the recruiting processes work. More information can be found on www.styrefagligmoteplass.no or www.elinhurvenes.com.

8. The Swiss case of women on boards of directors

Christine Wetli

In Switzerland women are still underrepresented on corporate boards of directors (Amacher, 2009; Ethos, 2011). In 2011, there were 10 percent women on boards of directors in Switzerland and during the following two years there has not been any significant change (Schillingreport, 2011, pp. 14–15). Almost one-third of the female board members are from abroad and 92 percent have a university degree compared to 88 percent of the male board members (Schillingreport, 2011, pp. 4–5).

Although there have been several attempts to introduce a gender quota, following the example of Norway (Bundesversammlung, 2003a), none of these has been successful. However, as this chapter tries to demonstrate, other measures are taken in order to increase the percentage of women on corporate boards of directors in Switzerland:

1. The IFPM Center for Corporate Governance of the University of St Gallen founded the Female Board Pool (FBP), which is 'a platform for the contact between experienced and future female board members and corporations' (Female Board Pool, 2011a, 2012; Institute for Leadership and Human Resource Management, 2006; 2011, p. 20).
2. From 2012 onwards, it is planned to publish an index listing the companies with the most women on their boards and in their top management teams.
3. Finally, the Center has also developed best-practice guidelines for small and medium-sized enterprises in which a certain representation of women on boards, depending on the size of the company, is recommended (IFPM Center for Corporate Governance, 2009).

Not only does this chapter explain the three measures trying to increase the representation of women on boards of directors in Switzerland, but it also discusses the several efforts at introducing a quota in Switzerland.

QUOTA ATTEMPTS

Switzerland has seen several attempts to introduce a gender quota legislation in publicly listed companies and government-owned companies. However, none of these has proven successful and there is no indication that the Swiss government will introduce a gender quota in the near future (Spencer Stuart, 2011).

The first attempt, in the form of a parliamentary initiative, took place in 2003 when a member of the Parliament suggested implementing a quota of 40 percent women on boards and in top management positions in publicly listed companies (Bundesversammlung, 2003a; Amtliches Bulletin, 2004). The initiative was declined, although the commission agreed that there were too few women on boards of directors and in the top management of such companies (Nationalrat, 2003). However, a quota regulation was not considered as an adequate instrument in order to remedy the underrepresentation of women on the board of directors (Nationalrat, 2003). Other criteria such as education and industrial know-how should be taken into account when it comes to the selection of board members (Nationalrat, 2003).

In the same year, another parliamentary initiative was submitted that asked for at least 30 percent women or men, respectively, on boards of directors of partly government-owned companies (Bundesversammlung, 2003b). This initiative was also dismissed at a later stage, as it was seen as too large a restriction on the autonomy of these types of companies, which compete after all with the private sector (Nationalrat, 2008).

Five years later, in 2008, another initiative was launched. Its objective was to have at least 30 percent women or men (as applicable) on boards of publicly listed and partly state-owned companies (Bundesversammlung, 2008). Again, the initiative failed (Nationalrat, 2009).

In the following year, in 2009, another motion demanding at least 40 percent women on boards (or men, respectively) in all companies with more than 200 employees was submitted (Bundesversammlung, 2009). The focus of the argument was that the financial crisis could have been partly avoided if there had been more women in top decision-making positions (Bundesversammlung, 2009). Again, this initiative failed, mainly because it was argued that the election of board members should remain in the responsibility of the general assembly (Bundesversammlung, 2009). Furthermore, the quota regulation would restrict companies in their selection process, which cannot be combined with the liberal company law in Switzerland (Bundesversammlung, 2009).

Given the fact that none of these efforts at legal quota regimes were successful, other non-legal measures may be more promising in increasing the percentage of women on boards of directors in Switzerland. In the following part of the chapter, such instruments are discussed.

FEMALE BOARD POOL

In 2011 at a meeting with leading European business schools, Viviane Reding, Vice-President of the European Commission, stated that: 'We need to start from the "bottom"; we need to ensure that women get the best training from the start so that they can climb up the corporate ladder … We need to create a pool of talented women, a pool of the next generation of female leaders … [and] business schools hold the key' (*Financial Times*, 2011). In this respect, she mentioned the Female Board Pool as an example of how business schools can take such actions (*Financial Times*, 2011).

The Female Board Pool, founded by Martin Hilb from the IFPM Center for Corporate Governance of the University of St Gallen, is a platform aiming to facilitate contact among experienced and future women board members and companies (Female Board Pool, 2011a; Amacher, 2009; Institute for Leadership and Human Resource Management, 2011). Today, the Female Board Pool is starting to operate in Luxembourg (Knott, 2011; www.femaleboardpool.eu). The objective of the Female Board Pool is to contribute to a significant 'increase of the percentage of competent and committed women at the Board of Directors level of corporations' (Female Board Pool, 2011b). 'This goal should be achieved by finding, promoting, connecting and matching female board members' (Female Board Pool, 2011b).

The Female Board Pool offers three main services (Female Board Pool, 2012; Institute for Leadership and Human Resource Management, 2006, 2011):

1. Board seminars for experienced and future female board members.
2. Female board network meetings for experienced and future female board members.
3. Offering female board candidates to companies based on an electronic information database which currently contains more than 400 members both from the Female Board Network of the IFPM Center for Corporate Governance and various Swiss companies.

BEST PRACTICE IN SMES

Following the encouragement of federal councillor Doris Leuthard, the IFPM Center for Corporate Governance has developed recommendations for the Direction and Control of Small and Medium-sized Enterprises (IFPM Center for Corporate Governance, 2009; Institute for Leadership and Human Resource Management, 2009). With regards to the constitution of the board the guidelines suggest that the board of directors 'should function as a team on the basis of culture of trust' (IFPM Center for Corporate Governance, 2009, p. 7). And as such, the guidelines recommend at least one female member in smaller enterprises, and two to three women board directors in larger companies. 'This is to assure more success relevant diversity in the decision-taking process' (IFPM Center for Corporate Governance, 2009, p. 7). These guidelines should help increase the percentage of women on boards of directors (Institute for Leadership and Human Resource Management, 2009).

CONCLUSION

As has been shown, quota legislations do not seem to work (as yet) for Switzerland. Hence other measures could be taken in order to increase the number of females in the corporate boardrooms. That is why the IFPM Center for Corporate Governance of the University of St Gallen has implemented various tools such as the Female Board Pool or the 'Best Practice' guidelines for small and medium-sized enterprises.

REFERENCES

Amacher, C. (2009) Der Weg in den Verwaltungsrat. *Women in Business*, Dec. 2009/Jan. 2010 (3): 30–34.

Amtliches Bulletin (2004) Parlamentarische Initiative Teuscher Franziska: Mehr Frauen in die Leitungen von Aktiengesellschaften, available from http://www.parlament.ch/ab/frameset/d/n/4705/112699/d_n_4705_112699_112700.htm (accessed 14 July 2011).

Bundesversammlung (2003a) 03.412 – Parlamentarische Initiative: Mehr Frauen in die Leitungen von Aktiengesellschaften, available from http://www.parlament.ch/D/Suche/Seiten/geschaefte.aspx?gesch_id=20030412 (accessed 14 July 2011).

Bundesversammlung (2003b) 03.440 – Parlamentarische Initiative: Mehr Frauen in Verwaltungsräten von Gesellschaften mit Bundesbeteiligungen, available from http://www.parlament.ch/D/Suche/Seiten/geschaefte.aspx?gesch_id=200 30440 (accessed 14 July 2011).

Bundesversammlung (2008) 08.510 – Parlamentarische Initiative: Mehr Frauen in den Verwaltungsräten, available from http://www.parlament.ch/d/suche/seiten/geschaefte.aspx?gesch_id=20080510 (accessed 22 December 2011).

Bundesversammlung (2009) 09.3067 – Motion: Frauen in alle Verwaltungsräte, available from http://www.parlament.ch/d/suche/seiten/geschaefte.aspx?gesch_id=20093067 (accessed 13 July 2011).

Female Board Pool (2011a) Home, available from http://www.female-board-pool.com/en.html (accessed 7 December 2011).

Female Board Pool (2011b) Our goal, available from http://www.female-board-pool.com/en/about-us/our-goal.html (accessed 7 December 2011).

Female Board Pool (2012) Unsere Leistungen, available from http://www.female-board-pool.com/de/unsere-leistungen.html (accessed 12 January 2012).

Financial Times (2011) Call to arms for Europe's women, available from http://www.ft.com/intl/cms/s/2/8850f164-f0cb-11e0-aec8-00144feab49a.html#axzz1hGZW8756 (accessed 22 December 2011).

IFPM Center for Corporate Governance (2009) Best Practice in SME, available from http://www.ccg.ifpm.unisg.ch/~/media/Internet/Content/Dateien/InstituteUndCenters/IFPM/BestPractice_en.ashx (accessed 22 December 2011).

Institute for Leadership and Human Resource Management (2006) Jahresbericht 2006, available from http://www.ifpm.unisg.ch/de/About+us/~/media/Internet/Content/Dateien/InstituteUndCenters/IFPM/Jahresbericht%202006.ashx (accessed 17 January 2012)

Institute for Leadership and Human Resource Management (2009) Jahresbericht 2009, available from http://www.ifpm.unisg.ch/de/About+us/~/media/Internet/Content/Dateien/InstituteUndCenters/IFPM/Jahresbericht%202009.ashx (accessed 22 December 2011).

Institute for Leadership and Human Resource Management (2011) Female Board Pool, available from http://www.ifpm.unisg.ch/de/Centers/Female+Board+Pool.aspx (accessed 22 December 2011).

Knott, R. (2011) Female Board Pool to be launched in Luxembourg, available from http://www.mega.public.lu/actualites/actu_min/2011/03/female_board_pool/programme.pdf (accessed 22 December 2011).

Nationalrat (2003) 03.412 n Mehr Frauen in die Leitungen von Aktiengesellschaften, available from http://www.parlament.ch/afs/data/d/bericht/2003/d_bericht_n_k12_0_20030412_0_20031103.htm (accessed 22 December 2011).

Nationalrat (2008) 03.440 n Pa.Iv. Hearing. Mehr Frauen in Verwaltungsräten von Gesellschaften mit Bundesbeteiligungen, available from http://www.parlament.ch/afs/data/d/bericht/2003/d_bericht_n_k12_0_20030440_0_20080403.htm (accessed 14 July 2011).

Nationalrat (2009) 08.510 n Pa.Iv. Roth-Bernasconi. Mehr Frauen in den Verwaltungsräten, available from http://www.parlament.ch/afs/data/d/bericht/2008/ d_bericht_n_k12_0_20080510_0_20090626.htm (accessed 2 December 2011).

Schillingreport (2011) Transparenz an der Spitze. Die Geschäftsleitungen und Verwaltungsräte der hundert grössten Schweizer Unternehmen im Vergleich, available from http://www.schillingreport.ch/upload/public/5/4173/schilling report_2011_D.pdf (accessed 7 December 2011).

Spencer Stuart (2011) Female Director Trends in Europe – 2011, available from http://www.spencerstuart.com/research/1551 (accessed 14 December 2011).

9. Boards and role models for supporting the climb upwards: Italy and Women Corporate Directors (WCD)

Cristina Finocchi Mahne

To increase the number of women on corporate boards, actions should focus on existing cultural constraints, boosting role models, favoring a change in the public depiction of women and reinforcing individual capabilities related to social capital tools.

The attention to female leadership is increasing worldwide. In developing countries, a more important role for women is considered to provide higher social stability and to limit the level of aggression in society. In developed economies, going through recession, executive female contribution is considered an opportunity to exploit in exiting the crisis. But in spite of recognizing the importance of a higher presence of women in top positions, the gender gap still exists in these posts around the world. Research (Soares et al., 2011) offers statistics showing that men still dominate: women held 51 percent of positions in the US labor force employed in management and professions, but only 14 percent of chief executive positions are held by women – with only 4 percent in Fortune 500 companies.

A study conducted for several years ('Women Matter' by McKinsey, 2012) highlighted how few women held top management and board positions in European companies. The study analyzed the trend of women's representation on corporate boards and executive committees four years on, from 2007 to 2011, in nine main European countries: Italy, Norway, the UK, Germany, France, Belgium, the Netherlands, Sweden and the Czech Republic.

In eight out of nine countries, there are now more women on corporate boards: 20 percent of board members in France, and 16 percent in Germany and the UK, for example, are women; compared, respectively, with 8, 11 and 12 percent in 2007. In the Netherlands, the figure stands at

19 percent, compared with 7 percent four years earlier. We expect that at least some of this effect is related to the introduction of legally binding quotas in several countries, including Norway, Belgium, France and Italy, and non-binding ones in others. In most countries, however, quotas have only recently been introduced and companies have several years to comply. Hence, quotas cannot be credited with all the progress to date. Prominent public debate has played a part too. Norway, which introduced a quota system in 2008, has the highest proportion of women sitting on its boards. Sweden, with the second-highest proportion, has no quotas. On average, women now hold 17 percent of the seats on the boards in these nine countries, 5 percentage points higher than in 2007.

But women's representation is lower where it perhaps matters most: on executive committees. On average, women now hold 10 percent of executive committee roles in the nine countries, compared with 4 percent four years ago. But in none of the countries has the percentage of women on these committees grown at the same rate as in corporate boards over the four-year period. Indeed, given current growth rates, the proportion of women sitting on Europe's executive committees will still be less than 20 percent by 2022.

Most discussion and analysis about women's representation in business focuses on boards and, to a lesser extent, on executive committees. What often goes unmentioned is the pipeline that can feed those positions. The problem is not only at the top: women are increasingly outnumbered as they rise through the ranks.

Among more than 1000 directors from around the world surveyed by Groysberg and Bell (2012), 45 percent of men versus 18 percent of women believed that the lack of women in executive ranks is the primary reason that the percentage of women on boards is limited. As the top reason why there were not more women on boards, women respondents cited that 'traditional networks tend to be male-oriented'.

The odds of advancement at the highest hierarchical posts for men are much higher than those for women. Research (McKinsey, 2012) shows that although in many, but not all, companies a fair share of women are being recruited, they become increasingly underrepresented as they move higher up the organization. This is a discouraging finding if it serves as any measure of future female representation on executive committees. It is worth asking the question why.

As Eagly and Carli (2007) point out, the conservative mindset does not take into sufficient consideration that the obstacles women face are socially constructed. Organizational structures and persistent stereotypes still support gender discrimination, and limit professional careers for women whose desire for leadership is equal to that of men, while role models work as source of inspiration with a transformational impact on an individual or team.

A recent extensive survey (Ernst & Young, 2012) of 1000 UK professional women shows that two-thirds believe they faced multiple barriers throughout their careers, rather than just a single ceiling on entry to the boardroom. Three out of four (75 percent) of those questioned said that they have few or no female role models within their organizations, with some respondents (8 percent) going as far as to say that a lack of role models had had a detrimental impact on their career to date. And therefore role models were identified as one of the key barriers. A lack of role models was a consistent theme across all the age groups polled.

For there to be a further boost to cultural change that can modify current stereotypes, there is a also need to work through good role models. They represent an effective tool for change in a challenging economic environment as they act at a subconscious rather than a rational level.

Having female leadership in key sectors makes the idea of female authority in that role more natural. This will happen all the faster if there are more women in top positions in the most powerful sectors, the ones that exercise most influence over the collective mindset: politics, the media and finance. Politics matters because it sets the path for future generations. The media is important because it influences peoples' attitudes and values. Finance is pivotal because it is the custodian of the resources that fuel growth.

Christine Lagarde, Managing Director of the International Monetary Fund, represents a significant example in terms of role models in this sector. But the current strong debate on having a woman in the management committee of the European Central Bank, while having no women in the top leading positions in the whole financial system, shows that there is still a long way to go.

Different sectors have leaks and blockages in different parts of the pipeline. In financial services, for example, almost half of all employees are women, but their representation shrinks by more than half at middle management level. By contrast, in those sectors where there are fewer women overall, such as transport and logistics as well as energy and basic materials, women have a relatively good chance of promotion to middle management and beyond. For example, women hold 11 percent of the places on the executive committees of the companies in the McKinsey study in energy and basic materials, the same as in consumer goods, despite these having proportionally fewer women in their organizations.

FEMALE STEREOTYPES, ROLE MODELS AND PUBLIC DEPICTION

President Richard Nixon, recorded on White House audiotapes made public through the Freedom of Information Act, when explaining why he would not appoint a woman to the US Supreme Court said, 'I don't think a woman should be in any government job whatsoever mainly because they are erratic. And emotional. Men are erratic and emotional, too, but the point is a woman is more likely to be.' In a culture where such opinions and stereotypes were widely held, women had virtually no chance of attaining influential leadership roles. Even though now there is substantial and recent scientific evidence against such prejudices (Barber and Odean, 2001; Eckel and Grossman, 2002; Levi and Li, 2010) women continue to be portrayed in this way in the media, where they are also underrepresented.

Recent research in the US (Lauzen, 2011) highlighted that women's occupations, determining the content of news and entertainment media, have consistently been characterized by a lower presence of women with little change in proportions over time. And women also have been underrepresented in screen roles. When films and television do depict female characters, they often reflect gender stereotypes. Women in films, particularly young women, are far more likely than men to be hyper-sexualized (Lauzen and Dozier, 2005).

Underrepresentation and negative depictions in media have broad societal effects. Trepte (2006) summarized several results as demonstrating that 'Media entertainment functions as a source of information on groups and their legitimate status.' How women are represented in media affects gender equality in general. It is important, then, to determine the causes of underrepresentation and stereotypical depiction and to develop practical approaches to improving the status quo. Mainly men seem to be entrusted with the public depiction of women and that needs to be changed.

As far as leadership in general is concerned, people view female leaders less favorably than male leaders. And as studies show (Burgess and Borgida, 1999; Heilman and Okimoto, 2007), success and likeability are positively correlated for men and negatively correlated for women.

Psychologists use the 'Big Five Personality Traits' (Barrick and Mount, 1991) to describe an individual's personality through five dimensions: extraversion, emotional stability, agreeableness, conscientiousness and openness to experiences. Eagly and Carly (2007) showed that the traits that contribute the most to effective leadership behavior (extraversion, openness to experience and conscientiousness) are similar in women and men, while women have a stronger degree of emotional intelligence and empathy than men, which helps in managerial tasks. Although men exhibit more risk-taking behavior, women are less likely to engage in unethical and criminal behavior. But where women are really weaker in comparison to their male colleagues is building social capital: networking and international relations are a key tool to climb the top and women need to reinforce individual capabilities related to those social capital tools.

ITALY: WHAT CHANGE BESIDES THE GENDER QUOTA LAW?

In Italy, the latest figures related to women's presence on corporate boards show that 9 percent of board members of listed companies are women, compared with 3 percent in 2007 and 5 percent in 2011 (Bank of Italy, 2012; Sacchi, 2012). A quite impressive increase was generated by the gender quota law, approved in 2011, while it remains quite surprising that there are no women chief executive officers (CEOs) among the most important companies listed on the Italian Stock Exchange which make up the FTSE MIB 40 index.

As far as role models in Italy are concerned, what has happened in the most influential sectors? In politics an important step in this direction was the appointment of three prominent and highly reputed women to key ministerial posts: Justice (Paola Severino, Ministro della Giustizia), Labor (Elsa Fornero, Ministro del Lavoro) and the Interior (Annamaria Cancellieri, Ministro degli Interni). And in particular the Minister of Justice, besides being a respected and successful lawyer, turned out to be the highest taxpayer in the Cabinet with an annual income of €7 million.

In finance, in the last 15 years the number of top positions held by women in the banking sector has risen from 2 percent to 7 percent. But still today 60 percent of banks in Italy have no women in significant positions. Their presence is much lower than in other sectors, and significantly lower than in other European Union (EU) countries, where the record is hardly impressive.

In the media, the current Chair of RAI, Italy's national state-owned broadcasting company, is a highly regarded woman who explicitly targeted a change in women's image as a goal for state TV. And in a country where there has never been a woman editor of the most important newspapers, for the first time currently two out of three major

Italian editorial groups are led by women (L'Espresso Group and Il Sole 24 Ore Group).

THE ITALIAN CHAPTER OF WOMEN CORPORATE DIRECTORS (WCD)

The Women Corporate Directors (WCD) represents an interesting example of how to develop and valorize a global female board member network that can effectively impact on social and business constraints in order to increase the number of women in the boardrooms.

WCD is the international membership organization and community of women corporate directors, comprising more than 2000 members serving on over 3500 boards in 54 chapters around the world. In 2012, WCD launched the Global Nominating Commission, a high-level task force of select corporate board nomination committee chairs and members from around the world, as well as CEOs, focused on proactively building diverse boards and candidate slates. This association represents a sophisticated social capital tool at international level. Susan Stautberg is WCD Co-Founder and Global Co-Chair.

The Italian chapter (co-chaired by myself and Prof. Marina Brogi,Vice Dean of the Faculty of Economics at Rome University La Sapienza, the largest in Europe, and member of WCD's Global Nominating Commission) is an example of a refined social capital tool related to governance, a female institutional and corporate perspective at the top, through a forceful convergence across the leading women in the country.

Among the 11 members of the steering committee, in addition to Co-Chairs, are the following:

- Elsa Fornero, first woman Minister of Labor;
- Anna Maria Tarantola, former first woman Deputy General Manager of the Bank of Italy, now President of Rai (Italy's national state-owned broadcasting company);
- Livia Pomodoro, first woman President of the Court of Milan;
- Carla Rabitti Bedogni, Professor of Financial Market Law at Sapienza and first woman member of Italy's Antitrust Authority;
- Lucia Calvosa, Professor of Commercial Law at Pisa University and Independent Director of Telecom Italia (approximately €15 billion market cap);
- Lucrezia Reichlin, Professor of Economics at London Business School and Independent Director of Unicredit (Italy's most international bank, approximately €20 billion market cap);

- Cristina Rossello, Lawyer, Independent Director at Mondadori (one of Italy's main publishing company, €300 million market cap);
- Luisa Spagnoli, CEO of Nicoletta Spagnoli (one of Italy's largest privately held fashion groups);
- Donatella Treu, CEO of Gruppo Sole 24 Ore (which publishes Italy's top business daily newspaper).

WCD members sit on boards representing 26 percent of the total market capitalization of the Milan stock exchange and that is a tremendous success considering that companies representing 35 percent of market capitalization have no women on their boards.

REFERENCES

Bank of Italy (2012) *Annual Report 2011*, pp. 118–120, available from http://www.bancaditalia.it/pubblicazioni/relann (accessed 7 January 2013).

Barber, B.M. and Odean, T. (2001) Boys will be boys: Gender, overconfidence and common stock investment, *Quarterly Journal of Economics*, 116(1): 261–292.

Barrick, M.R. and Mount, M. (1991), The big personality dimensions and job performance: A meta-analysis, *Personnel Psychology*, 44(1): 1–26.

Burgess, D. and Borgida, E. (1999) Who women are, who women should be: Descriptive and prescriptive gender stereotyping in sex discrimination, *Psychology, Public Policy, and Law*, 5(3): 665–692.

Eagly, A.H. and Carli, L.L. (2007) *Through the Labyrinth: The Truth About How Women Become Leaders*, Cambridge MA: Harvard Business Press.

Eckel, C. and Grossman, P. (2002) Sex differences and statistical stereotyping in attitudes toward financial risk, Working Papers published in *Evolution and Human Behavior*, 23(4): 281–295, University of Texas Richardson, available from http://papers.ssrn.com/sol3/papers.cfm?abstract_id=1843509.

Ernst &Young (2012) Survey: The glass ceiling is an outdated concept, available from http://www.ey.com/Publication/vwLUAssets/The-glass-ceiling-is-dead-as-a-concept-for-todays-modern-career/$FILE/FINAL_INFOGRAPHIC.pdf.

Groysberg, B. and Bell, D. (2012) *Third Annual Global Board of Directors Survey 2012*, Women Corporate Directors, New York: Heidrick & Struggles, available from http://www.womencorporatedirectors.com/associations/9942/files/2012_BOD_Survey_Report_FINAL.pdf .

Heilman, M. and Okimoto, T.G. (2007) Why are women penalized for success at male tasks? The implied communality deficit, *Journal of Applied Psychology*, 92(1): 81–92.

Lauzen, M.M. (2011) The celluloid ceiling: Behind-the-scenes employment of women on the top 250 films of 2010. White Paper, Center for the Study of Women in Television and Film, San Diego State University US, available from http://womenintvfilm.sdsu.edu/files/2011_Celluloid_Ceiling_Exec_Summ.pdf.

Lauzen, M.M. and Dozier, D. (2005) Maintaining the double standard: Portrayals of age and gender in popular films. *Sex Roles*, 52(7/8), San Diego State University US, available from http://link.springer.com/article/10.1007/s11199-005-3710-1#page-1.

Levi, M. and Li, K. (2010) Deal or no deal: Hormones and the mergers and acquisitions, *Management Science*, 56(9): 1462–1483.

McKinsey Research (2012) *Women Matter*, available from http://www.mckinsey.com/features/women_matter.

Trepte, S. (2006) Social identity theory, Working Paper, University of Hamburg, Hamburg, Germany, available from http://www.uni-hamburg.de/fachbereiche-einrichtungen/medienpsychologie/trepte_2006.pdf.

Sacchi, M.T. (2012) *Donne ai vertici nelle aziende*, Corriere della Sera book, Milan: Rcs Media Group.

Soares, R., Cobb, B., Lebow, E., Regis, A., Winsten, H., and Wojnas, V. (2011) *2011 Catalyst Census: Fortune 500 Women Directors*, Catalyst: New York.

10. Research and considerations regarding women on boards

Heather Foust-Cummings

In 2012, Catalyst celebrated the fiftieth anniversary of its founding. Established as an organization devoted to helping educated married women and mothers return to the workforce, Catalyst has seen progress over the years for women and advancement opportunities at work. Yet at the highest levels of corporations, women's rate of progress has not kept pace with other demographic developments. For example, in 2012, while women comprised more than 50 percent of the managerial and professional labor force in the United States (Catalyst, 2012a), they represented only 16.1 percent of Fortune 500 board directors (Soares et al., 2011). Indeed, over the past few years, women's representation on corporate boards has generally stagnated below 20 percent, not only in the United States (Catalyst, 2012b), but globally (Catalyst, 2011a).

The notable exceptions to women's less-than-stellar representation in the boardroom are in those countries where, through legislation or policy regulation, the state has intervened to establish quotas or targets that require certain types of companies to achieve some measure of gender diversity on their boards (Catalyst, 2012c). In these countries, significant change is apparent, as many chapters in this volume attest. In Norway, for example, representation of women on boards has surged to just over 40 percent (Catalyst, 2011a). In Australia, where the Australian Stock Exchange enacted a 'comply or explain' approach to increasing gender diversity on boards (Catalyst, 2011a), the percentage of women appointed to boards has increased far more rapidly than prior to the comply-or-explain policy taking effect (Australian Institute of Directors, 2012).

Catalyst's formal position on quotas is as follows: 'To compete and flourish in the global economy, business must leverage the talents of its very best women. The means may vary – the key is that it gets done. Until women achieve parity in business leadership roles, they will be marginalized in every other arena. Quotas are one proven strategy to boost diversity on top.' Regardless of one's opinion regarding quotas, targets, and voluntary efforts, the business case for getting more women into corporate leadership roles is clear: to compete and flourish in the global economy, companies must leverage the talents of all their employees. Firms cannot rely on old ways of doing business when the corporate landscape as well as the global economy has been, and continues to be, transformed (Pellegrino et al., 2011). Given this evidence, corporate leaders need to take a hard look at the teams they are assembling, the succession plans they are developing, the career-catapulting opportunities they are assigning, and the people they are sponsoring, as each of these factors plays a critical role in shaping the company's future. If there is little to no diversity among people getting the prime assignments, being sponsored (Foust-Cummings et al., 2011), appearing in the succession plan, assuming leadership roles and serving on the board, then the company and its future are placed at significant risk (Simkins et al., 2012).

Indeed, there is ample evidence that diversity, well managed, has many positive benefits for companies (Catalyst 2011b), ranging from greater engagement and satisfaction among employees (HR Solutions International, 2007) to teams' better problem-solving ability (Woolley et al., 2010) and increased creativity (Higgs et al., 2005). When it comes to corporate boards specifically, diversity similarly boasts benefits. Perhaps the greatest difficulty in establishing more fully the benefits of gender-diverse boards is the lack of such boards. Clearly, getting women into the boardroom continues to be a significant hurdle in countries and companies worldwide. Thus, specifying precisely how women's presence does, or does not, affect board tasks, outcomes and effectiveness largely remains to be seen. Research on this front will undoubtedly continue as boardrooms see the addition of women in more substantive numbers. Nevertheless, the proportion of women board directors has been linked to decreased levels of board conflict and increased quality of board development activities (Nielsen and Huse, 2010). Research also has shown that when women directors are present, men temper masculine behavior, and the boardroom environment becomes more effective (Singh, 2008). Moreover, research by Catalyst (Joy, 2008) and others (for example Matsa and Miller, 2011) has demonstrated a relationship between higher representation of women on boards and greater representation of women in companies' executive officer ranks. These findings, in particular, present compelling evidence for those concerned with increasing women's representation on boards and in corporate leadership, as well as those interested in establishing a more robust pipeline of diverse talent.

How do companies go about getting more women into boardrooms and positions of executive leadership and developing more robust talent pipelines? Catalyst believes that one of the keys to advancing women and building a better pipeline of diverse talent is men (Prime and Moss-Racusin, 2009). Men have a crucial role to play in developing broader talent pools, creating more inclusive workplace cultures, and championing well-qualified women by acting as sponsors, mentors, role models and inclusive leaders. However, Catalyst research indicates that many men are not aware of the gender inequities women face in the workplace (Prime and Moss-Racusin, 2009), which creates a significant barrier to men becoming more vocal advocates on behalf of women and for inclusion. Even when men do acknowledge that gender inequities in the workplace exist, men face other hurdles, such as feeling neither knowledgeable about gender issues nor confident in how to address them (Prime et al., 2012). These barriers suggest that opportunities for learning about gender gaps and building skills to address them are critical to empowering men to be advocates for gender equity in the workplace (Prime et al., 2012).

In spite of the hurdles women and men face in achieving more gender-equitable workplaces, Catalyst is encouraged by the recent momentum around the issue of getting more women onto boards. It feels to many observers that the momentum is shifting in favor of greater representation of women, which will benefit businesses by allowing them to be more responsive to and reflective of their clients, customers, consumers, and employees. And beyond making good business sense, greater gender balance on boards and in corporate leadership also is, quite simply, the right thing to do.

REFERENCES

Australian Institute of Directors (2012), Statistics, http://www.companydirectors.com.au/Director-Resource-Centre/Governance-and-Director-Issues/Board-Diversity/Statistics (accessed 6 February 2012).

Catalyst (2011a) Catalyst quick take: Women on boards, http://www.catalyst.org/publication/433/women-on-boards.

Catalyst (2011b) *Why Diversity Matters*, New York: Catalyst.

Catalyst (2012a) Catalyst quick take: US Women in Business, http://www.catalyst.org/publication/132/us-women-in-business.

Catalyst (2012b) Catalyst quick take: Women in US Management, http://catalyst.org/file/546/qt_women_in_us_management.pdf.

Catalyst (2012c) Increasing gender diversity on corporate boards: Current index of formal approaches, http://www.catalyst.org/publication/514/increasing-gender-diversity-on-boards-current-index-of-formal-approaches.

Foust-Cummings, H., Dinolfo, S. and Kohler, J. (2011) *Sponsoring Women to Success*, New York: Catalyst.

Higgs, M., Plewnia, U. and Ploch, J. (2005) Influence of team composition and task complexity on team performance, *Team Performance Management*, 11(7–8): 227–250.

HR Solutions International Inc. (2007) Attention to diversity pays off: A conversation with Murat Philippe, http://www.hrsolutionsinc.com/PDF/eBridges_Fall_07_final.pdf (accessed December 2012).

Joy, L. (2008) *Advancing Women Leaders*, New York: Catalyst.

Matsa, D.A. and Miller, A. (2011) Chipping away at the glass ceiling: Gender spillovers in the corporate leadership, RAND Corporation.

Nielsen, S. and Huse, M. (2010) The contribution of women on boards of directors: Going beyond the surface, *Corporate Governance: An International Review*, 18(2): 136–148.

Pellegrino, G., D'Amato, S. and Weisberg, A. (2011) The gender dividend: Making the business case for investing in women, Deloitte.

Prime, J., Foust-Cummings, H., Salib, E.R. and Moss-Racusin, C.A. (2012) *Calling All White Men: Can Training Help Create More Inclusive Workplaces?* New York: Catalyst.

Prime, J. and Moss-Racusin, C.A. (2009) *Engaging Men in Gender Initiatives: What Change Agents Need to Know*, New York: Catalyst.

Simkins, B.J., Lang, I.H. and Foust-Cummings, H. (2012) Does gender diversity on the board of directors improve risk governance? *Risk Watch*, Conference Board of Canada, pp. 14–17.

Singh, V. (2008) Transforming boardroom cultures in science, engineering and technology organizations, Resource Centre for Women in Science, Engineering and Technology, UK.

Soares, R., Cobb, B., Lebow, E., Regis, A., Winsten, H. and Wojnas, V. (2011), *2011 Catalyst Census: Fortune 500 Women Directors*, New York: Catalyst.

Woolley, A.W., Chabris, C.F., Pentland, A., Hashmi, N. and Malone, T. (2010) Collective intelligence: Number of women in group linked to effectiveness in solving difficult problems, *Science Daily*, 2 October.

11. Concluding remarks to Part II

Silke Machold

For the majority of countries, the right of women to vote and run for office is less than 100 years old. Oxford University only allowed women's admission in 1920 (www.ox.ac.uk), Cambridge followed even later in 1948 (Sutherland, 1994). The UN Convention on the Elimination of Discrimination against Women (also known as the International Bill of Rights for Women) did not come into force until 1981, and even today some countries have not yet signed up to the Convention. These examples show that it is only in fairly recent history that progress towards women's rights has been made, and much of that progress has been due to strong national and international movements advocating the rights of women.

In Part II, we have discussed a different kind of advocacy movement, specifically the various initiatives that are under way outside the immediate political arena to promote women on to boards. We focused in particular on the role of education, the creation of networks and networking opportunities, the provision of research and information, and the promotion of role models for women in leadership. These initiatives are in many obvious ways different from the women's rights advocacy movement, yet they all serve to publicize the debate and mainstream the practice of women on boards. In particular, we have argued that these various initiatives are essential parts of normative (professionalization) and mimetic (copying and replication) processes which in tandem with more formal approaches to gender diversity on boards bring about an institutionalization of the practice.

From the chapters in Part II, a number of lessons for practitioners emerge. First, promoting the case for women on boards is best done by also involving men. Hurvenes in Chapter 7 wrote 'Men had networks with other men, women had networks with other women, and there was simply not enough overlap between these.' The Professional Boards Forum she founded therefore deliberately set out to involve male and female actors, and the success of the initiative is evident to date in the recruitment of Forum participants to Norwegian ASA and UK FTSE 100 boards. Similar lessons about 'bringing men on board' are recounted by

Foust-Cummings (Chapter 10) in relation to talent management and the development of inclusive workplace cultures, and by Standal in Chapter 6 on training for board-level competences. Second, promoting the case for women on boards should not be seen in isolation; rather the topic is part of a broader agenda of women in leadership. Some scholars have noted that it is not so much a matter of women being confronted with a 'glass ceiling' but that women are experiencing numerous small and large obstacles in navigating through a maze in their efforts to attain leadership positions (Eagly and Carli, 2007). Finocchi Mahne and Foust-Cummings in Chapters 9 and 10, respectively, discuss strategies by means of which companies and other interested actors can help alleviate stereotypes and develop inclusive workplace cultures. Finally, much progress has been achieved through broad coalitions of actors – companies, membership-based and voluntary sector organizations, business schools and universities, and politicians. Whether it is in relation to developing networks, training for board members, increasing knowledge about the phenomenon, or lobbying for and evaluating formal policy approaches, the most impactful initiatives are those involving collaborative efforts. The contributors to Part II all highlighted different ways to operationalize such collaborative efforts to advocate for change and advance the case for women on boards.

REFERENCES

Eagly, A.H. and Carli, L.L. (2007) Women and the labyrinth of leadership, *Harvard Business Review*, 85(9): 63–71.
Sutherland, G. (1994) Emily Davies, the Sidgwicks and the education of women in Cambridge, in Mason, R. (ed.), *Cambridge Minds*, Cambridge: Cambridge University Press, pp. 34–47.

PART III

Norwegian board members: stories from the field

12. Characteristics and background of the Norwegian women directors

Morten Huse

Part III has two main objectives: (1) to explore the board compositional consequences of the Norwegian gender balance law; and (2) to provide background and illustrations about the women who have become board members in Norway. It contains the stories from some of the 'Golden Skirts', with emphasis on their own contributions, motivations and challenges. Part III contains stories from Ingvild Myhre, Merethe Lütken, Thorhild Widvey and Nini Høegh Nergaard. They represent different types of women who are now highly present and visible on corporate boards.

WHO ARE THE WOMEN ON BOARDS? MULTI-BOARD MEMBERS IN ASA COMPANIES

As one purpose of Part III is to explore board compositional conse-quences of the Norwegian gender quota law we decided to focus on the women that were introduced to the Norwegian boards in the period 2007–2010. Our particular attention was on the women often labelled the 'Golden Skirts'. The term the 'Golden Skirts' has received considerable attention in the Norwegian and later also the international press, as well as in research (Seierstad and Opsahl, 2011). Generally it has a negative connotation, and studies have been conducted to explore who the women on boards in Norway are, and how they have been selected (Heidenreich, 2010). Critical voices in the international press have been skeptical about the development of an elite group of prominent women that is replacing the 'old boys' network'. Table 12.1 illustrates that this may indeed be the case.

*Table 12.1   ASA multi-board memberships 2007, 2008, 2009 and 2010
(sum totals)*

	Women	Men
More than 16 (mean more than 4 on average)	8	2
13–16 positions	13	7
9–12 positions	27	39
5–8 positions	107	111

Table 12.1 shows the presence of multi-board memberships by women and men in the Norwegian publicly tradable companies (ASA companies). I have summarized the number of board positions during the years 2007, 2008, 2009 and 2010. I found that during these four years 1309 women had at least one year in a board position in an ASA company. Knowing that only 40 percent of the board members are women, it would be expected that in total there should be more men than women having multi-board membership. However, that is not the case. I found that eight women and only two men over these four years had, on average, more than four positions in ASA companies, and 21 women and only nine men had on average more than three ASA board memberships. One explanation for this finding may be the selection process. Since prior board experience is generally a criterion for becoming a board member, it makes the few women that have such experience more likely to get multiple appointments. Table 12.2 gives a picture of how multi-board membership by gender has been changing from 2000 till 2010.

Multi-board memberships have migrated from men to women, and the 'Golden Skirts' have replaced the 'old boys' network'. The 'old boys' network' is in the literature presented as an elite of present and previous managers that use their board memberships and interlocking directorates largely for intra-class purposes to protect their own privileges (Mace, 1971; Richardson, 1987; Useem, 1984). I analyzed the presence of interlocking directorates among the women with the most board positions. Two women were on three boards together, but they were not on a board with any of the other women. These two women are discussed later on. Among the women with an average of more than three board positions, no other women were on more than one board together. Only three women had more than two board positions with each other. This means that within the group of 'Golden Skirts' there are very few interlocks, and therefore no clear similarity to the 'old boys' network'.

Table 12.2 Gender change in multi-board memberships

	Multi-board directors 2000	Multi-board directors 2005	Multi-board directors 2010
Women	No women	Some 'Golden Skirts', family and business women	Professional independent (including the 'Golden Skirts'), family, officers and business women
Men	'Old boys' network', consultants, investors, lawyers	'Old boys' network', consultants, investors, lawyers	Women have replaced many multi-board men

Some of the women even indicated in interviews that they did not know any of the others.

DIFFERENT TYPES OF BOARD MEMBERS

A framework for understanding board composition is presented in Table 12.3. The framework has two axes based on independence and the profession. The profession axis is split by gender. Based on the corporate governance literature three main types of board positions can be identified (Baysinger and Butler, 1985; Burgess and Tharenou, 2002). Board members will typically have a board identity depending on which type they belong to (Hillman et al., 2008; Huse and Rindova, 2001). The first group, insiders and quasi-insiders, contains the positions held by persons with financial and/or psychological relations to the company leadership, including executive directors, consultants, family and friends, and business partners. The second group, stakeholder related directors, contains the positions held by persons with financial and/or psychological relations to the main external stakeholder or ownership groups. These will often be the investors, their representatives, family members and friends; sometimes also politicians. The last groups of board members will be those that are completely independent, i.e. those with no relations to either internal or external actors. On the other axis are persons who make their living as board members: the professional directors; and those that make a living out of their business, but have some additional board positions, that is, the business directors.

Table 12.3   Different types of board members

	Business directors – having board memberships in addition to other business activities		Professional directors – making a living solely from board memberships	
	Women	Men	Women	Men
Insider and quasi-insider. Limited scope to replace	Family	Entrepreneurs, friends, business relations, majority shareholders	Family, officers	Officers, consultants, lawyers, investors
Stakeholder related directors. Limited scope to replace	Investors, their employees and partners. Employee directors	Investors and their employees. Employee directors	Investors, majority shareholders and their partners and employees	'Gold Sacks'. Business angels, investors and majority shareholders
Independent directors. Replaceable	Entrepreneurs	CEOs, 'Old boys' network', experts	'Golden Skirts' and those in SMEs	Ex-CEOs, 'Old boys' network'

I used web descriptions to classify the various board members. Women as well as men exist in all six categories, and their characteristics are displayed in Table 12.3. In the categories I identify the typical descriptions of the 'old boys' network' as well as the 'Golden Skirts'. Both 'the old boys' network' and the 'Golden Skirts' are in the category of independent directors. There are some business directors in Norway who are independent directors, but only a handful of the 30 women with three or more board positions (based on the 2007–2010 average) can be classified as businesswomen, and only one or two of them as independent business women. The women with the most board positions in the Norwegian ASA companies are independent professional board members. This is the group of prominent women that I here label the 'Golden Skirts'. Only a few, if any, of the professional women board members are in the insider or stakeholder categories.

When exploring the transition in Norway based on the gender quota law, I found that the directors in board positions with insider or stakeholder-based motivations are difficult to replace. This means that the transition from men to women on boards required by the law has been almost exclusively in the group of independent directors. Few new board members in this period have been recruited among families and friends (Heidenreich, 2010). Table 12.3 indicates that 'the old boys' network' is replaced by the 'Golden Skirts'. The men with the most board positions are now those who are either themselves investors or investors' representatives, that is, the 'Gold Sacks'. Interestingly, it is the women who in practice will fill most of the seats as independent directors, and consequently who also will fill most of the seats on important board committees such as the auditing committee, nomination committee and compensation committee. This is a change from the past situation when women only obtained positions on the least-important committees (Bilimoria and Pederit, 1994).

CATEGORIES OF THE 'GOLDEN SKIRTS'

Who are then the 'Golden Skirts'? I used the list of the women with the most positions in the period 2007–2010 (Table 12.1). Among the 21 women having on average more than three positions, I found one women who was a major ship-owner and was also a board member or chair on her company's subsidiary boards. Two women had strong ties to the main owners of a group of investment companies, and they were board members in several of these companies. These two women were also the only women serving on several boards together. The companies they served on changed their form of incorporation in 2010. The remaining 18 multi-board women were considered as independent board members. Among them only three had a main position outside that of being a board member, but the main positions of these three women were entered before they became board members. In my analyses I thus considered them as professional board members together with the remaining 15. I conducted in-depth portrait interviews with all these women. The formal competencies and qualifications of these women were impressive, with respect to education as well as to practice, but I found that they differed in several ways. As a result of the interviews I categorized them based on: (1) length and amount of experience; and (2) degree of pragmatism or flexibility in behavior. This is displayed in Table 12.4.

Table 12.4   Who are the 'Golden Skirts'?

	Principle- and facts-oriented 'Golden Skirts'	Pragmatic business-oriented 'Golden Skirts'
Aspiring 'Golden Skirts' (less experience as decision-maker)	'The young, smart and clever that have facts on their fingertips, often having mentors' (around 40 years). Providing specialist advice to the management and the board.	'The ambitious and pragmatic women – using the opportunities given by the law' (50 years +). Mostly focusing on that formal corporate governance issues are followed.
Experienced 'Golden Skirts' (substantial experience as decision-maker)	'The iron fists that are used to fight – experience from top level politics' (50 years +). Focusing on issues and decision-making processes.	'The business experienced – being board members before the gender-balance law' (55 years +). Caring for the long-term development and value creation in the firm.

The result is a four-square matrix. In my analyses I categorized four women into each of the groups, and two women were classified as being in transition, that is, in the process of moving from one classification to another. The labels put on the various groups were: (1) the 'young, smart and clever'; (2) the 'ambitious and pragmatic'; (3) the 'iron fists that are used to fight'; and (4) the 'business experienced'. The 'young, smart and clever' are typically younger than the other groups, they have facts at their fingertips, they have typically been discovered by a mentor, and they emphasize the support of their husband and his professional network as influential in being recruited as board members. These women typically have the analytical skills, approaches and competencies of 'McKinsey' consultants. This group would have been larger if I only considered the positions in 2010. They consider themselves as persons who bring knowledge and facts to the board.

   The 'ambitious and pragmatic' are those who have the greatest number of board memberships. Their backgrounds vary (law, engineering, etc.), but they typically have no or only a limited background in executive business leadership. They typically saw the opportunity to make a living from being a board member as the gender quota law was introduced. They did not wait to be discovered, but actively sought opportunities to be visible and get board positions. The ambition of these women has been more to become a board member rather than to contribute to board behavior and company performance. However, typically they focus on board control tasks, risk aversion and corporate governance recommendations. There are many women with similar aspirations, but the ones described here have been the most successful.

Norway has a long tradition of women in top positions in politics. The 'iron fists that are used to fight' all have a background in top-level politics, often as ministers in the big and influential industry-related departments in the Norwegian Cabinet. However, it is not enough to have been a minister or a party leader, you also need to bring forth your aspiration for top-level business positions. These women bring their backgrounds from the political arena to the corporate boards. They know the political system. They also know how to use power techniques both inside and outside the boardroom, and they have a large network related to politicians, business leaders and bureaucrats. As board members the women in this category are typically crusaders, but they are also used by boards for their networks into the political systems.

The 'business experienced' 'Golden Skirts' had considerable business and board experience before the law was introduced, and with the quota law they were the first to be considered for additional positions. The educational and professional backgrounds of some of these women are really impressive. The women in this group are on average somewhat older than the women in the other groups, with a mean age of about 60 years. Their focus as board members was to contribute to value creation in the firm, and to strategic decision-making processes. They felt happy when they experienced that the company and its management were doing better because of their contribution.

Most of the women, except for those in the 'young, smart and clever' category, have been divorced, are single or without children. Most of the women are also finding that being a board member fits nicely into their personal and professional life, and it provides a good work–life balance. They argue that it is difficult to make a career in business. Many of them describe themselves as good at multi-tasking, and that they have needed to stow away the 'nice girl' ambition. However, many are also commenting that being a board member is much easier than being a top executive. The work load is usually more predictable, and they can more easily plan their time, take days off and combine it with the care for children, grandchildren or elderly parents.

Following these groups over the period 2007–2010 illustrates some interesting developments. Some of the women with the highest number of board positions in the beginning of the period were reducing the numbers of boards they were involved with. And there was one woman who did not have any board position in 2007, but who in 2010 had attained the highest number of positions on the ASA company boards. There were also some women who during the period became chief executive officers (CEOs) of other companies, and that led them to reduce the number of board involvements. About half of the women being interviewed were for various reasons negative about the quota law when it was introduced, but having experienced its implementation and results they all expressed a change in views since, and that they were positive and supported it. Through the interviews I observed a tendency that women in the three other categories were approaching the 'business experienced' category. This may indicate that in future, when the women on corporate boards become more experienced, we will see that they may approach the values and behavior of the 'business experienced' 'Golden Skirts'.

REFERENCES

Baysinger, B.D. and Butler, H.N. (1985) Corporate governance and the board of directors: Performance effects of changes in board composition, *Journal of Law, Economics, and Organization*, 1(1): 101–124.

Bilimoria, D. and Pederit, S.K. (1994) Board committee membership: Effects of sex based bias, *Academy of Management Journal*, 37: 1453–1477.

Burgess, Z. and Tharenou, P. (2002) Women board directors: Characteristics of the few, *Journal of Business Ethics*, 37(1): 39–49.

Heidenreich, V. (2010) Rekruttering til ASA-styrer etter innføring av kvoteringregelen, *Magma*, 13(7): 56–70.

Hillman, A.J., Nicholson, G. and Shropshire, C. (2008) Directors' multiple identities, identification, and board monitoring and resource provision, *Organization Science*, 19(3): 441–456.

Huse, M. and Rindova, V.P. (2001) Stakeholders' expectations of board roles: The case of subsidiary boards, *Journal of Management and Governance*, 5(2): 153–178.

Mace, M.L. (1971) *Directors: Myths and Realities*, Boston, MA: Harvard University.

Richardson, R.J. (1987) Directorship interlock and corporate profitability, *Administrative Science Quarterly*, 32: 367–386.

Seierstad, C. and Opsahl, T. (2011) For the few not the many? The effects of affirmative action on presence, prominence, and social capital of women directors in Norway, *Scandinavian Journal of Management*, 27(1): 44–54.

Useem, M. (1984) *The Inner Circle: Large Corporations and the Rise of Business Political Activity in the US and UK*, Oxford: Oxford University Press.

13. Stories from four Norwegian multi-board women

Nini Høegh Nergaard, Merete Lütken, Thorhild Widvey, Ingvild Ragna Myhre and Morten Huse

The label 'Golden Skirt' generally has a negative connotation. An objective in Part III has been to go beyond the surface of the multi-board women in Norwegian publicly tradable companies (ASA companies). We have tried to achieve this by taking a closer look at the profiles behind the figures and data on women on ASA companies in Chapter 12, and will follow this up in this chapter by presenting the stories of four of these women directors. Nini Høegh Nergaard, Merete Lütken, Thorhild Widvey and Ingvild Myhre all give presentations about their experiences at the Think Tank in Oslo. For comparative reasons in the following presentations their stories have been sorted to respond to six main questions. These are:

1. Who are you?
2. Why have you been interested in being a board member?
3. How and when were you recruited to boards in ASA companies?
4. What do you perceive to be your particular contribution to boards?
5. What is your perception of the gender balance law?
6. What are your most important lessons when working on boards?

NINI HØEGH NERGAARD

Who Are You?

My name is Nini Høegh Nergaard, I am 39 years old, married and the mother of two boys. I hold a law degree, but have never practiced as a lawyer. I worked in investment banking for six years before resigning to a more slow-paced family life. I live a suburban life at Snarøya, a peninsula on the Oslo Fjord and a suburb to Oslo. I often introduce myself as a 'stay-at-home mom'. I feel this describes my life, even though some people in the very egalitarian Norwegian society find this naive and ignorant. My family is the main focus at this time of my life. As a consequence, my board positions are my part-time work. I feel very lucky to have this job. I get to work with some really dedicated and intelligent people, without putting in the amount of hours required by company executives. I still have my free time, my flexibility and I am (most of the time) able to manage my own schedule. I currently work on three boards, down from seven last year. One company was sold, the other three boards I resigned from voluntarily.

Why Have You Been Interested in Being a Board Member?

I have always been the kind of person to get involved. At elementary school I was my class representative to the student board, and from there it went on. I have been involved in my yacht club, the National Sailing Association, and so on. While studying at the University of Oslo, I was involved in student politics. As part of this I was elected as a member of the board of directors of the Student Union. I later became the Chair of the board. The Student Union at that time employed 600 people and had revenues of around NOK 500 million. At the age of 25, to me, this was a great responsibility. It was also a great learning experience. The board of the Student Union is a political body, and I have never found myself in so many conflicts as I was while serving on this board. Managing the board meetings as the Chair was very demanding; it felt at times like juggling flaming torches. Still, filled with youthful energy, I survived and I felt I was doing something important. The seed for my future interest in board work was planted.

After having my second child I realized I was not willing to give what it takes to succeed as an investment banker. I might not even have what it takes, but that I was shielded from confronting. By resigning from my job I did feel I gave up on something that had been a major part of my life. I was always quite ambitious, and I was used to know what direction to take. Now I had no direction and the ambitions were gone. Around this time, in the spring of 2005, I was introduced to the course 'The Value Creating Board' at BI, Norwegian School of Management. I decided to apply. It felt like a smart thing to do, and something that could keep my mind from degeneration. Later, I discovered I thoroughly enjoyed the course and found it very interesting. I learned a lot, and I truly liked being back in an educational environment.

Later that same spring, I was asked to join the board of directors of a medium-sized privately owned technical consultancy company (an AS company). I was recommended by a former colleague at the board of the Student Union. I did not know the owner, nor anyone else involved in the company. After the interview I was asked to consider the position as the Chair of the board. I gladly, though somewhat nervously, accepted the offer, and I still enjoy working with this company.

How and When Were You Recruited to ASA Company Boards?

I have been recruited to ASA company boards through a combination of ownership positions and acquaintanceships. The first ASA board I was recruited to was in 2006, as the ASA companies were preparing for the gender balance regulations. In this company, my family had a long history of ownership. At this time smaller companies did not normally have a Nomination Committee, so my candidacy to this board was proposed by the chief executive officer (CEO). For the other ASA boards on which I serve or have served, the story is much the same. I have been fortunate to work with people who have suggested me to others as a potential board member.

I have never listed myself in any of the databases that have been constructed for female board candidates. I do not believe these databases are relevant. I find board members are recruited through other channels.

What Do You Perceive To Be Your Particular Contribution to Boards?

A board member's focus should always be on what is in the best interests of the company. To me this means that several different and at times conflicting interests need to be balanced. As a board member I think of myself as someone driving a car with one foot on the accelerator and one foot on the brakes. When accelerating I focus on the future and am trying to motivate the potential and the creativity of the management and my fellow board members. When braking, control, corporate governance and structure are what I focus on.

Since my background is quite varied and I have experience from several different industries and companies, I believe I can contribute in many ways. I take an analytic approach to the tasks ahead. I like to ask questions, both to clarify and to highlight other perspectives of a case. I believe dynamic discussions often lead to high-quality resolutions.

With this approach I am at times willing to work with companies where I do not necessarily know the industry very well in advance. In these cases, the industry competence will normally be secured through other board members. To fill in on my lack of knowledge, I study available information about the company, its competitors and the industry. For public companies (ASAs) there is normally quite a lot of information available.

I do not think board work is very glorious. In fact I think it is quite hard work. I do not make it my identity to be 'The Board Member'. I know I am up for election at least once a year. Therefore, I can only do my best – for the company. I am willing to take on fights when I think it is necessary, and I am willing to risk being the 'skunk' in the board room. And trust me, that is not fun.

How Have You Perceived/Do You Perceive the Law about Gender Balance?

All of my six ASA board positions I have been elected to after the law regulation on gender balance was introduced. It is fair to say the regulation has been a great opportunity for me. Still, I have mixed feelings towards the quota regulations. The liberal in me opposes using law regulations with penalties to reach political goals at the cost of the right of choice for the owners of private corporations.

The board of directors is the owners' forum, where the owners have elected their representatives. Often private owners will like to be present themselves. Private owners are (unfortunately) mostly men. I am not convinced this is a problem, but I do see that most of the arguments against the quota have proven invalid. Finding qualified women does not seem to have been a major problem. None of the ASA companies has failed to comply with the quota law, and I do not believe any owners have chosen unqualified board members for their companies. New ASA companies are still being formed. We have not seen a significant decline in profitability as a consequence of the gender balance regulation. What we have seen are more women with a wider variety of backgrounds serving on boards. We have also seen a general increase in focus on board work. And if not embraced, the quota law is now generally accepted.

Personally I have valued having female colleagues on my boards. This is especially true in times of conflicts. Though I may not have 'teamed up' with my female board colleagues, more women present has somewhat softened the tone. I think the board members now have a more varied background thanks to the increased number of women, and I think that the quota in combination with the Good Corporate Governance Statutes that have been introduced has resulted in higher-quality board work.

There is always the danger of boards becoming too big to be efficient. There are many interests that need to be balanced in addition to compiling wanted qualifications, and here the quota is but one of the considerations. Another is the rights of the employees in Norwegian companies to hold up to one-third of the seats of the board. A third is the requirement for independent board members.

When boards get too big, there is always a possibility that board decisions in reality are made outside of the boardroom. However, I believe the increased influence of women on the boards have had the opposite impact. I believe there were more informal structures before. I do not socialize with my female board colleagues, whereas in the 'old days' there was known to be a group of male executives in the larger Norwegian companies who were good personal friends and were alternating on each other's boards.

The terms 'Golden Skirts' and 'Quota Queens' are used to describe female equivalents to these groups of men. I find these terms both patronizing and untrue.

What Are the Most Important Lessons You Have Learned about Working on Boards – Focusing on ASA Boards?

I guess I have learned several lessons from working on ASA company boards. The main lesson is that it is hard work, and at times both stressful and unpleasant. I was once placed in a position where I was awarded option rights that immediately came in the money and could have given me a profit of several hundred thousand kroner. This was because of an offer on all shares of the company that was still undisclosed but known to the board at a time when the recommendation to the annual general meeting (AGM) to grant the options could still be amended. There was probably nothing illegal in the grant itself, but I did not think it was ethical to accept. Out of nine board members, there were three who declined to accept these options. A very unpleasant situation followed, with heated discussions and newspaper articles. In the end, a new AGM overturned the original grant of options, and the case solved itself. The lesson I learned from this is to never let go of my own ethical compass. It is tempting to accept free money, and it is hard to stand up for a view which also can make other people lose money, however undeserved the gain of the money was in the first place.

I have also learned there are times when I need to resign from a board. It is in my bones not to leave a task until it is done. However, as a board member I have learned to accept that there are times where I will never succeed with what I started off to achieve. There can be several reasons for this: it may be that the (other) owners do not share my views, or the management is not willing to change its ways, or I constitute a minority of the board in a case where I believe great values are at stake. In cases like these I have learned I need to resign from my board position. I sit on the board to influence, and when I cannot do so I should no longer sit there, no matter how hard it is to give up on an unaccomplished project. As a board member I value my independence and I guard my reputation as best as I can, and I think it is pivotal not to let money or pride ruin this.

MERETE LÜTKEN

Who Are You?

My name is Merete Lütken, I am 51 years old and live in Bærum, just outside Oslo. I am married with two children. I presently work as a non-executive board director, management consultant, speaker and writer. Later this year I am planning to publish a financial thriller from the boardroom. I also serve as chair of the board network together with Elin Hurvenes.

I have worked as a non-executive board director for more than a decade, but I did not start out with a plan to be a board professional. After studying psychology, marketing and business administration, I spent the first 20 years of my career working as a marketing and communications director and vice-president in several well-known Norwegian companies. These jobs provided me with valuable experience within strategy, business development, management and communication.

Why Have You Been Interested in Being a Board Member?

I got my first two board appointments while I was working as director of marketing and communication at the Norwegian public broadcaster, NRK. These directorships gave me an appetite for board work.

After 20 years in top management positions, I started my own company and engaged myself professionally in board work, as a public speaker, writing articles and working as a board member in a variety of companies and industries, from small start-up companies to medium-sized companies, and to listed companies.

I got interested in board work because I saw it as an opportunity to utilize my knowledge and experience, and network in a new arena, particularly since I had dedicated my career to developing successful businesses. I also thought it was about time more women entered the board room.

How and When Were You Recruited to ASA Boards?

Most of my directorships have been in industries I have prior work experience in, namely health, media and education. But I have also served on boards in technology and industrial companies. Nearly all my directorships have come as a result of my network, that is people who know me professionally have recommended me.

The major part of my directorships (12 boards), have not been in limited companies, and therefore are not a result of the law. But there is no doubt that the quota law has helped me to obtain board positions in three public limited companies (ASA boards). I was recruited to these boards in 2007, two of them through my professional network. One board position was a result of an interview I gave in the Norwegian business newspaper, DN. The head of the selection committee in a public limited company read it, and called me up.

What Do You Perceive To Be Your Particular Contribution to Boards?

I think my previous experience from board work and executive positions in a variety of industries has been a valuable contribution to the boards, and the fact that I cover a wide range of competences such as financial, strategic management and public relations.

My approach to board work is proactive and constructive with special emphasis on strategy and business development. I am equally concerned with value creation as with the control aspect of board work. I also focus on bringing structure, routines and governance to the board. These contributions are also emphasized in recommendations posted by board colleagues on my LinkedIn profile http://www.linkedin.com/pub/merete-l%C3%BCtken/3/a69/188.

Like many other board women I know, I am often the 'skunk in the room', not afraid to ask the difficult questions and challenge established truths. This is not always popular. Although it is important to be flexible and have social intelligence, it is important to remember that board work is not a popularity contest.

This became very clear to me a few years ago, when I was sued for 20 million Norwegian kroner, allegedly for breach of the Company Act and my board responsibilities, in a technology company I had left the year before. The accusations were completely unfounded. Luckily, I had saved all the documentation from this board position, and could prove that I had performed correctly. It turned out that the management of the company had been embezzling money, and the plaintiff was a black-mailer trying to extort money from the board members. He dropped all charges when he realized that he could not intimidate me.

This was a shocking experience that gave me a crash course in business law. Looking back I was probably too naive regarding corruption and economic crime. Although I checked out the company before I accepted the directorship – talked to the company lawyer and the chairman of the board, checked the board minutes and annual reports – this still was not enough. The experience has made me more concerned with risk management and more able and willing to ask 'the right questions'. Subsequently this has made me a better board member.

How Have You Perceived/Do You Perceive the Law about Gender Balance?

I think the quota law has increased the general awareness of qualified female board directors. The business case is obvious: including women increases the recruitment pool. A larger talent pool allows owners to pick the best of both men and women. The benefits of being able to increase the recruitment base by 50 per cent of the population should be obvious. For those who are still in doubt, I recommend a look at McKinsey's three-year-long study of women's contribution to value creation. You cannot make a clearer business case for greater diversity.

Instead of embracing this resource base, opponents of the quota law argue that the shareholders must be allowed to choose the board members they feel are best suited for the job, regardless of gender. I understand the owner's principal views, but it is not as if everyone that served on the boards before the quota law was brilliant, or the composition of the boards was optimal at any given time.

The Enron scandal and the financial crisis have led to an increased focus on board work and good corporate governance. This has emerged in parallel with the quota law. When the Act was introduced, the Norwegian companies had two choices: to expand the board in order to make room for women, or replace some men. The companies were forced to look at their board's competence and composition with new, critical eyes. Thus, the quota law has helped to accelerate the professionalization of the boards.

The polarization between the sexes is a diversion from what it really is all about: the development of a leadership that values, and manages to make use of, the world's talent pool, whether they are men or women. This applies not just in the boardroom but in all areas of business. In my opinion, the opposition to the quota law boils down to attitudes and resistance to change. Diversity is demanding and requires tolerance, maturity and leadership. It is easier to communicate with people who are similar to oneself, who you know and in whom you trust. It is also human to choose the path of least resistance. Suddenly the board of directors has to deal with women they do not know; that raises critical questions, and changes the dynamics in the boardroom. But the demand for diversity is not something that is going to disappear – on the contrary. In a globalized world the need for greater diversity in terms of nationality, background and cultural pressure becomes ever more evident. This is a trend that cannot be stopped.

How well the board works depends largely on the Chair. It is a demanding job that requires sufficient maturity, experience and sensitivity to control the interactions with the administration, the board and the owners, all within the framework of good corporate governance. The Chair must also be able to direct the increased diversity in the boardroom into a harmonious whole, not a harsh dissonance.

I think the quota law was necessary to get the company owners and selection committees to notice women and think in new ways. But the law has unfortunately not influenced the number of women in AS companies and family-owned companies. These companies represent the major bulk of Norwegian businesses. Although the quota law has been a success in the ASA companies, it has made little impact on the rest of Norwegian business.

What Are the Most Important Lessons You Have Learned about Working on Boards – Focusing on ASA Boards?

In my experience female board directors have three traits that can be viewed both as strengths and challenges. The first is that women seldom are major owners. This makes them independent and able to make ethical decisions. On the other hand, female directors might miss out on important information. This makes it more difficult for them to understand the power game between the owners, and there is a risk that not all decisions are made in the boardroom. The second is that women usually are more risk-averse than men. It is good to have a healthy scepticism, but that does not mean saying no to all risky projects. It is necessary to take and accept risks, in order to create development. The purpose of risk management is not to eliminate risk, but to understand the risk factors so that benefits can be exploited and negative aspects limited. This requires clarity as to what risks the company is prepared to take, and a system in place to manage these risks. Thirdly, women on boards are not afraid to ask questions, and want to examine an issue from different angles before making a decision. This might irritate some men but it is valuable, at least if the Chair of the board is a good team leader, and sees the benefit of discussions and diversity. The Chair is in fact crucial for the board's performance. Being a female board member can be very interesting and rewarding but also challenging, especially if you are the only woman on the board. It is certainly easier if there are at least two women on the board, what is referred to as the critical mass theory. A final point to remember is that board directors in Norway have a pretty insecure position. As a board member you are in economic terms responsible with your whole personal fortune. Many companies do not have board insurance, and the board remuneration is quite low. I therefore urge women to weigh the benefits and risk carefully, and perform a thorough due diligence of the company before taking on a directorship.

In my opinion there are nine key issues that women who aspire for board member should focus on:

1. It is flattering to be asked to sit on a board, but make sure to do your own due diligence of the company.
2. Role clarification between the owners, the board and the top management.
3. Understanding the power game and the owner's motives.
4. Clarify expectations: what do the owners expect, what kind of board do they want – a controlling board, a pro-forma board, a celebrity board or a value-creating board?
5. Know the industry, understand the business model, and the value and cost generators.
6. Seek information from a wider source than the CEO.
7. Familiarize yourselves with the Company Law Act and your board responsibility.
8. Pay special attention to risk management.
9. Never be afraid to voice your opinion. And if you disagree with the rest of the board on important issues, make sure it gets written down in the minutes.

Further information can be found through the following sources:

- Public Profile: http://www.linkedin.com/pub/merete-l%C3%BCtken/ 3/a69/188.
- Academic paper on board work in growth companies: http://www. magma.no/styrer-i-vekstselskaper-er-ikke-som-andre-styrer.
- Feature article on women on boards and the law about gender balance: http://e24.no/kommentarer/kvinner-i-styrer/3861927.

THORHILD WIDVEY

Who Are You?

I have grown up in the western part of Norway, and have always been 'Kjerringa mot strømmen', which translates as 'always swimming the opposite way', meaning somebody who holds a different opinion to that of others. I am 55 years old, and have had experience as a board member for the last 35 years. My first board experience was in a girls' choir. I have always seen myself as a leader. I am educated as a sports teacher, and have followed different courses at the Norwegian Business School, among them the BI master course 'The Value Creating Board'.

I have been in politics for many years, and as a 22-year-old I was elected into the municipal government. In 1989 I was elected to the Norwegian Parliament and was there for eight years. I left the Parliament because myself and my husband wanted to get international experience, and we moved to London.

In 2002, I was asked to join the Norwegian Government as Deputy Minister in the Ministry of Fishery, and later as Deputy Minister in the Ministry of Foreign Affairs. In June 2004, I became Minister of Oil and Energy.

Why Do You Want To Be a Board Member?

I like to work with companies at the board level, to help companies to fulfil their business potential. I like to work strategically and found that my knowledge was of interest to the companies. I have chosen to work with companies in the energy sector, because of my experience of working in this sector.

How and When Were You Recruited to ASA Boards?

The first year after I finished my tenure as Minister of Oil and Energy (in 2005), I received 70 phone calls with invitations to become a board member. Usually I have been asked by the nomination committee, the owners or by the CEO of the company. Recruitment consultants have also contacted me.

What Do You Perceive To Be Your Particular Contribution to Boards?

A big network, competence, knowledge and experience. It has been perceived positively that I have been in politics and that I have lived abroad. I am curious and want to create something, and I like to support and develop companies in movement.

How Have You Perceived/Do You Perceive the Law about Gender on Boards?

I believe in equality between women and men, and that women as well as men represent valuable thoughts, ideas, competences and knowledge. In order to recruit the best people to the board, you must choose among the best from both women and men. It is a waste of resources if only 50 percent of the competence of the world's population is used. Your selection pool is inevitably much smaller.

The law has contributed to more women in corporate boards. I must admit that the intentions have been met. I was not a supporter of the law as it was introduced, and did not have any involvement in it whilst I was in the Government.

The women now coming on to boards are much more conscious than the men in that they are there due to their qualifications, and not because they are quota'd in. I experience that the women coming on to the boards are very well prepared, and they really get into the various issues that are raised and discussed. They have not been afraid, and dared to ask the seemingly silly questions. Women have contributed to create a greater openness on the board. And the women contribute to a more relaxed atmosphere.

What Are the Most Important Lessons You Have Learned about Working on Boards – Focusing on ASA Boards?

The first lesson learned from working on boards is that all board members, women and men, must have a focus on what creates values in the company. The second point is that the board should consist of various types of experience, competence and knowledge. The third point is that all boards should have a good board Chairperson who considers all the board members. The Chairperson has responsibility that the whole spectrum of competences and knowledge that exists in the board will be used for the company's development. It is also important that the Chairperson is professional when it comes to leading the meetings. My experience is that we lose time, focus and motivation if you do not have a good Chairperson. The most important role for a board Chair is to make use of the other board members. Experience from leadership is an important knowledge aspect to bring into the boardroom.

INGVILD MYHRE

Who Are You?

I am from the northern part of Norway, and I am 53 years old. My background is that I have a Master of Science in telecom and fibreoptics from the Norwegian University of Science and Technology in Trondheim. My board experiences developed over the course of many years. Some of the most challenging boards I am a member of today are probably the Research Council of Norway and the Norwegian Pension Fund. Also I am board Chairperson of Simula Research. This firm has recently received an award as one of the leading technology-based research firms. I am board member of a number of companies, small as well as large, and including some that are listed on the Oslo Stock Exchange. I am working mainly with projects directed towards technology. Currently, I am also a partner of a consultancy partnership that works on board-related issues.

Why Do You Want To Be a Board Member?

Board work is demanding, challenging, and great fun. Being a board member gives me plenty and it is very exciting. However, it takes much time. You must be prepared to work evenings and parts of weekends. There have been periods when I have spent very little time with friends, but at the same time it is important to take care of the friendships that you have. It is, however, my family, my personal and private friends and networks that I want to protect.

How and When Were You Recruited to ASA Boards?

My road to the boardrooms has gone through having held positions as middle manager and manager. It was my boss at one stage who recommended me for a board position. I got my first board position in 1992 and that was in the Research Council of Norway. My boss was asked if he had somebody to recommend, and the Research Council were in need of women with a background in natural science and technology. At that time I was very young, but quite quickly I ended up in board positions in several of the largest and most important companies in Norway.

What Do You Perceive To Be Your Particular Contribution to Boards?

I have always taken the approach that I am contributing specific competences, whilst at the same time I am also continually learning from my board experiences. During the board meeting I do not feel the need to talk if I do not have anything to contribute.

I am not the auditor type in the boardroom, and am very clear on that. Of course, I read the figures, however my strongest areas are much more in relation to strategy and creativity. You are welcome to call my role supporting rather than controlling. I am supporting the CEO. For sure, I am not always as prepared as I should be, but please show me the person that has not been sinning on this point.

For several years I have had very substantial leadership experiences, and have seen things from many perspectives. That leadership experience has also been accumulated at the international level. I contribute to strategic thinking, the pros and cons in relation to a choice of various scenarios. But I am also very operative. I enjoy very much working with small entrepreneurial companies where you are there to help the entrepreneur develop new strategies. You know that when you enter such a firm that only one out of ten firms will succeed. And I am there to help it succeed. How can the board help this particular firm to succeed? And through many years I have established a comprehensive network.

How Have You Perceived/Do You Perceive the Law about Gender Balance?

Women have been recruited to boards through the networks known by men. Women often fall out of the career system when they are having children. I am trying to encourage mature and experienced women that have networks to remember to include the women that have been at home with children, and to challenge them continuously.

When the law was proposed I was at first against it. I did not want the same system of female quotas that we had in some of the disciplines at the Norwegian University of Technology. Women should not be second class as a result of quotas. However, many have been telling me that we need to start somewhere. I remember talking with an older and very experienced career woman. She took me aside and said: 'Ingvild, I am significantly older than you and I entered boardrooms before you, and none of us are actually in favour of the law. But at the same time we must admit that also the first times we were invited to boards it was due to the need of getting women to boards.' If there are qualified women out there then I am positive about the law.

The group of women that have been recruited to boards since the law is very diverse. There are many lawyers. I am not negative about and towards lawyers, but we have got some women with a law background into boards. Some may say that we have got too many appointments through family relations, on the basis of relationships to a certain family. We do not have any proper aristocracy in Norway, but we have got many heirs on to the boards. This is not wrong, but I think we also should have more women leaders in boardrooms. We do not really need any systematic mapping to find them, but only that we should be somewhat more conscious when we make our choices. There are many corporations that have many very clever women on their staff.

This is what we got with the quota law. I think that the law very clearly has not been unsuccessful or negative because I do not think that the boards have been worse off. But I think that we can invest greater efforts to find many more highly competent women, especially those with leadership experience and the type of competence that is not there yet.

I have been the only woman on several boards, and have never seen it as a negative when another woman is introduced to the boardroom. But at the same time it must not happen that women's alliances are being created. It happens that decisions are actually made before the board meeting, even in listed companies. However, in some companies this never happens. I can accept this if it concerns a family firm, but not if the company is listed.

What Are the Most Important Lessons You Have Learned about Working on Boards?

I try to ask myself: has this been a good board meeting? If the company management has not got anything from the board meeting then it has not been a good board meeting. In many ways it is more fun to work in small entrepreneurial firms than in large listed companies. Then you can use yourself more. You may influence more. In small firms you depend more on the competence present among the board members. This means that the boards that are working best are those that use the knowledge and skills available in the board. The boards that are the best are those that are good at using board evaluations, that is, board evaluations are not to be made for their own sake, but for how they contribute to the board and the company.

The largest potential for improvement in Norwegian boards is to develop a greater awareness of the competences that are needed around the board table, from both men and women. This is one of the main responsibilities of the board Chair.

14. Concluding remarks to Part III

Morten Huse

The public debate about the Norwegian gender balance law often refers to an American study about the perception of it by investors (Ahern and Dittmar, 2012). The study shows how investors on the stock exchanges reacted when companies announced that a woman was elected. They reported that investors did not like the law. The authors reported that the women directors had 'significantly less CEO experience and were younger, more highly educated, and more likely to be employed as a non-executive manager'. Interesting, but not very surprising. Investors and stock exchanges are typically not in favor of governmental interventions, and we also know that the most important criterion for becoming a board member traditionally has been prior experience as a board member or a chief executive officer (CEO). In Norway, only about 2 percent of CEOs were women before the gender balance law, and only 6 percent of board members were women. Inevitably, the women that were introduced as board members had to have different backgrounds. Finally, it is not very surprising as the Norwegian corporate law generally requires that all board members are non-executive. We have in Part III explored board compositional characteristics of the Norwegian gender balance law, and illustrated who the women are that became board members in Norway.

The immediate consequence of the law was that women already in board positions received more invitations to such posts, and Norway has more multi-board women than multi-board members. The Norwegian women directors typically had a form of double independence, and without creating their own network, they broke the 'old boys' network'. While the women obtained the independent positions, the remaining men kept the executive or investor positions.

The women making a living from being board members because of the law have in the press been labeled as the 'Golden Skirts', while most of the remaining men are on boards are called the 'Golden Sacks' because they are or represent investors. In Part III we developed a four-square matrix with four ideal types of the 'Golden Skirts'. We found substantial differences, but also some similarities. In general, the women were formally more highly educated than the men.

The four ideal types of women were the advisors (the 'young, smart and clever', having facts at their finger-tips), the controllers (the 'ambitious and pragmatic' women using the opportunities given by the law), the decision-makers (the 'iron fists that are used to fight', with experience from top-level politics) and the value-creators (the 'business experienced' ones having been board members before the law came into force). Following the 'Golden Skirts' over a four-year period we found some developments. Some of the women became CEOs of other companies, some women moved from one ideal type to another, and some simply reduced their board involvements. The women typically moved from the three first ideal types to the fourth (the value-creators).

Chapter 13 contains the stories from some of the women board members, with emphasis on their own contributions, motivations and challenges. The chapter contains stories from Ingvild Myhre, Merethe Lütken, Thorhild Widvey and Nini Høegh Nergaard. They represent different ideal types of women that are now highly present and visible on corporate boards. Their stories are summarized in Table 14.1.

Table 14.1   The stories of four women board members

	Nini Nergaard	Merethe Lütken	Thorhild Widvey	Ingvild Myhre
Who are you?	39 years, law degree, 'stay-at-home mom'	51 years, consultant, speaker and writer	55 years, politics	53 years, from business, engineer
Why a board member?	Always interested – a way of channeling energy	Started a board career after 20 years in management positions – an arena to utilize knowledge, experience and networks	Always been on boards	Challenging, exciting and fun

Table 14.1 continued

	Nini Nergaard	Merethe Lütken	Thorhild Widvey	Ingvild Myhre
How and when recruited?	Recommended by colleagues, ownership links and acquaintances	Results of networks – recommend- ations	Received 70 phone calls with invitations in 2005 when period as Minister of Oil and energy ended, usually asked by the CEO	Was middle manager and was recommended by her boss
Your particular contribution on boards?	Analytic approach, willing to be the 'skunk'	Previous experience on boards and as executive, also bringing structures, routines and governance to the boards, being the 'skunk'	Big network, competence, knowledge and experience, has been living abroad	Contributing to creativity and strategic thinking in the boardroom
Perception of the gender balance law?	Arguments against the law have proven invalid	The business case is obviously positive – competence and diversity	The intentions of the law have been met	Was against, but became positive, there was a need to get women on boards
Lessons from working on boards?	It is hard work – sometimes stressful and unpleasant	Differences between men and women, the importance of the chairperson, weigh risks carefully	Every board member must focus on what creates value, a good chairperson is the one that makes the other board members perform	Collaborate with the executives to contribute to the long-term value creation of the company

Some similarities and differences among the women are displayed in the table. The four women are examples of the four ideal types. They have different backgrounds, have various motivations to work on boards, and they make different contributions. Their main lessons from working on boards also vary. The main similarity is that today they all are positive about the law, even though three of them were negative when the law was introduced.

I have in this unique perspective from the field learned something about the women who are recruited to boards as a result of the Norwegian gender balance law. I have gone beyond much of the stereotypical thinking that there is only one type of women who is generally qualified for board positions. I have seen how different they are, and this must be recognized when arguing about the business case for women directors and the success of the Norwegian law.

REFERENCE

Ahern, K.R. and Dittmar, A.K. (2012) The changing of the boards: The impact on firm valuation of mandated female board representation, *Quarterly Journal of Economics*, 127(1): 137–197.

PART IV

Lessons from research on gender on boards

15. Women on boards: what we know, what we do not yet know and how we should further advance knowledge

Katrin Hansen

Two recent developments have prompted researchers to investigate the phenomenon of women on boards and associated dynamics and outcomes in boardrooms. On the one hand, there has been an intense political, economic and social discourse on women on boards, resulting in the introduction of quota laws and other formal devices in some countries. On the other hand, there has been increased public interest in corporate governance as a result of the 2008 crisis, associated with an awareness of ethical dilemmas and weaknesses in solving those in large firms' management and the subsequent debate on corporate social responsibility. This formed the background against which scholars that had been invited to the 2011 Think Tank on women on boards presented their insights, conclusions and suggestions.

Before I introduce the contributions from these scholars, a short overview is given on the recent developments in the field of research on women on boards. To structure the field I use three different lenses. First, I distinguish two perspectives from which boards and especially women on boards are approached and outcomes evaluated. Those are ethical–moral considerations and the business perspective. Second, I discuss the respective features of quantitatively oriented and qualitatively oriented studies and their interplay. Third and finally, I differentiate three levels that constitute the foci of investigations, namely the macro level (society, economics), the meso level (corporations, boards), and the micro level (individuals, micro-foundations), and suggest further research that involves multi-level designs.

Two distinct perspectives of approaching the women on boards phenomenon can be identified: ethical–moral and economic considerations. Ethical–moral considerations focus on the societal level as well as the individual level. From a society's perspective, gender equality, justice and the participation of historically discriminated social groups are criteria for investigating and evaluating the share and the position of women on boards of corporations and other important institutions such as non-profit health and social care organizations, universities, and political parties. Giving voice, power as well as income to those groups are central issues in this debate, and constitute one research stream (see Heidenreich, Chapter 17 and Seierstad, Chapter 20, in this volume).

Ethical–moral considerations are also discussed from an individual's perspective. Board positions are very attractive in that they often generate high income and the potential to exert strong influence on management decisions. Moreover they provide opportunities for personal development and the building of symbolic capital (Bourdieu, 1985 [1998]).

These considerations throw the spotlight on boards of large, and politically and economically important and influential organizations, such as Fortune 500, FTSE 100 or Dax corporations. These top groups have been the topic of many research projects such as Oehmichen et al. (2010), Holst & Wiemer (2010), Egon Zehnder International (2010), Ruhwedel (2011), Board Academy (2011) and Catalyst (2011a, 2011b), to name but a few recent studies. The research here tends to combine the societal perspective with a discussion of the business case by using data from the largest firms.

Economic considerations aim on building a business case. From this perspective, women on boards, or diversity of boards in a broader sense, is interpreted as a strategic resource (Hillman et al., 2007; Ladegård, Chapter 21 in this volume) which under certain conditions generates positive effects on board process, behaviors, and overall board performance and effectiveness (Nielsen and Huse 2010a; Huse and Solberg, 2006; Erkut et al., 2008). Huse's concept of the 'value creating board' (Huse, 2007), and the associated model, can be used nicely to further investigate the contribution women as board members make to board performance (see Torchia, Chapter 18 in this volume; Huse, 2008; Huse et al., 2009). Seierstad further discusses 'utility' arguments and argues that: 'Over the last few years, financial instability has affected both countries and companies globally. This has given a renewed focus that highlights the need for further strategies to challenge the persistent trend of vertical sex segregation' (Seierstad, Chapter 20 in this volume).

The business case is also pursued by researchers in the world's leading consulting groups (e.g. McKinsey, 2007, 2008, 2009, 2010, 2012; Ernst & Young, 2012), and their focus often goes beyond women on boards to include women in top management positions in general. Catalyst as an international Think Tank provides a database to support discussions on the business case. Their recent study finds that: 'Companies with sustained high representation of women board directors (WBD) (three or more WBD in at least four of five years) significantly outperform those with sustained low representation (zero WBD in at least four of five years)' (Carter & Wagner, 2012, p. 1). The range of performance differential is quite remarkable according to Catalyst: 84 percent on ROS (return on sales), 60 percent on ROIC (return on invested capital), and 46 percent on ROE (return on equity) in the period 2004 to 2008. Nevertheless, the authors point out that 'These studies have examined historical data and revealed statistically significant correlations. The studies do not however, establish or imply causal connections' (Carter & Wagner, 2012, p. 3).

These considerations lead to a discussion on the methods that are used to research women on boards. Catalyst and most of the consultancies' studies are quantitatively oriented, and distinct patterns and relationships without necessarily revealing mediating factors, interdependencies, or underlying mechanisms and processes. Boerner et al. (2012) conclude from their meta-analysis on research on gender diversity that an agreed-upon and complex enough framework is still lacking. They propose that future research should investigate mediating and moderating variables related to the processing of task relevant information in a team or organization, which can be influenced by conflict, cohesion, commitment and in general by the normative fit between tasks and gender as perceived by the actors involved.

Indeed, we have to question whether statistically significant correlations represent causalities. To explore direct and indirect effects of the presence of women directors on boards, to understand board dynamics with their intended and non-intended outcomes, to highlight positive and vicious cycles, we need additional insights that can be gained by using qualitative methods. This is particularly required in instances where individual intent, group dynamics and social relations are involved, and where the phenomena are constructed and reconstructed in discourses. Bührmann, in Chapter 22 in this volume, argues that: 'we do not know much about the impact of these developments, just as we do not know how different processes and practices interact and what are their potential effects on the number of women on board'. Nevertheless, research on these questions is ongoing, and in this chapter and the other chapters in Part IV we will show how to learn more about these complexities.

In general, only a combination of quantitative and qualitative methods enables us to paint a full picture. This can be represented as an ongoing cycle of gaining insights from both methodological approaches, proceeding through different phases and with different aims and functions. The methods can be employed relatively independent from one another across several studies, or loosely yoked in a combination of individual studies, or indeed closely knit in a single study. In the narrower sense, this 'mixed approach' pursues the aim of 'confirming, cross-validating, or corroborating findings within a single study' (Creswell, 2003, p. 217) and thus meets the idea of triangulation (Flick, 2011). Figure 15.1 gives an overview of the specific tasks of each methodological approach in the phases of the research process as a whole.

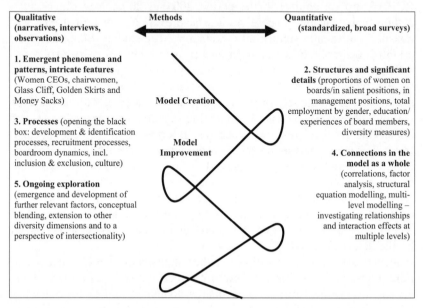

Figure 15.1   Research cycles

Most of the contributions to Part IV use quantitative methods. Two chapters focus on the identification of compositional patterns in the field of boards. Heidenreich (Chapter 17) presents results from the board member survey in Norwegian public limited companies, whereas Moore (Chapter 16) bases her analysis on secondary data with the aim of measuring 'the effectiveness and success of the drive to increase the representation of women on boards around the world'. Both authors analyse structures and compositional features and thereby open the field to qualitative research on underlying processes, and more complex quantitative tests of interdependencies and relationships.

Ladegård (Chapter 21) uses survey data to gain knowledge on how women directors experience their influence, participation and access to information from other board members. The study aims to understand 'women directors' own experiences about the presence of conditions for effective task performance on the board on which they hold a present position'. Those experiences can be interpreted as a mediating factor between the presence of women on boards and boards' effectiveness, and therefore Ladegård's contribution can be positioned on level four, visualized as shown in Figure 15.1. A similar approach is taken by Torchia whose chapter:

> addresses the question of whether an increased number of women directors results in the build-up of critical mass that substantially contributes to firm innovation. By identifying different minorities of women directors (one woman, two women and at least three women), I test whether, and to what extent, they could have an impact on the level of firm innovation. (Torchia, Chapter 18)

However, instead of testing a direct effect between presence of women directors and levels of innovation, Torchia provides a finer-grained analysis by testing for the mediating effects of board task performance, specifically board strategic tasks.

The third lens used is highlighting three different levels of focus of research on women on boards. Macro-level studies focus on society and/or economics, and mainly investigate board compositional issues and their implications. Catalyst is one of the organizations that provide international research and comparative data. One strand of its publications involves a global overview of comparative data on women on boards, including female chairpersons (Catalyst, 2011a). A second strand entails the documentation and analysis of political and legal activities across the globe (Catalyst, 2011b; see also Part V).

Aside from the international comparative studies, in Part IV we can also identify more detailed research at country level, and the following chapters take a closer look at such studies in Germany and Norway. In Germany, the German Institute for Economics (DIW) provides ongoing analysis on the structures of the most important corporations' boards. Holst and Wiemer (2010) give an overview on the development and current situation in Germany. They conclude that the predominance of men on the supervisory boards of Germany's largest private sector companies has created a 'male monoculture' there. Weckes (2011) investigates board structures of the Dax corporations with particular emphasis on gender relations, but also on the relations between employer and employee representatives, thereby pursuing an intersectional approach. FidAR as an activist organization (see Part V) started empirical research on women on executive and supervisory boards in Germany in 2011, and provides a continually updated list of the top 160 DAX corporations' ranking based on the documented number of women on their boards.

Turning to Norway, the Institute for Social Research in Oslo is an important source of research. Heidenreich's chapter exemplifies research at macro-level, analyzing consequences of the quota legislation on the board composition in Norwegian PLCs (see also Heidenreich and Storvik, 2010). Heidenreich (Chapter 17 in this volume) sums up the results from this research as follows: 'Educated and professional women have entered the boardrooms through the traditional recruitment channels to boards, that is, professional social networks. The women are independent and in general seem to be younger than the male board members. Among the board chairs, men are still in a striking majority.'

The results of research at the macro level are delivering important insights on the structures and trends in the field. However, the antecedents and consequences (individual, team or business related) of those structures are typically addressed by research at the meso and micro levels.

Research at the meso level may focus on the company and/or the boards as the unit of analysis, the latter being interpreted as a business entity with certain functions, tasks and outcomes, or as a team for a group dynamics perspective. Many of these studies conceptualize boards implicitly or explicitly as value-creating entities with different roles, certain tasks and interwoven processes. Some focus on relating certain board characteristics and specific board processes to financial performance of the corporation. I start with one example of the latter approach.

He and Huang (2011) ground their study in a business case and use financial performance of the firm as their outcome variable. They 'consider boards as human groups on the uppermost echelon of corporations' (2011, p. 1119), and investigate tacitly formed informal hierarchies based on directors' deference for one another. As He and Huang point out: 'A clear hierarchical order provides clear guidance about, for example, when to speak, how to speak, and with whom to talk, making board interactions smoother and more effective' (2011, p. 1122). They suggest three internal contingencies: (1) the rank of the firm's chief executive officer (CEO) in the board informal hierarchy; (2) the overall rank composition of a board; and (3) the size of a board. As external contingencies the authors consider past firm performance and environmental dynamics. He and Huang (2011) found that age, tenure and gender on their own are not significant predictors of financial performance. Instead, competence and influence seem to play a more important role in building informal hierarchies which, if they are quite clear to board members, seem to be positively related to financial performance. This is especially the case in a dynamic industry, in firms that have performed more poorly in the past, and in smaller boards with a middle-ranked board composition. The question of what constitutes perceived competence and influence is still left open in He and Huang's paper. Nevertheless, it shows (again) that gender per se should not be overestimated as a performance driver on boards.

A broader concept of performance is developed by Huse's model that emphasizes the need to understand boards as value-creating entities in which internal and external stakeholders interact (Huse, 2007). Analyzing Norwegian firms, Nielsen and Huse (2010a) find that women directors influence board strategic involvement through their contribution to board decision-making. This influence depends on women directors' professional experiences and the different values they bring to the board. The authors identify the perception of women as unequal board members as a limitation for their potential contribution to board decision-making. Further the authors show the impact of the chairperson's gender on the level of women's contribution to board decision-making (Nielsen and Huse, 2010b). In another paper, Huse et al. (2009) combine diversity dimensions, specifically gender, and status as employee- or employer-elected board member. They found that the contributions of women and employee-elected board members varied depending on the board tasks studied (see also Tacheva and Huse, 2006). They found that board effectiveness was positively influenced when the employee-elected board members were considered to have certain knowledge and information different from the other board members. From this the authors conclude that backgrounds and experiences of the board members should be taken into consideration when researching the implications of diversity, that is, the interplay between demographic and task-related diversity (see also Torchia et al., 2011).

Bolsø et al. (Chapter 19 in this volume) support the argument about the importance of board members' background broader than gender:

> According to our informants, when it comes down to the decisions they have to make as members of a corporate board, men and women are similar in very particular ways. They all have to take markets into consideration, they have to answer to owners, shareholders and company administrations. They belong to the same privileged social class, and are educated and trained in the same schools. They are managing large economic and socially important resources,

and both men and women will have to do that in accordance with shared ideas about what it means to manage in a responsible way. If they do not, there is no seat for them at the table.

Oehmichen et al. (2010) pursued a similar research question in German supervisory boards. They found an increasing acceptance of women board directors by their male colleagues if the latter could build on previous experiences of collaboration with female colleagues. Nevertheless, this holds only concerning women perceived as hierarchically equal. Thus, further research should be dedicated to analyzing what constitutes a perception of somebody being hierarchically equal in a boardroom setting, a question which requires multi-level modeling as will be shown in Chapter 23 in this volume.

Westphal and Stern (2007) analyze processes on US boards and in particular the likelihood to attain additional board appointments by use of provision of advice and information to CEOs and ingratiatory behavior toward peer directors. They show differences in relation to social groups:

> ethnic minorities and women are rewarded less than male Caucasians on the director labor market for engaging in a given level of advice giving or ingratiatory behavior (that is, they improve their chances of receiving a board appointment less by engaging in these behaviors), and they are punished *more* for engaging in monitoring and control behavior. (Westphal and Stern, 2007, p. 283)

They mark this as a 'subtle form of social discrimination in the corporate elite' (Westphal and Stern, 2007), which should be taken into consideration in research on social capital, a concept which in itself spans analysis at macro, meso and micro levels.

Torchia's chapter in this volume is another exemplar of research at the meso level. Pursuing the research question: 'Does an increased number of women on corporate boards result in a build up of critical mass that substantially contributes to firm innovation?' she concludes that, yes, this may be the case. Under certain conditions:

> attaining critical mass – going from one or two women (a few tokens) to at least three women (consistent minority) – makes it possible to enhance the level of firm innovation. Moreover, the results show that the relationship between the critical mass of women directors and the level of firm innovation is mediated by board strategic tasks. (Torchia, Chapter 18)

This is supported by Ladegård's study, who finds that:

the ratio of women on a board has impact on their experienced participation and influence. When the ratio of women increases on a board, each individual women director perceives that she has more influence. Although we have no 'objective' measures of each director's influence on board decisions, I suggest that the individual experiences are relevant indicators of real influence. Hence, a better gender balance may enable the women directors to perform their job on the board more effectively. (Ladegård, Chapter 21 in this volume)

In Ladegård's contribution, we can identify a combination in the levels of analysis, namely board processes at meso-level and individual women directors' perceptions and experiences at the micro-level.

We present in Part IV selected contributions from a group of international scholars. Their different approaches in terms of disciplinary underpinning, methodological stance and level of analysis allow us to understand and learn more about different facets of the same phenomenon. We start with Dorothy Perrin Moore (Chapter 16) who supplies a conscientiously investigated comprehensive overview on the situation of women on boards worldwide viewed from an US perspective. This is followed by Chapter 17 by Vibeke Heidenreich in which she presents the results from the first Norwegian board member survey conducted in the wake of the introduction of the gender quota regulation. Mariateresa Torchia's Chapter 18 also has an empirical setting in Norway, and she shows the importance of critical mass of women in boards, and involvement in decision-making on firm outcomes.

Agnes Bolsø et al. (Chapter 19), Cathrine Seierstad (Chapter 20) and Gro Ladegård (Chapter 21) delve even deeper into (micro) processes on boards. Seierstad explores views from women directors and their opinions of quotas. Ladegård investigates processes in Norwegian boards from an actor's point of view focusing on women's perceptions of their influence on board-decisions. We close Part IV with Andrea D. Bührmann's reflections on recent research activities on women on boards of directors from a sociologist point of view. She frames women on board research as an 'intersectionally inspired, transdisciplinary research field investigated by different quantitative and qualitative methods'. This is completely in line with the intention of this book.

REFERENCES

Board Academy (2011) Aufsichtsräte Deutscher Großunternehmen, available from http://www.board-academy.com/cms/upload/studien/BA_AR-Studie_ 2011.pdf (last accessed 8 March 2012).

Boerner, S., Keding, H. and Huettermann, H. (2012) Gender diversity und organisationserfolg – Eine kritische bestandsaufnahme, *Zeitschrift für Betriebswirtschaftliche Forschung*, 64: 37–70.

Carter, N.M. and Wagner, H.M. (2012) The bottom line – corporate performance and women's representation on boards (2004–2008), available from http://www.catalyst.org/publication/479/the-bottom-line-corporate-performance-and-womens-representation-on-boards-20042008 (last accessed 2 February 2012).

Catalyst (2011a) *Women on Boards*, available from http://www.catalyst.org/publication/433/women-on-boards (last accessed 2 February 2012).

Catalyst (2011b) *Increasing Gender Diversity on Boards: Current Index of Formal Approaches*, available from http://www.catalyst.org/publication/514/increasing-gender-diversity-on-boards-current-index-of-formal-approaches (last accessed 2 March 2012).

Creswell, J.W. (2003) *Research Design*, 2nd edn, Thousand Oaks, CA, USA; London, UK; and New Delhi, India: Sage.

Egon Zehnder International (2010) European board diversity analysis 2010. Is it getting easier to find women on European boards? available from http://www.womens-forum.com/uploads/assets/resource/73_file.pdf (last accessed 2 March 2012).

Erkut, S., Kramer, V.W. and Konrad, A.M. (2008) Critical mass: Does the number of women on a corporate board make a difference? in Vinnicombe S., Singh V., Burke R., Bilimoria D. and Huse M. (eds), *Women on Corporate Boards of Directors: International Research and Practice*, Cheltenham, UK and Northampton, MA, USA: Edward Elgar, pp. 222–232.

Ernst & Young (2012) Mixed leadership, available from http://www.ey.com/Publication/vwLUAssets/Mixed_Leadership/$FILE/Mixed%20Leadership%20 2012.pdf (last accessed 2 March 2012).

Flick, U. (2011) *Triangulation. Eine Einführung*, 3rd edn, Wiesbaden: VS Verlag für Sozialwissenschaften.

He, J. and Huang, Z. (2011) Board informal hierarchy and firm financial performance: Exploring a tacit structure guiding boardroom dynamics, *Academy of Management Journal*, 54(6): 1119–1140.

Heidenreich, V. and Storvik, A.E. (2010) Rekrutteringsmønstre, erfaringer og holdninger til styrearbeid blant ASA-selskapenes styrerepresentanter, Tabellrapport fra surveyundersøkelse ISF Rapport, Institute for Social Research Oslo.

Hillman, A.J., Shropshire, C. and Cannella, A.A. (2007) Organizational predictors of women on corporate boards, *Academy of Management Journal*, 50(4): 941–952.

Holst, E. and Wiemer, A. (2010) Zur Unterrepräsentanz von Frauen in Spitzengremien der Wirtschaft. Ursachen und Handlungsansätze, DIW Discussion Paper 1001, available from http://ideas.repec.org/p/diw/diwpp/dp1001.html (last accessed 5 November 2010).

Huse, M. (2007) *Boards, Governance and Value Creation*, Cambridge: Cambridge University Press.

Huse, M. (2008) Women directors and the 'black box' of board behavior, in Vinnicombe S., Singh V., Burke R., Bilimoria D. and Huse M. (eds), *Women* on Corporate Boards of Directors: International Research and Practice, Cheltenham, UK and Northampton, MA, USA: Edward Elgar, pp. 140–151.

Huse, M., Nielsen, S.T. and Hagen, I.M. (2009) Women and employee-elected board members, and their contributions to board control tasks, *Journal of Business Ethics*, 89(4): 581–597.

Huse, M. and Solberg, A.G. (2006) Gender related boardroom dynamics: How women make and can make contributions on corporate boards, *Women in Management Review*, 21(2): 113–130.

McKinsey (2007) Gender diversity, a corporate performance driver, available from http://www.mckinsey.de/html/publikationen/women_matter/2007/women_matter_01.asp (last accessed 8 March 2012).

McKinsey (2008) Female leadership, a competitive edge for the future, available from http://www.mckinsey.de/html/publikationen/women_matter/2008/women_matter_02.asp (last accessed 8 March 2012).

McKinsey (2009) Women leaders, a competitive edge in and after the crisis, available from http://www.mckinsey.de/downloads/publikation/women_matter/women_matter_3_brochure.pdf (last accessed 8 March 2012).

McKinsey (2010) Women at the top of corporations: Making it happen, available from http://www.mckinsey.de/html/publikationen/women_matter/2010/women_matter_4.asp (last accessed 8 March 2012).

McKinsey (2012) *Making the Breakthrough*, available from http://www.mckinsey.de/downloads/publikation/women_matter/20120305_Women_Matter_2012.pdf (last accessed 8 March 2012).

Nielsen, S. and Huse, M. (2010a) Women directors' contribution to board decision-making and strategic involvement: The role of equality perception, *European Management Review*, 7(1): 16–29.

Nielsen, S. and Huse, M. (2010b). The contribution of women on boards of directors: Going beyond the surface, *Corporate Governance: An International Review*, 18(2): 136–148.

Oehmichen, J., Rapp, M.S. and Wolff, M. (2010) Der Einfluss der Aufsichtsratszusammensetzung auf die Präsenz von Frauen in Aufsichtsräten, *Zeitschrift für Betriebswirtschaftliche* Forschung, 62: 503–532.

Ruhwedel, P. (2011) Aufsichtsratscore. Studie zu Effizienz, Besetzung und Transparenz deutscher Aufsichtsräte, available from http://www.ruhwedel.com/fileadmin/data/ruhwedel.com/downloads/Peter_Ruhwedel_Aufsichtsrats-Score.pdf (last accessed 8 March 2012).

Tacheva, S. and Huse, M. (2006) Women directors and board task performance: Mediating and moderating effects of board working style in boards and governance, *Best Paper Proceedings*, European Academy of Management, May, pp. 103–120.

Torchia, M., Calabrò, A. and Huse, M. (2011) Women directors on corporate boards: From tokenism to critical mass, *Journal of Business Ethics*, 102(2): 299–317.

Weckes, M. (2011) Geschlechterverteilung in Vorständen und Aufsichtsräten in den 160 börsennotierten Unternehmen (Dax-30, M-Dax, S-Dax, Tec-Dax), available from http://www.boeckler.de/pdf/mbf_gender_2011.pdf (last accessed 8 March 2012).

Westphal, J.D. and Stern, I. (2007) Flattery will get you everywhere (especially if you are a male Caucasian): How ingratiation, boardroom behaviour, and demographic minority status affect additional board appointments at US companies, *Academy of Management Journal*, 50(2): 267–288.

16. Women on boards: the United States in a global comparison

Dorothy Perrin Moore

The key focus of the 2011 Women on Board Conference at the Norwegian School of Management BI was how to measure the effectiveness and success of the drive to increase the representation of women on boards around the world. The discussion started with the Norwegian business case, tracing the earlier efforts to increase the number of women on corporate boards from fewer than 7 percent of the seats to the mandated goal to fill at least 40 percent of the seats on the boards of directors of public companies with women and similarly at least 40 percent of the seats with men. By 2010, this had been largely achieved.

The Norwegian model had a far-reaching impact. Finland, with a present-day board representation of 23.4 percent, enacted a requirement that women constitute at least 40 percent of board members in companies wholly owned by the state, an objective achieved in the spring of 2006; and in 2010, a corporate governance code that required public companies to have representation from both genders on the board of directors. Sweden (23.9 percent women on corporate boards) enacted a corporate governance code in 2008 for public companies requiring them to strive for equal gender distribution on boards. An equality law introduced in Spain in 2007 required public companies with more than 250 employees to 'develop gender equality plans with clear implications for female appointments to the board', with the objective that by 2015 they would represent at least 40 percent of board members. Joining Iceland, Finland, Denmark and Ireland in mandating quotas, the French Parliament gave final approval to a law requiring large companies to have at least 40 percent female board members within six years. In Italy, where women have only a 6.8 percent representation, the Italian lower house approved a 30 percent quota for corporate boards and the Senate passed an amended version of the law. Rejecting quotas, but clearly making gender equality a priority, the British government endorsed the conclusions of a report it had commissioned that stated that by 2015 women should make up at least 25 percent of the boards of the largest British firms. Similarly, the Australian government mandated that by 2013 all companies with 100 or more employees must report their gender statistics to the Equal Opportunity for Women in the Workplace Agency (Moore, 2012).

In the United States, the fact that by the beginning of the twenty-first century female customers controlled over 80 percent of personal and family expenditures and made 75 percent of purchasing decisions made it clear to many that companies could benefit from the insights of female board members. While research findings were mixed, there was sufficient evidence to strongly suggest that adding highly qualified and motivated women to corporate boards in sufficient numbers to be effective yielded positive results. According to S&P GovernanceMetrics, for example, US companies with a board membership of at least 22 percent women showed the highest board performance; companies with 13 percent, the lowest. Catalyst reported that companies with three or more women on their boards increased their return on equity 112 percent. But women made up only 15.7 percent of the corporate board membership of publicly traded US companies of all sizes in 2010. To be innovative and competitive US firms needed to work to bring women into more corporate board rooms in greater numbers to contribute to firm innovation, elevate strategic planning and enhance productivity.[1] Is this taking place? How does the US compare to Norway, the leading advocate and role model nation for women on boards?

Given the differences in the society and culture (the Norwegian population is relatively homogenous, the United States is far more diverse), legal structures and the political and economic systems (large sectors of the Norwegian economy, especially energy, are wholly or partially state-owned), developments have taken a different path. To begin with, for reasons deeply embedded in society, there is little likelihood a US government would go further than offering such encouragement as the regulation adopted by the Securities and Exchange Commission (SEC) in February 2010, that public companies and mutual funds must disclose whether or not diversity is considered when directors are named and, if so, how the policy will be implemented and its effectiveness evaluated. For the reasons discussed below, there is no foreseeable possibility that any administration would mandate gender diversity on the boards of companies where stock is publically held. Influences in the USA include cultural, social and economic factors, the sheer numbers of people and businesses large and small, the complex diversity of US society, the large number of women moving into private ownership, and the 'lessons' learned from the decades of civil rights advancement.

The key word in the SEC regulation is diversity. On New Year's Day 2012, the resident US population topped 312 million. In the 2010 census, one person out of every four had put themselves in a designated minority category such as Black or African-American (13.6 percent of the population), Native American (1.7 percent), Native Hawaiian/Pacific Islander (0.4 percent), Some Other Race (7.0 percent) or the fastest-growing categories of Hispanic or Latino (16.3 percent) and Asian (5.6 percent).[2] With regard to gender, since the beginning of the twenty-first century, women have held nearly half of all managerial and executive positions (48.1 percent) and accounted for more than one-half (52.8 percent) of the employed professionals.[3] In part, this was because women now made up well over half of the enrolments in two-year institutions, four-year colleges and graduate programs and were now earning more than half of all Bachelor's, Master's and Doctoral degrees and a fraction less than half of all professional degrees. These gains did not come because women were taking the places of men, as the number of men earning degrees also increased, but because women were enrolling in programs of higher education in greater numbers.[4]

The strongest forces driving the dramatic changes in the market and advancement opportunities for women and minorities over the last 40 years were the impact of the Equal Employment Opportunity and Affirmative Action programs whose full effects began to slowly penetrate the economy in the 1970s and 1980s (Konrad and Linnehan, 1999). Initially debated over matters of race – sex was added to the proposed bill by an opponent who was trying to kill it by making a joke – this legislation had been severely contested and in its final form specifically rejected the use of quotas except in cases of proven discriminatory hiring and promotion practices. Among the reasons were the complexities involved in dealing with the numerous ethnic, socio-economic, and marginalized groups as well as gender and the inevitable backlash from males who would feel they were being pushed out.

The business landscape is equally diverse. For some time, many of the largest US companies had been moving in the direction of increasing the number of women on their boards. In 2010, some 19.4 percent of the board members of the Fortune 100 companies were women. But among the companies in the Fortune 1000 the disparity was striking. Nearly one-third of these firms had a 20 percent or greater board representation of women. But a plurality of these companies (33 percent) had only one woman board member and 18 percent had no women board members.[5]

To focus solely on the Fortune 500s and 1000s can be misleading. The largest group of US businesses, more than 99 percent, have 500 employees or fewer and are considered small businesses.[6] In this huge cluster are found the family-owned firms, the expanding number of home-based businesses, sole proprietorships and limited liability companies. The important statistics here are that 'Enterprises that are at least 51 percent owned by women account for 29 percent of all companies in the United States'. Women not only have staying power but start businesses at 1.5 times the national rate, and are now estimated to own just over 8.1 million firms.[7] This leads directly to the suggestion that in addition to examining the status of women on corporate boards in any given society, one needs to also examine the presence and percentage of women business owners, the sizes of their firms and their impact on the economy. Two current developments are interacting worldwide, simultaneously. One is characterized in the special task force on women in the economy published in the *Wall Street Journal* (April 2011) which reports that half of the global growth in women entrepreneurs comes from the developing world. The second is highlighted in the *Global Entrepreneurship Monitor (GEM) 2010 Women's Report* which lists the 22 high-income, innovation-driven economies and notes that the US is one of the two most highly internationalized innovation-driven countries (Kelley et al., 2011).

Here is how they fit together. Innovation-driven economies have the advantages of a base of ongoing research and development, knowledge intensity and an expanding service sector that provides a great potential for innovative entrepreneurial opportunity. This does not mean that the effects on women and men are equal. The proportion of women entrepreneurs within the GEM group is not high overall. Socialization, fields of educational attainment and push and pull economic factors all play a role. According to the GEM 2006 report, the highest ratios of female entrepreneurial participation are in Belgium and Switzerland, with ratios of around 80 women to 100 men, and in the United States with a ratio of 85 to 100. In the US, the growth in female entrepreneurship is strongly influenced by opportunity as well as necessity in times of economic instability, and the fact that women maintain smaller firms. As a result, the two most distinct groups of women entrepreneurs today consist of the 'Careerpreneurs' and the 'Mompreneurs'. 'Careerpreneurs' are the women with corporate experience and ambition, predominantly mid-career, who are most likely to succeed in running the businesses they start. The 'Mompreneur' group is drawn from the more than 72 percent of mothers (predominately young) participating in the US workforce for whom technological innovations make possible the part-time, private business ownership that gives them the flexibility they need to balance work and family (Moore, 2012). By contrast, Norwegian women are an entrepreneurial minority, which is why the Norwegian government formulated an action plan with the objective that women would represent at least 40 percent of all entrepreneurs by 2013.

Finally, with regard to corporate boards in the US, groups of citizens, consumers, stockholders and a number of advocacy groups led by women who currently serve on corporate boards have led to the creation of the '2020 Women on Boards Campaign'. With the support of more than 28 non-profit strong and strategically placed organizations as well as corporate sponsors, this strong advocacy group has now gone national with the aim of having a 20 percent or greater representation of women on public boards by 2020.[8] At the end of January each year a list of those companies meeting the 2020 challenge are posted for wide circulation around the globe. Publicity does bring a lot of attention for the need for change, and especially among organizations that heavily depend on the consumer dollar.

NOTES

1. Catalyst (2011). US Women in Business. Pyramids, citing Catalyst, 2010 Catalyst Census; Fortune 500 Women Board Directors (2010); Catalyst, 2010 Catalyst Census Fortune 500 Women Executive Officers and Top Earners (2010). Retrieved from http://www.catalyst.org/publication/132/us-women-in-business; Globewomen Issue No. LXXX. (Dec. 17, 2010). Retrieved from http:globewomen.org.
2. US Census Bureau (Dec. 29, 2011). Census Bureau Projects U.S. Population of 312.8 Million on New Year's Day. Retrieved Jan. 1, 2012 from http://www.census.gov/newsroom/releases/archives/ population/cb11-219.html; 2010 Census Race Alone or In Combination. Retrieved Jan. 1, 2012 from http://2010.census.gov/news/releases/operations/cb11-cn125.html.
3. Department of Labor, Bureau of Labor Statistics, Current Population Survey. Civilian labor force participation rate 16 yrs or over in April, 2011. Retrieved from http://www.bls.gov/cps/
4. U.S. Department of Education, National Center for Education Statistics. Higher Education General Information Survey. Degrees and other formal awards conferred. Surveys 1976–1977 and 1980–81; and 1989–1990 through 2007–08. *Educational data system compilations survey* (Prepared June, 2009). Tables 278, 285, 288, 291, 292, 294. Retrieved from http'//nces.ed.gov/programs/digest/2009menu_tables.asp; *The Chronicle of Higher Education Almanac Issue 2010–2011.* (Aug. 27, 2010). LVII, 1, 26–31.
5. Governance Metrics (March 8, 2011); Catalyst C-News. (Aug. 2011). Changing work places, changing lives, *3*(7); Governance Metrics (March 8, 2011); Catalyst (2011). U.S. Women in Business. Pyramids, citing Catalyst, 2010 Catalyst Census; Fortune 500 Women Board Directors (2010); Nanivadekar, M. (2010). Overview: Women's leadership in the global context. In K. O'Connor (ed.), *Gender and Women's Leadership: A Reference Handbook* (pp. 293–303); Soares, R., Combopiano, J., Regis, A., Shur, Y. and Wong, R. (2010). Women on boards; 2010 Catalyst Census: *Fortune 500 Women Board Directors*(Catalyst, 2010), pp. 1–16. Retrieved from http://www.catalyst.org/publication/433/women-on-boards.

6. U.S. Census Bureau (2008). Table 2a. Employment Size of Employer and Non-employer Firms Retrieved from http://www.census.gov/econ/smallbus.html; U.S. Small Business Administration FAQs: Advocacy Small Business Statistics and Research. Retrieved from http://web.sba.gov/faqs/faqIndexAll.cfm?areaid=24
7. The American Express OPEN State of Women-Owned Businesses Report – *A Summary of Important Trends, 1997–2011. (2011).* Report prepared by Womenenable. Retrieved from http://media.nucleus.naprojects.com/pdf/WomanReport_FINAL.pdf
8. 2020 Women on Boards Campaign. Retrieved on Dec. 31st, 2011 from http://www.2020wob.com/.

REFERENCES

Kelley, D.J., Brush, C.G., Greene, P.G. and Litovsky, Y. (2011) *Global Entrepreneurship Monitor 2010 Women's Report*, Center for Women's Business Research, Babson, available from http://gemconsortium.org/article.aspx?id=185.

Konrad, A. and Linnehan, F. (1999) Affirmative action: History, effects, and attitudes, in G. Powell (ed.), *Handbook of Gender and Work*, Thousand Oaks, CA, USA; London, UK; and New Delhi, India: Sage Publications, pp. 429–452.

Moore, D.P. (2012) Women on board – the business case, *WomenPreneurs: 21st Century Success Strategies*, New York, USA: Routledge.

17. Consequences of the Norwegian gender quota regulation for public limited company boards

Vibeke Heidenreich

INTRODUCTION AND BACKGROUND

This chapter presents the first board member survey done in the wake of the introduction of the gender quota regulation to Norwegian public limited companies (PLCs) (Heidenreich and Storvik, 2010). In December 2003, after a prolonged period of intense discussions, the political demand for more women corporate board members led to the gradual introduction of gender quotas for most of Norway's leading companies, including all listed companies. The gender quota regulations were formulated as new paragraphs in the existing Company Laws: § 6-11 in the law covering the public limited companies (PLC) and § 20-6 in the law covering state-owned private limited companies (Ltd). The gender quota regulation also applies for the boards of other kinds of municipal and state owned companies, but does not apply to private limited companies (Ltd).

The corporate boards of the companies affected by the regulation are obliged to have a balanced representation of men and women. The gender quota regulation is often referred to as the 40 percent rule. Actually, the minimum requirements for gender representation vary between 33 percent for boards with three members, up to 50 percent in boards with two, four or six members. For boards with five, seven, nine or more members, the minimum requirement is 40 percent or more. The regulation also applies for the election of the employees' representatives, except in companies where more than 80 percent of the employees are either men or women.

The Norwegian gender quota regulation was put into effect for state-owned companies on 1 January 2004, for new PLCs on 1 January 2006, and for existing PLCs on 1 January 2008. There are now just under

350 PLCs and close to 1200 other companies affected by the gender quota regulation (Business Register, 2010; State Ownership Report, 2010).

The Company Acts apply identical sanctions for breach of their diverse rules and that is forced dissolution. Consequently, a company that does not have a legal board, despite several warnings that give the company an opportunity to correct the matter, will be subject to forced dissolution.

In the late 1990s, when debate sparked off in Norway, no reliable statistics covering the presence of women in the board rooms existed. However, a mapping suggested that women occupied 6 percent of the board positions (ECON, 2003). After the introduction of the gender quota regulation, the proportion of women rapidly increased until reaching 40 percent (Figure 17.1).

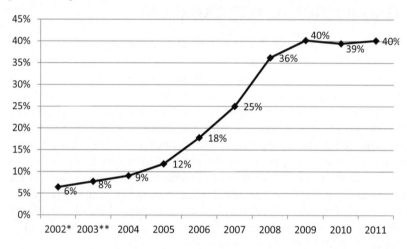

Sources: 2002*: ECON Rapport (2003); 2003**: calculated mean between 2002 and 2004; 2004–2011: Statistics Norway

*Figure 17.1   Proportion of women on Norwegian PLC boards (2002–
          2011)*

In order to extend our knowledge of the board composition in the wake of the gender quota regulation, a survey was carried out during the autumn of 2009. Questionnaires went out to 1411 board members of PLCs in Norway. The response rate was 62 percent. Among the 880 respondents, 42 percent were women.

RESULTS

Position on the Board

A gender hierarchy persists within the boards. Only 3 percent of the women in the survey are board chairs, while 32 percent of the men have this position. Eight percent of the women and 9 percent of the men report being board deputy. The employee representatives are more often male (19 percent of the men) than female (11 percent of the women).

Age Distribution

There are considerably more young women than men among the respondents. Nineteen percent of the women are 40 years old or younger (men 8 percent). Only 6 percent of the women are 60 or older, compared to 29 percent of men. Many newly recruited women board members tend to be relatively young. In addition, new and young women board members are probably not replacing the 'old boys' but the young men, who are either not getting board positions in the first place, or are substituted by women to meet legal demands.

Educational Attainment

The education level of the board members is generally high, with more than 70 percent having four years or more of university education. Women board members' educational level are somewhat higher than for the men; this mainly correlates with age as the older men seldom have higher education compared to women the same age.

Type of Education

The differences between men and women board members when it comes to types of education are relatively small. Fifty percent of both men and women are educated in business management. The men tend to be more often educated within science and technology, most likely as graduate engineers, and the women are somewhat more often lawyers. This reflects the main patterns of gender differences in educational backgrounds.

Main Occupation

Men more often than women report being a partner or self-employed, while women more often report being a manager at some level. Unfortunately, participants' privacy protection, monitored by the by the Data Inspectorate, prevented us from asking on what organizational level participants were managers.

Ownership Interests

More women (77 percent) than men (45 percent) report not having major ownership interests in the company (including their family). Similarly, more men (56 percent) than women (23 percent) report representing an investor or major shareholder, or being major shareholders themselves. Consequently, more women board members than men board members can be described as 'independent' of the company in question.

Changes in the Functioning of the Board

The most widespread opinion among the board members is that nothing much has changed as a result of the quota reform. This is a particularly widespread response among the men (60 percent). Women more than men (20 percent and 12 percent respectively) say that the functioning of the board has improved. A minority of the men (11 percent) says that the functioning of the board has worsened or become more problematic. Two women agree on this. The largest proportion of the women respondents (44 percent) do not know whether the quota reform has led to changes in the board work, or they report that the reform did not touch upon the company of which they were serving as a board member. The board members with positive experiences were asked what improvements they had noticed. There are only marginal differences between the men and the women. Most frequently they either say that more women in the boards has led to new perspectives being offered or that there are more discussions around the issues on the board agenda. The few persons who are negative to the reform and its consequences, mostly men, believe that the new women lack the necessary competence.

Recruitment Procedures

There are no indications that headhunters or databases are more commonly used in recruiting women board members, or are being more commonly used than before the introduction of the quota regulation. The election committees apparently manage to recruit the necessary number of women board members by their own effort. We see no indications either that more women are being recruited from the private social networks of owners, managers and nomination committee members. Few women report having family affiliations to major shareholders and few women report being recruited through a social network of friends or family. Women are recruited to boards in the same way as men, that is, through their professional and social relations.

CONSEQUENCES

Decrease in the Number of PLCs

At the same time as the gender quota regulation was implemented, there was a major drop in the number of PLCs. When the law was passed in 2003, there were 554 PLCs, whereas in 2010 there were only 339 (Business Register, 2003, 2010). About 100 companies re-registered from public limited to private limited companies in 2007. What is the reason for this drop – are companies evading the gender quota?

A closer examination reveals that this may be too hasty an assumption. One main reason for the rise in re-registrations relates to a change in the legislation covering trade with securities in 2007. Until then, financial companies trading securities had to be registered as PLCs. From 2007 onwards this was no longer necessary, and a number of companies chose to change their formal status to private limited company, a status less demanding when it comes to a wide scope of regulations including accounting and claims to compulsory equity. An anonymous survey that the Institute for Social Research conducted with chief executive officers (CEOs) and board leaders with a representative sample of 108 of all 126 companies re-registering from PLC to private limited company (Ltd) in 2007 and 2008 also indicated that the quota arrangements were not the main reason for re-registering of companies. The main reasons given were that it was more convenient or practical to be a private limited company (60 percent); that it was possible to register as a private limited company as a consequence of the change in the Norwegian law covering financial companies and requirements to their formal status (36 percent); and that the company had restructured (36 percent). Very few respondents mentioned the quota law as a direct reason for re-registering the company from PLC to Ltd during 2007 and 2008.

Women in Other Top Positions

There is a striking stability in the gender composition of private limited company boards, the proportion of women being at 17 percent (Statistics Norway). The proportion of women CEOs is increasing slowly and is now 7 percent in the PLCs and 14 percent in the Ltds (Statistics Norway). The gender quota regulation can indirectly help to explain the stability in the boards of private limited companies, as well as the stability in the proportion of women CEOs in PLCs and Ltds. Because the demand for women to the PLC boards has increased, the supply of women available to fill other top positions may have decreased correspondingly. The most visible and experienced business women are in a situation where they can choose between several bids to attractive board positions. On the other hand, the display of competent women board members could inspire businesswomen to career climbing, as the highest positions of trust now seem more open to them.

'Golden Skirts'

Recent network analyses indicate that the gender quota regulation has led to an increase in persons with multiple board memberships and that this goes both for men and women; however, more for men than women (Seierstad and Opsahl, 2011). How can we explain the increase of multiple board memberships as an effect of the quota law? A main reason for the increase among women is probably an effect of the perceived limited supply of women candidates with the relevant qualifications and experience. The most experienced and visible women candidates get many offers to sit on company boards. In accepting these offers, there is a tendency that a few very experienced women monopolize the board positions.

A main reason for the increase of men with multiple board memberships is probably that it is the most powerful men that remain on the board, while the least experienced men have been substituted by women to fill the gender quota requirements. This tendency of power concentration questions the democracy argument for the quota law. On the one hand, the gender quota regulation has opened the boardroom and women's access to power in Norwegian economic life in a way and to an extent which we have never seen before. Simultaneously, board memberships are concentrated on fewer persons as an effect of the quota law. Whether this reflects a transition problem and an adjustment to the requirements in the law, or a new tendency of concentration of power in economic life, is too soon to say.

CONCLUSION

This chapter offers a comparison of men and women PLC board members in the wake of the introduction of the gender quota regulation to boards, and looks at what effects this regulation has on the companies and the boards affected concerning recruiting and functioning. The main results can be summed up in the following. Educated and professional women have entered the boardrooms through the traditional recruitment channels to boards, that is, professional social networks. The women are independent and in general seem to be younger than the male board members. Among the board chairs, men are still in a striking majority. In the Norwegian public debate the quota reform has been little discussed after it was implemented. The main impression is that it is widely accepted and that more women in the boards have not engendered large modifications in how boards work. On the other hand, there is little evidence so far pointing in the direction of the gender quota regulation as a major promoter of more access for women to a wider scope of positions of power in economic life.

REFERENCES

Business Register (2003) http://www.brreg.no/statistikk/2003/fore1.html (last accessed 20 December 2011).
Business Register (2010) http://www.brreg.no/organisasjon/aarsmelding/ (last accessed 20 December 2011).
ECON Rapport (2003) Kvinner og menn med styreverv, Prosjekt nr. 37660, Oslo: ECON.
Heidenreich, V. and Storvik, A.E. (2010) Rekrutteringsmønstre, erfaringer og holdninger til styrearbeid blant ASA-selskapenes styrerepresentanter. Tabell-rapport fra surveyundersøkelse, *ISF Rapport 2010*, 11, Oslo: Institute for Social Research.
Seierstad, C. and Opsahl, T. (2011) For the few not the many? The effects of affirmative action on presence, prominence, and social capital of female directors in Norway, *Scandinavian Journal of Management*, 27(1): 44–54.
State Ownership Report (2010) http://www.eierberetningen.no/2010/index.php?seks_id=5330&element=Del (last accessed 20 December 2011).
Statistics Norway (n.d.), www.ssb.no, diverse statistics.

18. Women directors and corporate innovation: a critical mass perspective

Mariateresa Torchia[1]

INTRODUCTION

Drawing on the critical mass theory (Granovetter, 1978; Kanter, 1977a, 1977b, 1987), this chapter addresses the question of whether an increased number of women directors results in the build-up of critical mass that substantially contributes to firm innovation. By identifying different minorities of women directors (one woman, two women and at least three women), I test whether, and to what extent, they could have an impact on the level of firm innovation. Moreover, I explore how women directors contribute to the level of firm innovation by looking at boards as decision-making groups performing different tasks (Forbes and Milliken, 1999; Robinson and Dechant, 1997). Specifically, I analyse whether, and to what extent, the contribution of women directors to the level of firm innovation could be mediated by board strategic tasks.

The key research questions are: (1) Is there a critical mass to reach ('three women directors') to have a bearing on the level of firm innovation? (2) Do board strategic tasks mediate the relationship between the critical mass of women directors and the level of firm innovation? To address these questions, the chapter statistically tests the effects that different sizes of minority group (one woman, two women and three women) could have on firm organizational innovation. Moreover, the mediating role of board strategic tasks is tested. Tests were conducted on a sample of 317 Norwegian firms.

The selection of the country is critical since Norwegian legislation makes Norway one of the few countries in the world with a sufficient number of companies where gender diversity can be said to have been taken beyond tokenism and thus enabling us to select a good number of companies in the independent variables of one, two or three women directors.

THEORETICAL FRAMEWORK

The arguments for a higher number of women in corporate boards are numerous (Burke, 1997; Carver, 2002; Cassell, 2000; Huse, 2005; Singh et al., 2006) but in many countries, women who serve as board members are still tokens (Daily and Dalton, 2003; Kanter, 1977a, 1977b; Singh et al., 2001; Terjesen et al., 2009).

Drawing on the critical mass theory, I build on research on the minority and majority influence on group decision-making as well as on tokenism theories. In particular, I look at women directors as a minority subgroup within a larger group. In this regard, for decades research has studied the effects of majority and minority influence in small groups. These studies demonstrate that the majority exerts more influence in a group of people than minorities do, by virtue of their greater numbers (Asch, 1951, 1955; Tanford and Penrod, 1984). Minorities are easily marginalized when their presence in a larger group is modest. Due to their under-representation in the group, they are viewed as a symbol or a token (Kanter, 1977a, 1977b).

However, when the size of the minority group increases to the point that it is no longer a token minority, the perspective of its members and the nature of the relations between the minority and majority changes qualitatively (Etzkowitz et al., 1994). Critical mass theory (Kanter, 1977a, 1977b, 1987; Granovetter, 1978) in particular suggests that the nature of group interactions depends upon size. When the size of the subgroup reaches a certain threshold or critical mass, the subgroup's degree of influence increases.

It does not, however, suggest what number represents the critical mass. To answer this question, I use Asch's (1951, 1955) studies and experiments, leading to the definition of a threshold that represents critical mass. These studies suggest that when an individual is faced with the unanimous opinion of three people, they feel pressure to conform to the others. The Asch experiment demonstrates that the effectiveness of group pressure increases markedly when the group size is three, but further increases in group size add little to the overall effect. In accordance, other studies suggest that three usually represents the tipping point (critical mass) influencing the group setting (Bond, 2005; Nemeth, 1986; Tanford and Penrod, 1984). Drawing on the preceding arguments, recent studies of women on corporate boards (Erkut et al., 2008; Konrad et al., 2008) suggest that the critical mass of women directors is reached when boards of directors have 'at least three women'.

While these studies help to identify the critical mass of women directors, empirical tests are still required to strengthen its overall validity of corporate board studies. This chapter thus fills a gap in the literature, using arguments from critical mass theory and testing the validity of the 'at least three women' critical mass of women directors. Specifically, I test the relationships between different minorities of women directors (one woman, two women, at least three women) and the level of firm innovation.

HYPOTHESES FORMULATION

Women may differ from men in several aspects in this sphere. Some scholars argue that women can add unique perspectives, experiences and working styles compared to their male counterparts (Daily and Dalton, 2003; Huse and Solberg, 2006). Women are generally considered to have more wisdom and diligence than many male board members (Huse and Solberg, 2006). They are also able to create a good atmosphere in the boardroom, representing diversity, different values and women's issues (Bilimoria and Huse, 1997). Indeed, they may bring different values (Selby, 2000), knowledge and expertise (Hillman et al., 2002) to boards, thus positively influencing the level of organizational innovation. Drawing on critical mass arguments, it is to be expected that the contributions of women directors become more pronounced once there are 'at least three women' in the boardroom. In order to test the validity of the critical mass arguments, I also test the impact that different sizes of minority groups (one woman, two women) may have on firm organizational innovation. The expectation is that boards with one woman or two women have no impact on the level of organizational innovation. Hence, the influence of women directors on organizational innovation becomes pronounced when they reach the size of at least three. Therefore, I formulate the following three hypotheses:

Hypothesis 1a: There is no relationship between one woman director and the level of firm organizational innovation.

Hypothesis 1b: There is no relationship between two women directors and the level of firm organizational innovation.

Hypothesis 1c: There is a positive relationship between the critical mass of women directors (at least three women) and the level of firm organizational innovation.

Recent literature has investigated, through a value chain approach, how the various board tasks contribute to the value creation process (Huse, 2007; Huse et al., 2005). It was found that the greatest degree of board contribution to innovation is through strategic involvement. In fact, the studies suggest that board strategic involvement has a positive impact on firm innovation. Accordingly, I formulate the following hypothesis:

Hypothesis 2: Boards' strategic tasks mediate the relationship between the critical mass of women directors and the level of firm organizational innovation.

Figure 18.1 summarizes the research model and hypotheses formulation.

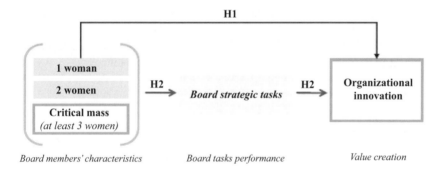

Figure 18.1   Research model and hypotheses on the effects of critical mass of women

METHODS

Data Collection and Sample

This study is based on a unique survey conducted among Norwegian companies during the winter 2005–2006 and the first half of 2006 (Huse, 2009). The hypotheses were tested on CEO responses, with an overall response rate of 33 percent. I selected 317 firms.

Measures

The dependent variable (organizational innovation) was measured with several items on a seven-point Likert-type scale (7 = fully agree, 1 = fully disagree).

The number of women directors is the independent variable. The sample was divided into four groups considering the number of women. In particular, the first group included firms with boards without any women; the second had only one woman, the third had two women directors and the last had 'at least three women directors'. I used three dummy variables: one woman (assuming value '1' if boards had only one woman, '0' otherwise); two women (assuming value '1' if boards had two women, '0' otherwise); at least three women – critical mass (assuming value '1' if boards had at least three women, '0' otherwise).

The mediating variable (board strategic tasks) was measured with several items on a seven-point Likert type scale (7 = fully agree, 1 = fully disagree).

I control for different variables influencing the level of firm organizational innovation, including firm size, industrial sector board size, CEO and chairperson tenure, CEO and chairperson gender, the length of board meetings, and director's knowledge and competence.

Analyses

I statistically tested the effects that the different sizes of the minority group (one woman, two women and three women) could have on firm organizational innovation. Moreover, the mediating role of board strategic tasks was tested using Baron and Kenny's (1986) mediating model. The hypotheses were tested using multiple linear regressions.

RESULTS

Pearson's correlation analyses were performed and the results are reported in Table 18.1 and Table 18.2 summarizes the results from the hypotheses testing.

Table 18.1 Correlation matrix (317 firms)

	Mean	S.D.	1	2	3	4	5	6	7	8	9	10	11	12	13	14
1. Firm size	437.2	891.4	–													
2. Industrial sector	0.39	0.48	0.06	–												
3. Board size	7.12	1.22	0.34**	0.04	–											
4. CEO tenure	6.82	5.95	0.01	0.01	0.03	–										
5. Board Chair tenure	4.77	5.35	–0.05	0.01	–0.07	0.18**	–									
6. CEO gender	0.95	0.23	0.05	0.03	–0.04	0.07	0.11	–								
7. Board Chair gender	0.93	0.25	0.01	0.05	0.07	–0.12*	0.09	0.11	–							
8. Length board meetings	3.95	1.88	0.18**	0.02	0.09	0.09	0.01	0.01	0.03	–						
9. Knowledge and competence	5.04	0.96	0.03	–0.01	–0.07	–0.06	0.01	0.03	0.17**	0.03	–					
10. One woman	0.28	0.45	–0.14*	–0.01	–0.25**	–0.09	–0.04	0.15**	0.11*	–0.01	0.11*	–				
11. Two women	0.27	0.44	0.04	–0.02	0.07	0.03	–0.01	–0.14*	–0.18**	–0.07	–0.19**	–0.38**	–			
12. At least three women (critical mass)	0.19	0.39	0.15**	0.06	0.39**	–0.03	–0.04	–0.02	–0.06	0.07	–0.05	–0.31**	–0.30**	–		
13. Board strategic tasks	5.13	1.40	0.21**	0.08	0.18**	0.15**	–0.08	0.01	–0.02	0.26**	0.18**	0.01	–0.09	0.15**	–	
14. Organizational innovation	4.09	1.30	0.27**	0.05	0.13*	0.04	–0.04	–0.12*	0.10	–0.03	0.05	–0.03	0.03	0.09	0.27**	–

Note: ** Correlation is significant at the 0.01 level (2-tailed); * Correlation is significant at the 0.05 level (2-tailed)

Table 18.2   Regression analysis (317 firms)

	Model 1	Model 2	Model 3
Control and independent variables	Organizational innovation	Board strategic tasks	Organizational innovation
Firm size	0.23***	0.15**	0.20***
	(0.06)	(0.06)	(0.06)
Industrial sector	0.19	0.17	0.15
	(0.17)	(0.17)	(0.17)
Board size	−0.028	0.01	−0.04
	(0.08)	(0.08)	(0.08)
CEO tenure	0.09	0.20*	0.04
	(0.11)	(0.11)	(0.12)
Board Chair tenure	−0.06	−0.18	−0.02
	(0.11)	(0.12)	(0.12)
CEO gender	−0.93**	−0.46	−0.81**
	(0.39)	(0.38)	(0.39)
Board Chair gender	−0.74*	−0.08	0.76*
	(0.39)	(0.39)	(0.38)
Length board meetings	−0.51*	1.10***	−0.75**
	(0.30)	(0.30)	(0.30)
Knowledge and competence	−0.06	0.25***	−0.01
	(0.09)	(0.08)	(0.08)
One woman	0.28	0.28	0.24
	(0.23)	(0.23)	(0.22)
Two women	0.31	0.17	0.28
	(0.24)	(0.24)	(0.24)
Critical mass (at least three women)	0.50**	0.72***	0.37
	(0.27)	(0.27)	(0.27)
Board strategic tasks			0.22***
			(0.06)
Adj R2	0.14	0.15	0.18
F Change	2.9***	4.71***	3.81***

Notes: Standard errors are in parentheses. The levels of significance are: * < 0.1; ** < 0.05; *** < 0.01.

Hypotheses 1a and 1b were supported, suggesting that if the size of the minority group is one woman or two women directors there will be no effects on the level of firm organizational innovation. Hypothesis 1c was supported, showing a positive and significant relationship between the critical mass of women directors ('at least three women directors') and the level of firm organizational innovation (0.50; p <0.05). Hypothesis 2 was supported, suggesting that board strategic tasks mediate the relationship between the critical mass of women directors and firm organizational innovation.

DISCUSSION AND CONCLUSION

The results from hypotheses 1a and 1b suggest that there are no relationships between a certain size of the minority group (one woman or two women directors) and the level of firm organizational innovation. Indeed, when there is only one woman, she conforms to the majority group's ideas and behaviors. She is assumed to be a token and is perceived as representing an entire demographic group. Hence, she is stereotyped by the majority group (Kanter, 1977a, 1977b). Hypothesis 1b is also supported. Consequently, having two women directors does not make any significant difference. Once the number of women directors increases from a few tokens (one woman, two women) to a consistent minority ('at least three women'), they are able to effectively influence the level of organizational innovation (hypothesis 1c). Having 'at least three women directors' makes boards more heterogeneous and allows majority–minority interactions and processes to take place, thereby enabling the overall board to take high-quality decisions.

Finally, my findings show that hypothesis 2 is also supported, showing that women directors contribute to firm organizational innovation by the intervening (mediating) effects of board strategic tasks. The mediating role of board strategic tasks requires that the critical mass of women directors positively impacts on board strategic tasks, in turn influencing the level of firm organizational innovation.

NOTE

1. The chapter is based on Torchia et al. (2011).

REFERENCES

Asch, S.E. (1951) Effects of group pressure upon the modification and distortion of judgment, in Guetzkow, H. (ed.), *Groups, Leadership and Men*, Pittsburgh, PA: Carnegie Press.

Asch, S.E. (1955) Opinions and social pressure, *Scientific American*, 193(5): 31–35.

Baron, R.M. and Kenny, D.A. (1986) The moderator–mediator variable distinction in social psychological research: Conceptual, strategic and statistical considerations, *Journal of Personality and Social Psychology*, 51(6): 1173–1182.

Bilimoria, D. and Huse, M. (1997) A qualitative comparison of the boardroom experiences of US and Norwegian women corporate directors, *International Review of Women and Leadership*, 3(2): 63–73.

Bond, R. (2005) Group size and conformity, *Group Processes and Intergroup Relations*, 8(4): 331–354.

Burke, R.J. (1997) Women on corporate boards of directors: A needed resource, *Journal of Business Ethics*, 16(9): 37–43.

Carver, J. (2002) *On Board Leadership*, San Francisco, CA: Jossey-Bass.

Cassell, C. (2000) Managing diversity in the new millennium, *Personnel Review*, 29(3): 268–274.

Daily, C.M. and Dalton, D.R. (2003) Women in the boardroom: A business imperative, *Journal of Business Strategy*, 24(5): 8–10.

Erkut, S., Kramer, V.W. and Konrad, A.M. (2008) Critical mass: Does the number of women on a corporate board make a difference?, in Vinnicombe, S., Singh, V., Burke, R., Bilimoria, D. and Huse, M. (eds), *Women on Corporate Boards of Directors: International Research and Practice*, Cheltenham, UK and Northampton, MA, USA: Edward Elgar, pp: 222–232.

Etzkowitz, H., Kemelgor, C., Neuschatz, M., Uzzi, B. and Alonzo, J. (1994) The paradox of critical mass for women in science, *Science*, 266(5182): 51–54.

Forbes, D.P. and Milliken, F.J. (1999) Cognition and corporate governance: Understanding boards of directors as strategic decision-making groups, *Academy of Management Review*, 24(3): 489–506.

Granovetter, M. (1978) Threshold models of collective behavior, *American Journal of Sociology*, 83(6): 1420–1443.

Hillman, A.J., Cannella, A.A. and Harris, I.C. (2002) Women and racial minorities in boardroom: How do directors differ? *Journal of Management*, 28(6): 747–763.

Huse, M. (2005) Accountability and creating accountability: A framework for exploring behavioural perspectives of corporate governance, *British Journal of Management*, 16(1): 65–79.

Huse, M. (2007) *Boards, Governance and Value Creation: The Human Side of Corporate Governance*, Cambridge: Cambridge University Press.

Huse, M. (2009) *The Value Creating Board: Corporate Governance and Organizational Behaviour*, London, UK and New York, USA: Routledge.

Huse, M., Minichilli, A. and Schoening, M. (2005) Corporate boards as assets for operating in new Europe: The value of process-oriented boardroom dynamics, *Organizational Dynamics*, 34(3): 285–297.

Huse, M. and Solberg, A.G. (2006) Gender related boardroom dynamics: How women make and can make contributions on corporate boards, *Women in Management Review*, 21(2): 113–130.

Kanter, R.M. (1977a) *Men and Women of the Corporation*, New York: Basic Books.

Kanter, R.M. (1977b) Some effects of proportions on group life, *American Journal of Sociology*, 82(5): 965–990.

Kanter, R.M. (1987) Men and women of the corporation revisited, *Management Review*, 76(3): 14–16.

Konrad, A.M., Kramer, V.W. and Erkut, S. (2008) Critical mass: The impact of three or more women on corporate boards, *Organizational Dynamics*, 37(2): 145–164.

Nemeth, C.J. (1986) Differential contributions of majority and minority influence, *Psychological Review*, 93(1): 23–32.

Robinson, G. and Dechant, K. (1997) Building a business case for diversity, *Academy of Management Executive*, 11(3): 21–25.

Selby, C.C. (2000) From male locker room to co-ed board room: A twenty-five year perspective, in Burke, R.J. and Mattis, M.C. (eds), *Women on Corporate Boards of Directors: International Challenges and Opportunities*, Dordrecht: Kluwer, pp. 239–251.

Singh, V., Vinnicombe, S. and Johnson, P. (2001) Women directors on top UK boards, *Corporate Governance: An International Review*, 9(3): 206–216.

Singh, V., Vinnicombe, S. and Terjesen S. (2006) Women advancing onto the corporate board, in Bilimoria, D. and Piderit, K.S. (eds), *Handbook on Women in Business and Management*, Cheltenham, UK and Northampton, MA, USA: Edward Elgar, pp. 304–329.

Tanford, S. and Penrod, S. (1984) Social influence model: A formal integration of research on majority and minority influence processes, *Psychological Bulletin*, 95(2): 189–225.

Terjesen, S., Sealy, R. and Singh, V. (2009) Women directors on corporate boards: A review and research agenda, *Corporate Governance: An International Review*, 17(3): 320–337.

Torchia, M., Calabro, A. and Huse, M. (2011) Women directors on corporate boards: From tokenism to critical mass, *Journal of Business Ethics*, 102(2): 299–317.

19. Gender-balanced corporate boards

Agnes Bolsø, Hilde Bjørkhaug and Siri Øyslebø Sørensen

In an article about the rise of women appointed to corporate boards in the UK, Tom Bawden optimistically notes that female membership is now edging up to 13.3 percent (Bawden, 2011). Norway's legal quota of 40 percent women is in the same paper said to provide 'mixed blessings' for the country's 'Golden Skirts' – a derogatory expression used repeatedly by the *Guardian*, this time by Mark Lewis – serving in its boardrooms. Norway's quota has brought the country to the very top of world indices of gender equality, although these of course can reflect legal rather than social and economic equality.

A possible increase in company value production was one of the central arguments when the law was debated in the Norwegian Parliament in 2003. Numerous factors contribute to the profitability of a business. It is analytically difficult to isolate the economic effect of an increased number of women on a board, and most likely it is impossible. A great deal of research has proved inconclusive: female participation seems to be correlated with financial loss based on some data sets and gain in others. There are good reasons to think that the bottom line primarily depends on other factors than the genitals of the board members. In spite of this, a 'corporate feminism' in which the concern for the bottom line was a key argument overshadowed more traditional gender equality arguments when the quota bill was passed. The rhetoric relies on a dubious economic analysis, but this does not undermine the significance of the 40 percent law: it is important for other reasons than the economic.

In a joint research project funded by the Norwegian Research Council, we have interviewed board members, chairs of boards and members of election committees about their experiences in the transition period up to the present. There are no indications that the decisions being made are different than before, but the way they are made seems altered. Board-room work is of better quality and the board functions better as a collegium when there is a gender balance. What seems clear is that gender diversity improves the boardroom working environment. A greater female representation seems to have an effect on the climate for and process of decision-making, but not necessarily on the decisions that are actually made by the board. It is a little nicer, the preparation material is a little tidier and more comprehensive, the processes a little more formal. It is often said that board work has become more professional.

Some might find it surprising that the decisions largely remain the same. Women are thought to be more caring, more socially responsible and also more aware of environmental issues than men. Surely, that has to affect the actual decisions that are made? No, not necessarily. According to our informants, when it comes down to the decisions they have to make as members of a corporate board, men and women are similar in very particular ways. They all have to take markets into consideration, they have to answer to owners, shareholders and company administrations. They belong to the same privileged social class, and are educated and trained in the same schools. They are managing large economic and socially important resources, and both men and women will have to do that in accordance with shared ideas about what it means to manage in a responsible way. If they do not, there is no seat for them at the table.

Women are now on the boards in significant numbers and they are not passively present. They have formed networks and are actively administering their share of the power to make decisions. The law allowed women through the glass ceiling – and what if we say that is satisfying in itself? That it failed to increase profits (in a period of global recession) is in our opinion no reason to say that the law was unsuccessful. As long as access to the table is more equitably possible and has led to more professional procedures, the lawmakers have no reason to worry. Unless one begins questioning the economic system as such, of course, but that is another question.

REFERENCE

Bawden, T. (2011) Number of women appointed to FTSE 100 boards doubles, *The Guardian*, 1 July.

20. Gender quotas on corporate boards in Norway, necessary but not ideal

Cathrine Seierstad

The lack of women on corporate boards has over the last few decades become a key concern globally for states, corporations, policy-makers and researchers (Huse, 2007, 2009; Seierstad and Opsahl, 2011; Teigen, 2003; Terjesen et al., 2009; Vinnicombe et al., 2008). In particular, the use of quotas to increase the share of women in positions of power and influence, although controversial and debated, is a timely concern. This has been predominantly visible in terms of corporate boards in the private sector, an area where equality strategies have previously been avoided. Norway was the first country to introduce a gender representation law in 2006. It had a two-year implementation period, and required boards of directors to have at least 40 percent representation of each sex by January 2008. Recently, other countries, such as France, Spain, the Netherlands, Iceland, Belgium and Finland have followed similar paths. In addition, softer initiatives have been introduced in a variety of other countries such as the UK, Sweden, Canada and Australia. Moreover, the European Union (EU) is closely watching the gender balance on European boards, open to the possibility of strategies at the EU level if the share of women does not increase further. This chapter builds on data from a larger study (Seierstad, 2011) and explores views from women directors that have benefitted from the use of quotas on boards in Norway. In particular, this chapter discusses women directors' opinions on quotas.

THE USE OF AFFIRMATIVE ACTION STRATEGIES TO CHALLENGE VERTICAL SEX SEGREGATION

Political strategies aiming to reduce and ultimately eradicate vertical sex segregation and the preferential selection of men over women for powerful positions, in order to get more equal and democratic societies and take advantage of all the human resources, are found worldwide.

Nevertheless, although equality is the political goal for many countries, there is divergence over why and how to achieve this. Chang (2000) stated that there are mainly two areas where state intervention into the characteristics of women's labor force participation is likely to take place: equality of access (such as affirmative action – AA) and substantive benefits. AA can include both liberal and radical strategies. Radical (or hard) strategies are the focus of this study and are, according to Taylor-Carter et al. (1995), characterized by the underrepresented group being granted an employment opportunity as long as the minority group meets the minimum qualifications for the job. Examples of radical strategies are minimum representation and quotas as well as earmarking of positions.

THE AFFIRMATIVE ACTION DEBATE

Several understandings, arguments and views both for and against radical equality strategies such as quotas exist. The debate generally revolves around two interrelated issues: arguments about justice, individual and social; and arguments about utility (Hernes, 1987; Teigen, 2000; McHarg and Nicolson, 2006).

From the individual justice perspective, one of the key lines of argument is related to prevention and compensation (Reskin, 1998). As put forward by Reskin (1998): 'affirmative action does not replace one form of favouritism with another; it replaces cronyism with objective personal practices'. Hence, if discrimination against certain groups exists, strategies can be used to balance this. Thus, equal treatment is secured by favoring women candidates when qualifications are about the same (Teigen, 2003, p. 50). The argument is that as a result, AA will cancel the institutionalized or unconscious discrimination that exists and thereby promote integration as a democratic value (Teigen, 2003, p. 50). Nevertheless, from the individual justice point of view you also find several arguments against the use of AA. One line of arguments is related to the principle of non-discrimination and equal treatment. The argument is that AA is a form of discrimination for those not benefiting (Reynolds, 1992). This again is built around the idea that you should be judged by individual qualities and not group characteristics, hence ethical individualism (Elster, 1992, p. 195). Thus one of the key critiques of AA is that it might discriminate against people that belong to a majority group (Lynch, 1997).

From the social justice viewpoint, the key underlying principle is the idea of an equal society. One essential argument is related to democracy and that the use of quotas is necessary, so that as long as women represent half the population they should have a right to half the seats of power, a claim of a more equal society (Dahlerup, 2002). One viewpoint is that AA is just reparation for historical injustice, and now it is women's turn. Teigen (2003, p. 66) made a convincing point, arguing that the 'social justice strategy argues for gender balance in terms of pure demand for justice, and the focus is then transferred from individual rights to groups based on social differences. The claim is, that it is evidently unfair that power and resources are predominantly possessed by men.' Nevertheless, also from the social justice point of view, there are several arguments against the use of AA. One is related to the contra effects: it might be the case that too much time and energy are actually spent debating AA in relation to the outcomes of these procedures, and then the consequences of these debates might include an increase in negative attitudes towards both AA and the groups that these regulations are designed to favor (Young, 1990).

Utility justifications focus on the benefits of AA and the business case for equality. The statement is that women as such have special contributions to make. Hence, the key of the resource argument is the focus on the organizational advantage gained by including women (Hernes, 1987; Helgesen, 1990). Teigen (2003, p. 66) argued that 'the utilitarian strategy stresses gender complementarity, and the special contribution of women in male dominated fields. This argument of difference aims at creating a shift of focus, from affirmative action as a tool to prevent discrimination towards seeing affirmative action as a tool for organisational enhancement by recruiting women.' Furthermore, human capital argument states that since the total potential of a population is about evenly distributed between men and women, the few women in high-status positions implies that the talent potential is not fully utilized (Hernes, 1987). Nevertheless, there are also strong arguments against the use of AA from a utility point of view. Malleson (2003) pointed to the danger of difference arguments and the danger of essentialism. Noon (2007, p. 776) raised an important concern, taking the position that a potential problem with the business case and utility arguments can be that employers might actually fail to recognize the benefits of diversity as they only have short-term goals. Another critique of AA from the utility point of view is related to the potential problem that diversity might not 'add value' and might not be beneficial from a business perspective for the organization, hence, it is a dangerous argument (Noon, 2007).

AFFIRMATIVE ACTION AND THE CURRENT TRENDS

Over the last few years, financial instability has affected both countries and companies globally. This has given a renewed focus that highlights the need for further strategies to challenge the persistent trend of vertical sex segregation. Huse et al. (2009, p. 581) illustrated that in the private sector this unstable economic environment has given renewed awareness to areas of corporate social responsibility (CSR) and corporate governance, as well as the composition and roles of boards of directors (BODs). Consequently, gender representation and the inclusion of women and employee-elected members on boards are central in contemporary debates (Huse et al., 2009). In addition, the rhetoric on the subject of women, leadership and occupational sex segregation has developed. In particular, this has affected how masculinities and femininities are perceived. As argued by Lewis and Simpson (2010, p. 166) 'while the discourse of merit places an emphasis on the similarities between men and women, an equally strong discourse of difference gives prominence to women's distinct feminine characteristics'. The recent financial crisis has therefore given new prominence to arguments which emerged in the 1990s that women possess qualities and characteristics necessary for organizational success in the twenty-first century (Lewis and Simpson, 2010). Consequently, they made the important point that 'whether women are conceptualised as similar or different from men, the suggestion is that organisational success is now possible in ways that were previously unsupportable' (2010, p. 166). Hence, the current debates in terms of both justice and utility as well as the economic climate have given a renewed focus and importance to the debate of vertical sex segregation and how to change this persistent trend. Moreover, the debates of using AA are complex and the rationales for using (or avoiding) it differ. In particular, countries and sectors have different histories in terms of using AA and patterns vary between and within countries. Therefore, it is also important to locate the research within its wider political, social, cultural and historical context

The use of gender quotas within the private sector in Norway has been controversial and debated. In particular, strong and conflicting opinions from the media, politics and the private sector challenged Norway's image as an equal country. Nevertheless, although arguments were raised by the opposing side, both in politics and other areas of society, the Norwegian government argued for introducing gender representation rules based on several reasons related to justice and utility (Norwegian Government, 2008). From a justice point of view the government argued for democracy, as equality between the sexes, a fairer society, and a more even distribution of power between the sexes were important factors for introducing the law. Additionally, several arguments along the lines of utility and the business case were used. One argument is that the legislation is important for the Norwegian economy. In particular, the demand for gender balance on company boards ensures that Norway makes use of all the human resources in the country, not just half of them. As women take higher education to a greater extent than men, it is important to use this talent and make use of their competence in terms of human capital and educational power. In addition, business-case arguments related to diversity as having a positive impact on companies' bottom lines were used (Norwegian Government, 2008).

METHOD

This study explores women directors' views and experiences of using AA to increase the share of women on boards and draws on both secondary and primary data. Secondary data are used to situate the discussion of using quotas to challenge vertical sex segregation in Norway. Primary data are used to capture views and experiences of Norwegian women directors. This study draws on 22 semi-structured in-depth interviews with Norwegian women directors (four with experience from boards not affected by the gender representation law, and 18 currently holding directorships on one or more PLC boards) in order to get insights into their views and experiences of the gender representation law.

DISCUSSION AND CONCLUSION

Maybe surprisingly, this study found strong support for the use of radical strategies on boards. The women directors referred to homosocial reproduction (Kanter, 1997) and organizational barriers (Acker, 2006a, 2006b), not merit, for them not having directorships before the law was introduced. Hence, this study revealed that women express preference for radical AA despite a context that has prioritized this form of action. Interestingly, this contradicts findings from other studies, such as Cockburn (1989, p. 217) who identified how in the British context she found little support for radical equal opportunity within organizations where she in fact found that 'women spoke bitterly of the disadvantage of women, black people of racism, but there was nonetheless a powerful dislike of the idea of favouritism, of moving the goal posts to make things easier for one's own particular group'. In this study, the most negative of the participants to the gender representation law in Norway were women with the least powerful positions. This might indicate that gendered barriers are more profound the higher up the career ladder you are, as the most senior women are the ones most inclined to see the need for AA and the more likely to have experienced discrimination. In addition, women at level one tend to be younger and may not have yet met the gender constraints faced by their older counterparts. Therefore for them the belief in the Norwegian equality project has not been shaken.

In terms of the rationale used by participants for their support of AA, it was apparent that the majority of participants used utility or a mix of utility and individual justice arguments. Human capital arguments had particular salience among the participants and the idea of merit was important. In addition, as the women directors have 'proven' to be competent, few of the arguments related to lack of human capital, as was visible in the national debate before the introduction of quotas had been justified. Moreover, after the introduction of the gender representation law, the national media debate has not questioned women's competence and the law has been accepted. In particular, some of the participants stated that new competences have entered boardrooms and there is a renewed focus on quality and corporate governance. This indicates that utility lines of arguments have wide support after the introduction of the law. Nevertheless, it was also apparent how structural factors such as homosocial reproduction and organizational barriers in the private sector highlighted a need for also focusing on justice case arguments. In particular, the idea of using AA as a way of creating a level playing field in an area with gender barriers was highlighted. In a way, participants justified using quotas from a justice point of view in order to maximize utility.

Although utility arguments were found to have particular support among the participants, there are dangers from an equality and feminist perspective for relying too heavily on utility arguments. Consequently, this study supports the point made by Noon (2007) for also keeping justice arguments as it can be dangerous only to focus on utility. As argued by Noon (2007, p. 781):

> the business case might rest upon this by providing an additional economic rationale, but in the absence of a rationale (or a rationale that might argue against equality initiatives) the moral base remains firm. The argument for the moral case based on the human rights of all employees and job seekers must not be abandoned for the current fashion of diversity and the business case.

Until recently, the leading approach to equality in Europe has been of a liberal nature and countries such as the UK have traditionally been skeptical about the use of radical strategies. Nevertheless, as put forward by Noon (2010, p. 737), 'it is difficult to see how radical change might occur without greater state intervention'. Based on stories from participants, this study supports the argument suggested by Noon (2010, p. 737) that there is a need to rethink the use of radical strategies. In fact, recently the academic as well as political debates globally have highlighted the need for and opened the possibility of taking more radical steps to challenge vertical sex segregation. Hence, the Norwegian use of radical strategies in the private sector has received attention from both policy-makers and academics. Countries such as Iceland, the Netherlands, France, Belgium, Finland and Spain have introduced similar gender representation strategies on corporate boards; while countries such as the UK, Sweden, Canada and Australia have taken softer approaches; and more countries are debating what approaches to take.

Findings from this study are important as they demonstrate how some of the key criticisms of using radical strategies have been unjustified, which gives way to the use of these types of strategies to change imbalance and improve equality in the labor market, both from a justice and utility point of view. In particular, benefits are identified in terms of the individual level for women directors gaining opportunities; the meso level for companies taking advantage of a wider pool of candidates; as well as the macro level where stereotypes can be challenged and women role models are emerging in an area that women have been excluded from, and companies are taking advantage of all the human resources that exist.

To conclude, this study found strong support for the use of radical strategies to challenge vertical sex segregation in the private sector using utility and individual justice rationales. Nevertheless, although the study found widespread support for quotas among women directors, the use of these kinds of strategies are not unproblematic; hence quotas are currently seen as necessary but not ideal – an imperfect strategy in an imperfect world.

REFERENCES

Acker, J. (2006a) *Class Questions: Feminist Answers*, Lanham, MD: Rowman & Littlefield Publishers.

Acker, J. (2006b) Inequality regimes: Gender, class, and race in organizations, *Gender and Society*, 20(4): 441–464.

Chang, M.L. (2000) The evolution of sex segregation regimes, *American Journal of Sociology*, 105(6): 1658–1701.

Cockburn, C. (1989) Equal opportunities: The short and long agenda, *Industrial Relations Journal*, 20(3): 213–225.

Dahlerup, D. (2002) Three waves of feminism in Denmark, in G. Griffin and R. Braidotti (eds), *Thinking Differently: A Reader in European Women's Studies*, London, UK and New York, USA: Zed Books, pp. 341–350.

Elster, J. (1992) *Local Justice: How Institutions Allocate Scarce Goods and Necessary Burdens*, Cambridge: Cambridge University Press.

Helgesen, S. (1990) *The Female Advantage: Women's Ways of Leadership*, New York: Doubleday.

Hernes, H. (1987) *Welfare State and Women Power – Essays in State Feminism*, Oslo: Norwegian University Press.

Huse, M. (2007) *Boards, Governance and Value Creation: The Human Side of Corporate Governance*, Cambridge: Cambridge University Press.

Huse, M. (2009) *The Value Creating Board – Corporate Governance and Organizational Behavior*, London: Routledge.

Huse, M., Nielsen, S.T. and Hagen, I.M. (2009) Women and employee-elected board members, and their contributions to board control tasks, *Journal of Business Ethics*, 89(4): 581–597.

Kanter, R.M. (1977) *Men and Women of the Corporation*, New York: Basic Books.

Lewis, P. and Simpson, R. (2010) Meritocracy, difference and choice: Women's experiences of advantage and disadvantage at work, *Gender in Management: An International Journal*, 25(3): 165–169.

Lynch, F.R. (1997) *The Diversity Machine*, New York: Free Press.

Malleson, K. (2003) Justifying gender equality on the bench: Why difference won't do, *Feminist Legal Studies*, 11: 1–24.

McHarg, A. and Nicolson, D. (2006) Justifying affirmative action: Perception and reality, *Journal of Law and Society*, 33: 1–23.

Noon, M. (2007) The fatal flaws of diversity and the business case for ethnic minorities, *Work, Employment and Society*, 21: 773–784.

Noon, M. (2010) The shackled runner: Time to rethink positive discrimination?, *Work, Employment and Society*, 24(4): 728–739.

Norwegian Government (2008) Representation of both sexes on company boards, (accessed 10 October 2009).

Reskin, B. (1998) *The Realities of Affirmative Action*, Washington, DC: American Sociological Association.

Reynolds, W.B. (1992) Affirmative action and its negative repercussions, in Orlans, H. and O'Neill, B. (eds), *Affirmative Action Revisited. Annals of the American Academy of Political and Social Science*, Newbury Park, CA: Sage, pp. 38–49.

Seierstad, C. (2011) Exploring the Norwegian paradox of vertical sex segregation – strategies and experiences in politics, academia and company boards, PhD Thesis, University of London.

Seierstad, C. and Opsahl, T. (2011) For the few not the many? The effects of affirmative action on presence, prominence, and social capital of female directors in Norway, *Scandinavian Journal of Management*, 27(1): 44–54.

Taylor-Carter, M.A., Doverspike, D. and Cook, K. (1995) Understanding resistance to sex and race-cased affirmative action: a review of research findings, *Human Resource Management Review*, 5(2): 129–157.

Teigen, M. (2000) The affirmative action controversy, *NORA Nordic Journal of Women's Studies*, 8(2), 63–77.

Teigen, M. (2003) *Kvotering og kontrovers: Om likestilling som politikk*, Oslo: Universitetet i Oslo.

Terjesen, S., Sealy, R. and Singh, V. (2009) Women directors on corporate boards: A review and research agenda, *Corporate Governance: An International Review*, 17: 320–337.

Vinnicombe, S., Singh, V., Burke, R., Bilimoria, D. and Huse, M. (eds) (2008) *Women on Corporate Boards of Directors: International Research and Practice*, Cheltenham, UK and Northampton, MA, USA: Edward Elgar.

Young, I.M. (1990) *Justice and the Politics of Difference*, Princeton, NJ, USA and Oxford, UK: Princeton University Press.

21. Legitimacy, inclusion and influence: investigating women directors' board experiences

Gro Ladegård

From a resource-dependence perspective, a board's major role is to provide the firm with needed resources, such as advice and counsel to management, reputation and legitimacy, and external ties or social networks (Hillman et al., 2000; Hillman and Dalziel, 2003; Lynall et al., 2003). The opponents to the quota rule in Norway did express concerns regarding a lack of sufficiently competent women to fill 40 percent of the director positions. For instance, business leaders and employer organizations warned that a lack of women with relevant management experience would lead to reduced performance, authority and legitimacy of Norwegian boards, resulting in the reduced competitiveness of Norwegian industry in international markets (Hoel, 2008). Thus, there were strong indications that women were regarded as an out-group in the business elite context (Singh and Vinnicombe, 2004; Tsui et al., 1992) and that the contributions women could make to corporate boards were in question.

Studying reactions to the quota rule on the Oslo Stock Exchange, Nygaard (Nygaard, 2011) found that the public limited companies (PLCs) subject to the quota did experience positive and significant cumulative abnormal returns (CAR) on stock subsequent to the introduction of the rule, but only in firms with low information asymmetry. Low information asymmetry was defined as publicly available information sufficient to perform an effective monitoring role for outside directors (Nygaard, 2011, p. 3). As 83 percent of female directorships in PLCs in Norway are outside directors (Staubo, 2010), it appeared that in firms where the newly appointed women had sufficient information to perform effective monitoring, the firms' value increased. This indicates that there was no loss of legitimacy nor authority of the PLC boards after the quota rule was implemented. Based on these recent findings, it may be questioned whether the contributions of women directors on corporate boards are dependent not only on their individual competence, but also on the presence of other conditions, such as productive group processes, for the ability to do the job effectively. As earlier research has shown that minorities in a group may face barriers that potentially reduce the likelihood for their viewpoints to be incorporated into group decisions (Hambrick et al., 1996; O'Reilly et al., 1989; Westphal and Milton, 2000) we need more knowledge on how gender balance may affect these processes.

In this chapter I focus on women directors' own experiences of the presence of conditions for effective task performance on the board on which they hold a present position. In addition to the publicly available information that is necessary for effective monitoring performance, internal informal information is also suggested to be crucial for the ability to perform the board tasks effectively. I investigate whether the women directors perceive that they receive sufficient information in general, or if they feel that information is withheld from them. I further address the women's access to informal social interaction between board members that may provide them with rich, internal information. Another condition for effective task performance is suggested to be active participation in discussions on the board, and that the board members are welcomed to bring forward divergent points of view during discussions. Thus, I address whether the women directors assert their opinions and feel free to do so, or if they practice self-censorship when they have deviant points of views. Finally, an obvious prerequisite for effective performance for a director is to have influence on decisions on the board, and I investigate this through asking the women directors about the perceived strength of their influence on board decisions.

As mentioned above, the public discourse around the implementation of the quota law indicated that women are regarded as an out-group in the business elite context. Not only are they a minority in power positions, but they are probably also subject to stereotyping based on traditional gendered social roles – a stereotypical women may be quite different from a stereotypical business manager. Thus, women do not 'fit in', in general. The social consequences of a minority status in groups are discussed within social identity theory. According to this theory, individuals construct social identities based on various characteristics, where salient demographic characteristics such as gender, race and age form a primary basis for categorization (Jackson, 1992). Through the social identity-forming process, the demographic minority may then be categorized as an out-group by the majority (or in-group). This categorization implies that the majority develop a coherence and confidence that reinforce their own self-esteem and self-perception (Ashforth and Mael, 1989; Tajfel and Turner, 1986). In a board context, there is evidence that members of the in-group on a corporate board have a tendency to assess the behavior of others in the in-group more positively, compared to the same behavior in the out-group (Singh and Vinnicombe, 2004). Thus, the out-group is considered as less competent, and will probably have less authority and less legitimacy than the in-group. Being an out-group may have several consequences, regarding both attitudes and behavior on the board. For example, in a study by Nielsen and Huse (2010) the gender of the respondent had an impact on the assessment of women's contributions to decision-making, with male respondents rating women directors' contributions significantly lower than did female respondents. Further, perceptions of women as unequal board members were significantly associated with lower ratings of their contribution to decision-making.

The main objective of the present study was to gain knowledge on how the women directors experience their influence, participation and access to information from the other board members, that is, internal legitimacy, authority and competence. Do they get heard, and do they have influence in decision processes? Do they get the information they need to do their job effectively, and are they included in social networks among male directors? We investigated these questions through a survey (completed in 2009) of 458 women directors, of whom 112 were chairpersons. The respondents were directors on boards in PLCs (6.3 percent), ordinary limited companies (Ltds) (62.2 percent) and other firms (e.g. non-governmental organizations, 31.5 percent). The proportion of women on the boards that the respondents represented ranged from 11 percent to 100 percent. Some of the results from this survey, along with detailed methods information, are also reported in Elstad and Ladegård (2010).

The objective here is not only to give an overview of women directors' experiences in general on these issues, but also to see if directors on the PLC boards have different experiences than those on other boards, and, further, whether the legitimacy, authority and perceptions of competence differ on boards with few versus many women. Table 21.1 is an overview of the sample and gives a picture of characteristics of the boards from which the respondents reported in the survey.

We see from the table that the average women to men ratio is similar on the boards of all three types of firms, nor is the board size very different, although the limited companies (which are mostly family-owned firms in Norway) on average are smaller than the others. As boards without women are excluded from the sample, the average women ratio on Ltds is larger here than in the population of these firms in Norway (the average women ratio on PLCs in Norway is now 38

Table 21.1   Characteristics of the boards and the respondents in the sample

Firm category	Board tenure (on the present board)	Position of respondent	Average board size	Average women to men ratio
PLC	2.5	Chairperson 7% Member 93%	6.4	0.43
Ltd	4.5	Chairperson 29% Member 71%	4.8	0.44
Other	3.4	Chairperson 19% Member 81%	6.9	0.44

percent). The average ratio of women on boards of ordinary limited companies was 16.9 percent in 2009 (Statistics Norway, 2009). The women directors on PLC boards have fewer years of tenure than the others (on average 2.5 years), which means that they were probably appointed when the quota rule was implemented in 2007. Fewer of the women directors on PCL boards serve as chairpersons, although 7 percent is above my expectations, as the average tenure is relatively low. This indicates that chairing a board is not impossible even in 'quota boards'. Recent statistics from Oslo Stock Exchange show that the proportion of women chairpersons on PLC boards had risen to 10 percent in 2012 (Haugnes, 2011), which is interesting as the position as the chair is not subject to the quota rule.

LEGITIMACY, INCLUSION AND INFLUENCE

In the present study, the women were asked about three issues: (1) their assertiveness on expressing divergent opinions in board discussions which is an indicator of their perceptions of internal legitimacy; (2) inclusion into the in-group through sufficient information access and informal networking; and (3) perceived influence in decision processes. The results are shown in Table 21.2. All scales range from 1 (never/very seldom) to 5 (always/very often).

Table 21.2   Mean score of board process variables (standard deviations in parentheses)

Type of firm	Board process variables			
	Assertiveness	Information access	Informal networking	Perceived influence
PLC	3.86 (0.26)	3.93 (0.61)	2.12 (0.88)	4.20 (0.41)
Ltd	3.73 (0.54)	4.18 (0.70)	2.72 (1.33)	4.37 (0.57)
Other	3.69 (0.47)	4.08 (0.64)	2.35 (1.13)	4.28 (0.60)

The results show that the women directors are assertive in expressing their opinions, including divergent points of view. There is no difference between the directors on PLC boards and other boards. Thus, the assumption derived from social identity theory about out-groups – that women directors may conform with the majority and suppress their own viewpoints – does not hold for any type of board.

Further, the women directors socialize to some degree outside the boardroom and seldom experience that information is a barrier against doing an effective job. However, social interaction and information sharing is stronger in the Ltds and other firms than in the PLCs. A plausible explanation to this may be that there is information asymmetry in the PLCs so that less information is available for external directors than for internal directors (Nygaard, 2011), especially because external directors socialize less than internal. As the Ltds and other firms to a larger extent are family firms and are composed of insiders that also include women insiders, the directors on these boards will probably have access to more information and have more informal social interaction.

Regarding influence, the women directors perceive their influence as quite strong, and there are no statistical differences between the three groups of firms. The women feel that they are being listened to, their opinions are taken seriously and they are included in decisions on the board. However, the degree of gender balance is to some degree affecting these experiences. A regression analysis of the four dependent variables of assertiveness, information access, networking and influence on the women to men ratio on the board showed that if the ratio increased, the directors experienced more information access, social interaction and influence, although the effects of increased ratio were quite small (beta coefficients were 0.12, 0.17 and 0.14, respectively, p ≤ 0.05). Assertiveness, however, was not affected by the women to men ratio on the boards. This shows that a critical mass of women do benefit the women's abilities to function effectively on a board (Konrad et al., 2008).

DISCUSSION

The quota rule forces a constraint on decisions regarding board composition in PLCs, which according to standard economic theory could lead to less optimal compositions. Nygaard (2011) found that, contrary to many expectations, the PLCs increased stock value after the implementation of the rule. He suggests that this may be explained as an effect of an increased proportion of external directors on these boards, and that the boards' compositions prior to the rule were not optimal. In line with agency theory, the monitoring performance of a board increases when external directors are appointed, provided that sufficient information is publicly available. The present results support this view, as they indicate that the women directors on PLC boards have no less legitimacy and influence than women directors in other companies, but slightly less information and social networking.

Overall, there are no indications that the quota rule has reduced the competence or the legitimacy of the boards in general. The women directors report their own behavior as assertive and active, they have influence on decisions and participate in informal socializing outside the boardroom. Further, they do not experience out-group attitudes towards themselves as a group. They feel they are being respected and listened to, and they are included in information sharing and social interaction with other members on the board.

However, the results also indicate that the ratio of women on a board has impact on their experienced participation and influence. When the ratio of women increases on a board, each individual woman director perceives that she has more influence. Although we have no 'objective' measures of each director's influence on board decisions, I suggest that the individual experiences are relevant indicators of real influence. Hence, a better gender balance may enable the women directors to perform their job on the board more effectively.

REFERENCES

Ashforth, B.E. and Mael, F. (1989) Social identity theory and the organization, *Academy of Management Review*, 14(1): 20–39.

Elstad, B. and Ladegård, G. (2010) Women on corporate boards: Key influencers or tokens? *Journal of Management and Governance*, 16(4): 595–615.

Hambrick, D.C., Cho, T.S. and Chen, M.J. (1996) The influence of top management team heterogeneity on firms' competitive moves, *Administrative Science Quarterly*, 41(4): 659–684.

Haugnes (2011) Kvinnelige styreledere stormer inn på børsen, available from www.aftenposten.no/jobb (accessed 1 February 2012).

Hillman, A.J., Cannella, A.A. and Paetzold, R.L. (2000) The resource dependency role of corporate directors: Strategic adoption of board composition in response to environmental change, *Journal of Management Studies*, 37: 235–255.

Hillman, A.J. and Dalziel, T. (2003) Boards of directors and firm performance: Integrating agency and resource dependence perspectives, *Academy of Management Review*, 28(3): 383–396.

Hoel, M. (2008) The quota story: Five years of change in Norway, in Vinnicombe, S., Singh, V., Burke, R.J., Bilimoria, D. and Huse, M. (eds), *Women on Corporate Boards of Directors*, Cheltenham, UK and Northampton, MA, USA: Edward Elgar.

Jackson, S. (1992) Consequences of group composition for the interpersonal dynamics of strategic issues processing, in Dutton, J., Huff, A. and Shrivastava, P. (eds), *Advances in Strategic Management*, Greenwich, CT: JAI Press, pp. 345–382.

Konrad, A.M., Kramer, V. and Erkut, S. (2008) Critical mass: The impact of three or more women on corporate boards, *Organizational Dynamics*, 37(2): 145–164.

Lynall, M.D., Golden, B.R. and Hillman, A.J. (2003) Board composition from adolescence to maturity: A multitheoretic view, *Academy of Management Review*, 28(3): 416–431.

Nielsen, S. and Huse, M. (2010) Women directors' contribution to board decision-making and strategic involvement: The role of equality perception, *European Management Review*, 7(1): 16–29.

Nygaard, K. (2011) Forced board changes: Evidence from Norway, NHH Sam discussion paper, Sam 5 (March).

O'Reilly, C.A., Caldwell, D.F. and Barnett, W.P. (1989) Work group demography, social integration, and turnover, *Administrative Science Quarterly*, 34: 21–37.

Singh, V. and Vinnicombe, S. (2004) Why so few women directors in top UK boardrooms? Evidence and theoretical explanations, *Corporate Governance: An International Review*, 12(4): 479–488.

Statistics Norway (2009) Bedrifter og føretak, available from http://www.ssb.no/naeringsliv (accessed 14 December 2009).

Staubo, S. (2010) Do female directors increase board independence? Mimeo, Oslo: Norwegian School of Management.

Tajfel, H. and Turner, J.C. (1986) The social identity theory of intergroup behavior, in Worchel, S. and Austin, W.G. (eds), *Psychology of Intergroup Relations*, Chicago, IL: Nelson-Hall, pp. 7–24.

Tsui, A.S., Egan, T.D. and O'Reilly, C.A. (1992) Being different – relational demography and organizational attachment, *Administrative Science Quarterly*, 37(4): 549–579.

Westphal, J.D. and Milton, L.P. (2000) How experience and network ties affect the influence of demographic minorities on corporate boards, *Administrative Science Quarterly*, 45(2): 366–398.

22. Lessons from previous research on women on boards for future research

Andrea D. Bührmann

'Women on boards' is a very complex and heterogeneous research subject. This has been pointed out in several studies. Basically they show that in the top European companies, women as members of boards are underrepresented (see Catalyst, 2011).

Norway is still at the top of the table and has 37.9 percent women on boards. Portugal, Italy, Greece, Spain, Belgium and France have more than doubled the number of women on boards from 2004 to 2010 (see European Professional Women's Network, 2012), whereas Germany, with 8.5 percent women on boards, remains almost at the bottom of the table.

Different developments have taken place in Europe designed to improve the numbers of women on boards and in top leadership roles. The quota legislation and the introduction of corporate governance codes together with equal access legislation currently are perceived as having a significant impact, as well as increased shareholder and media scrutiny of board membership. However we do not know much about the impact of these developments, just as we do not know how different processes and practices interact and what are their potential effects on the number of women on board.

Based on these macro-level data, studies from economic, (social) psychological, sociological and political perspectives have already discovered new insights about women on boards. On an individual level, supply- and demand-side explanations are given. Some scholars assume a certain educational background as well as individuals' knowledge, skills, abilities and other characteristics, for example Ployhart and Moliterno (2011, p. 128) speak of knowledge, skills, abilities and other characteristics (KSAOs) as relevant for becoming a board member. Networking, sponsorship and mentoring seem to be also important for a successful career. Moreover, a few researchers propose that a certain *habitus* – which in its simplest usage could be understood as a certain pattern of thinking, acting and perceiving or tasting (Bourdieu, 1977) – is important for gaining a top management position. Others highlight the constraining effects of cultural beliefs about gender on self-assessment of task competence and emerging career-relevant aspirations (Correll, 2004).

Most researchers highlight the organizational level and point to the role of the 'right' composition or compilation of the board (for the following, see also Hansen et al., 2012). Board composition is often studied as a reflection of the needs of the shareholders and the firm, and the competences needed are explained as a function of the board's roles (Daily et al., 2003). There are two different perspectives: the agency perspective, where the major role of the board is to monitor or control the managers of the firm (Hillman and Dalziel, 2003), and the resource-dependence perspective, where the board's major role is to provide the firm with needed resources, such as advice and counsel to management, reputation and legitimacy, and external ties or social networks (Lynall et al., 2003). Huse (2005) indicates the need to balance internal, external and strategic focus to gain a more adequate image of a value-creating board. Ployhart and Moliterno (2011), focusing on the board's compilation, draw attention to the heterogeneity of lower-level phenomena. This modus of board recruitment could be understood as a process which is focusing on diversity and on the optimization of the whole board's human capital instead of just adding a person with a profile identical to the one of the person who has left. Extending this perspective, Beckmann and Phillips (2005) argue that the demographic composition of an organization's exchange partner can influence the demographic composition of a focal organization, and Dencker (2008) points out that women's promotion rates are higher than men's during corporate restructuring. Access and advancement barriers are the central points of critiques and the integration of women is perceived as the main object. Important concepts here are 'critical mass' (Erkut et al., 2008), 'faultlines' (Lau and Murnighan, 1998) or the 'stereotype threat' (Roberson and Kulik, 2007), 'tokenism' (Kanter, 1977) and their cultural foundations (Turco, 2010), as well as the 'glass cliff' (Ryan and Haslam, 2007), 'glass wall' (Hymowitz, 2006) and 'glass ceiling' (Cotter et al., 2001).

And finally, some researchers also investigate the impact of the gender and welfare arrangements, or the debates in media, the so-called inter-discourse (Ashcraft, 2007). Others take a neo-institutional perspective beyond the traditional economic view to understand why so many businesses end up having the same organizational structures even though they evolved in different ways, and how institutions shape the behavior of individual members.

According to the state of the art as sketched out here, further research on women on boards should be trans-disciplinary oriented, using a multi-method research design and an intersectional perspective. These challenges will be exemplified and explained below.

TRANS-DISCIPLINARY RESEARCH ORIENTATION

As identified earlier, the research field 'women on boards' crosses the boundaries of several disciplines, including economics, sociology and (social) psychology; it seems to be a 'boundary object'. To identify further relevant research problems scholars of different backgrounds should work together and build up trans-disciplinarity. That includes different attributes (Nowotny et al., 2003):

- Researchers from different disciplines and practitioners (that means here, for instance, members of the top management teams, candidates but also lobbyists) should interact in an open dialogue, allowing for impact from each perspective and relating them to each other. Even research problems should be formulated from the very beginning through a dialogue among a large number of different actors and their perspectives.
- Therefore trans-disciplinarity aims to build up a framework which is not reducible to elements of traditional single disciplinary structures. Rather, it is in the context of application that new lines of intellectual endeavor emerge and develop, so that one set of conversations and instrumentation in the context of application leads to another and another, and so on.
- Researchers and practitioners should develop a form of institutionalized responsibility in order to have accountability vis-à-vis other actors involved, instead of having only individual ethics.
- Because trans-disciplinary oriented research perceives knowledge as transgressive, institutional boundaries between society and research are no longer respected. Consequently 'good' science is characterized by value integration. However, scientific excellence is and remains the basis of producing good and reliable new knowledge.

MIXED-METHODS RESEARCH DESIGN

The research field 'women on boards' has to be explored with various methods, in order to combine the already mentioned different research levels. Statistical methods can underpin research at the macro level to find out, for example, how many women and men are in top management positions and what educational, ethnic and/or social background they have. On an individual level, we need in-depth interviews to find out what top managers think about their own careers, whereas expert interviews are needed for research on recruitment processes. Yet, to understand how board members work together, we need more reconstructive methods such as ethnographic case studies, social network surveys and, most notably, discourse analyses of social conventions. For researchers highlight the central role of conventions in shaping economic activities; they understand social conventions as a set of agreed and accepted rules, which provide actors with resources to coordinate their actions. In a way, conventions reflect what is acceptably or what is viewed as 'normal' behavior, in this instance for women on boards. Conventions are seen neither as naturally given nor as effects of rational choices. Instead, they are viewed as socially constructed in discourses (Solow, 1985). Thus, discourse analyses can contribute to a better understanding of, for instance, why successful male top managers are seen as 'real' men, and successful female top managers have to deal with the question of whether they are womanly enough or not. To summarize, by combing different methods and creating mixed-methods research designs, new insights will most probably be generated.

INTERSECTIONAL RESEARCH PERSPECTIVE

Up until now the literature about women on boards has paid only limited attention to other forms of differences in their own right, or in how they intersect with gender. Recent studies typically examine the experience of 'token' women infiltrating higher-level, male-dominated work (for an exception to this see Stainback and Tomaskovic-Devey, 2009). Yet, we should be aware of the danger of universalizing the experiences, perspectives and interests of white, heterosexual Western professionals with a bourgeois background. Since gender is only one among many overlapping mechanisms that produce relations of power, it is increasingly unacceptable to theorize it as a discrete phenomenon. Because gender does not work in isolation, gender-only frames for doing research on women on boards are insufficient. Intersectional approaches are needed that make clear how gender mingles with other differences such as race, class and age, to name but a few, amid the convoluted demands of organizations. With respect to this we need an intersectional research perspective in order to examine 'the relationships among multiple dimensions and modalities of social relationships and subject formations' (McCall, 2005).

In summary, previous studies made clear that 'women on boards' is a very complex and heterogeneous subject. Accordingly, it should be seen as an intersectionally inspired, transdisciplinary research field investigated by different quantitative and qualitative methods. In doing research in this way, serendipitous discoveries and 'uncoveries' (Merton and Barber, 2004 [1958]) would become more likely. That means the 'fairly common experience of observing an *unanticipated, anomalous and strategic* datum which becomes the occasion for developing a new theory or for extending an existing theory' (Merton, 1968, p. 157).

REFERENCES

Ashcraft, K.L. (2007) Appreciating the work of discourse: Occupational identity and difference as organizing mechanisms in the case of commercial airline pilots, *Discourse and Communication*, 1: 9–36.

Beckman, C.M. and Phillips, D.J. (2005) Interorganizational determinants of promotion: Client leadership and the attainment of women attorney, *American Sociological Review*, 70: 678–701.

Bourdieu, P. (1977) *Outline of a Theory of Practice*, Cambridge: Cambridge University Press.

Catalyst   (2011)   http://www.catalyst.org/file/525/qt_women_in_europe.pdf (accessed 14 December 2011).

Correll, S.J. (2004) Constraints into preferences: Gender, status, and emerging career aspirations, *American Sociological Review*, 69: 93–113.

Cotter, D.A., Hermsen, J.M., Ovadia, S. and Vanneman, R. (2001) The glass ceiling effect, *Social Forces*, 80(2): 65–81.

Daily, C., Dalton, D. and Cannella, A. (2003) Corporate governance: Decades of dialogue and data, *Academy of Management Review*, 28(3): 371–383.

Dencker, J.C. (2008) Corporate restructuring and sex differences in managerial promotion, *American Sociological Review*, 73: 435–476.

Erkut, S., Kramer, V. and Konrad, A.M. (2008) Critical mass: Does the number of women on a corporate board make a difference? in Vinnicombe, S., Singh, V., Burke, R., Bilimoria, D. and Huse, M. (eds), *Women on Corporate Boards of Directors: International Research and Practice*, Cheltenham, UK and Northampton, MA, USA: Edward Elgar, pp. 222–232.

European Professional Women's Network (2012) Women on boards, available from http://www.europeanpwn.net/index.php? article_id=8 (accessed 14 December 2011).

Hansen, K., Ladegård, G. and Bührmann, A.D. (2012) What constitutes a preferred board room candidate? An explorative study in Germany and Norway, paper presented at EURAM Annual Conference, Rotterdam.

Hillman, A.J. and Dalziel, T. (2003) Boards of directors and firm performance: Integrating agency and resource dependence perspectives, *Academy of Management Review*, 28(3): 383–396.

Huse, M. (2005) Accountability and creating accountability, *British Journal of Management*, 16(5): 65–80

Hymowitz, C. (2006) The glass wall: Women are succeeding in executive ranks, but mostly in select industries, *Wall Street Journal*, February.

Kanter, R.M. (1977) *Men and Women of the Corporation*, New York: S. & M. Nielsen.

Lau, D.C. and Murnighan, I.K. (1998) Demographic diversity and faultlines: The compositional dynamics of organizational groups, *Academy of Management Review*, 23(2): 325–340.

Lynall, M.D., Golden, B.R. and Hillman, A.J. (2003) Board composition from adolescence to maturity: A multitheoretic view, *Academy of Management Review*, 28(3): 416–431.

Nowotny, H., Scott, P. and Gibbons, M. (2003) Introduction: 'Mode 2' revisited: The new production of knowledge, *Minerva*, 41(3): 179–194.

McCall, L. (2005) The complexity of intersectionality, *Signs*, 30(3): 1771–1800.

Merton, R. (1968) *Social Theory and Social Structure*, New York: Free Press.

Merton, R.K. and Barber, E. (2004 [1958]) *The Travels and Adventures of Serendipity: A Study in Sociological Semantics and the Sociology of Science*, Princeton, NJ: Princeton University Press.

Ployhart, R.E. and Moliterno, T.P. (2011) Emergence of the human capital resource: A multilevel model, *Academy of Management Review*, 36(1): 127–150.

Roberson, L. and Kulik, C.T. (2007) Stereotype threat at work, *Academy of Management Perspectives*, 21(2): 24–40.

Ryan, M. and Haslam, S.A. (2007) The Glass Cliff: Exploring the dynamics surrounding the appointment of women to precarious leadership positions, *Academy of Management Review*, 32(2): 549–572.

Stainback, K. and Tomaskovic-Devey, D. (2009) Intersections of power and privilege: Long-term trends in managerial representation, *American Sociological Review*, 74: 800–820.

Turco, Catherine J. (2010) Cultural foundations of tokenism: Evidence from the leveraged buyout industry, *American Sociological Review*, 75(6): 894–913.

23. Concluding remarks to Part IV

Katrin Hansen

For many years Huse and colleagues have dedicated their work to 'opening the black box' of boards and understanding the dynamism in relations outside and inside the boardroom. The core of this approach relates to the meso level but boards are perceived as embedded in dynamic contexts and the characteristics of the individual actors are acknowledged as well. Therefore, this stream of research is opening up to a multi-level perspective. As mentioned above, particularly the call for considering deep-level diversity as more important than gender per se redirects the focus onto micro-level phenomena, or 'microfoundations' (Zahra and Wright, 2011), which are embedded in social constraints with concomitant effects on meso and macro levels. These interactions are also shown by Ladegård in Chapter 21 regarding individual women's perceptions in board settings shaped by board compositional factors and the Norwegian quota law.

An even more explicitly multi-level approach has recently been presented by Ployhart and Moliterno (2011) who provide an original and ground-breaking contribution to human capital research by developing a multi-level model on the emergence of human capital. Wong et al. (2011) pursue a comparable approach in their research on top-management teams (TMTs) in investigating the interplay between TMTs socio-cognitive characteristics and organizational variables in affecting social performance. They develop the construct of 'team-level integrative complexity', viewing this cognitive style as a relatively stable characteristic of teams which arises from integratively complex individuals and/or diversity in perspectives and group social processes (Wong et al., 2011, p. 1209). Integrative complexity can be interpreted as a certain aspect of human capital valuable not only in TMTs but also on boards.

Ployhart and Moliterno (2011) discuss human capital with its unstable components (e.g. knowledge) and stable components (values, attitudes) at individual and unit/group level. They propose that unit-level human capital is not merely the sum of the individual human capital (labeled 'composition') but the result of a process called emergence, where individual human capital interacts and merges to create a different measure at the unit level (labeled 'compilation'). This approach has clear resonance in the boardroom context (see Hansen et al., 2012). Analyzing board profiles and valuable competencies from a compilation perspective requires the consideration of level interdependencies: optimizing human capital on the meso level can be achieved by selecting new and different candidates, providing the existing team with additional resources, instead of just filling an opening by replacing a leaving person with a similar one. The evaluation of the candidate then is based on their individual characteristics, and their contribution to the dynamic improvement of the group-level human capital.

In this dynamic process, habitus can become a crucial factor, as several recent studies discuss. Habitus, based on individuals' endowment with sets of capitals, can be interpreted as a generative structure providing and reinforcing specific dispositions but not determining actions (Vaara and Fay, 2011; Voronov and Vince, 2012). Hermann (2004) shows the mediating character of habitus between the individual and the field. She creates the label 'career habitus' to characterize a certain structure of cultural, economic and, above all, social capital that shows a strong impact on career development particularly concerning high-ranking positions (such as boards). A certain habitus may signal taken-for-granted competence to recruiters and board members, and it nurtures trust (Hansen et al., 2012). Maclean et al. (2010) discuss how habitus may explain individual access to power elite positions such as executive and non-executive directorships. They propose that status tends to reproduce itself through habitus, and that habitus reflects a disposition, a tacit knowledge of how to 'get on'. The quality of showing the 'right habitus' to become a defendable candidate to business elite positions is also indicated by Hamori (2010) in her study on search firms, although she does not explicitly mentioning the concept of habitus.

The preceding discussion and contributions identify an increasing body of research on women on boards. Moreover, useful concepts from neighboring fields provide further research opportunities. One interesting example of this kind is the proposition by Zahra and Wright (2011) to use a 'Multilevel Entrepreneurship Research Framework' (p. 77), which combines context, activities and micro-foundations, among those multiple and interrelated micro-processes that create and influence activities and structures in upper echelons:

> While detailed and messy, such research offers a promising direction toward explaining variety in opportunities, organizing principles and processes, and outcomes from pursuing more or less the same types of opportunities.

Mapping, deciphering, capturing, and cataloging these micro-foundational variables compel us in turn to pay special attention to context, generating rich opportunities for theory building and testing. (Zahra and Wright, 2011, p. 78) Referring to Figure 15.1 in Chapter 15, the state of model improvement has been reached. We have accumulated substantial knowledge on structures, activities and outcomes. Future research on women on boards of directors can and shall rely on existing models with their core focus on the value-creating board. These models can be further refined on the micro level by integrating micro-processes connected to gender and diversity, and on the meso level by mapping and modeling the complexity of mediating and moderating factors. On the macro level, I suggest a further consideration of social gender arrangements and cultural specifics from an intersectional perspective on the one hand, and a comprehensive analysis of the societal discourse on justice and utility on the other hand, thereby relying on a combination of quantitative and qualitative methods. To thoroughly explore these research issues, multi-level approaches should be pursued and a variety of methods, including those mixed-method designs, applied.

REFERENCES

Hamori, M. (2010) Who gets headhunted – and who gets ahead? The impact of search firms on executive careers, *Academy of Management Perspectives*, 24(4): 46–59.
Hansen, K., Ladegård, G. and Bührmann, A.D. (2012) What constitutes a preferred board room candidate? An explorative study in Germany and Norway, paper presented at EURAM Annual Conference, Rotterdam.
Hermann, A. (2004) *Karrieremuster im Management. Pierre Bourdieus Sozialtheorie als Ausgangspunkt für eine genderspezifische Betrachtung*, Wiesbaden: Deutscher Universitäts-Verlag.
Maclean, M., Harvey, C. and Chia, R. (2010) Dominant corporate agents and the power elite in France and Britain, *Organization Studies*, 31: 327–348.
Ployhart, R.E. and Moliterno, T.P. (2011) Emergence of the human capital resource: A multilevel model, *Academy of Management Review*, 36(1): 127–150.
Vaara, E. and Fay, E. (2011) How can a Bourdieusian perspective aid analysis of MBA education? *Academy of Management Learning and Education*, 11(1): 27–39.
Voronov, M. and Vince, R. (2012) Integrating emotions into the analysis of institutional work, *Academy of Management Review*, 37(1): 58–81.

Wong, E.M., Ormiston, M.E. and Tetlock, P.E. (2011) The effects of top management team integrative complexity and decentralized decision making on corporate social performance, *Academy of Management Journal*, 54(6): 1207–1228.
Zahra, S.A. and Wright, M. (2011) Entrepreneurship's next act, *Academy of Management Perspectives*, 25(4): 67–83.

PART V

Policy implications at the international level

24. Policy approaches to gender diversity on boards: an introduction to characteristics and determinants

Silke Machold and Katrin Hansen

The debate on women in corporate boards has been intense. Part IV identified current research findings on the case for women on boards at different levels of analysis. Taken together, these findings make a compelling argument for increasing the number and overall proportion (or critical mass) of women on corporate boards. The key question, however, is how best to achieve this from a policy perspective. Broadly speaking, there are two approaches. The first one, and one which is gaining momentum in national policy debates, is to mandate women's representation through a legal quota regime. The second approach involves creating environments conducive to promoting female representation on boards, and using codes of corporate governance to encourage companies to reflect on their practices and policies towards gender diversity on boards. And, of course, countries may chose to ignore the issue altogether. Before introducing the contributions in Part V, it is therefore apposite to reflect on these approaches, both within a broader political economy, legal regimes and economic development debate, as well as in relation to the experiences with these approaches to date.

Political economists have long been interested in the extent to which market-based economies differ in their institutional and coordination structures, and whether and how such differences translate into variances in economic performance (Hall and Soskice, 2001). This 'varieties of capitalism' perspective contrasts liberal market economies (LMEs) at one end of the spectrum with coordinated market economies (CMEs) at the other (Hall and Soskice, 2001; Hall and Gingerich, 2009), with some scholars adding mixed-market economies (MMEs), a group which shares some similarities with the CMEs (Hall and Gingerich, 2009). Countries grouped in these categories are broadly aligned in their underpinning economic coordination mechanisms, that is, market coordination (LMEs) versus strategic coordination of key actors and institutions (CMEs and MMEs) (Hall and Gingerich, 2009). Aligned with this coordination approach to classifying national political economies are political economy categorizations regarding a country's economic or industrial policy approach (Chang, 1996). The latter go beyond coordination problems of firms to also consider the role of the state as an actor in resource allocation. Here, one end of the spectrum is characterized by a neo-liberal ideology, central to which is the belief that markets rather than the state will ensure efficient allocation of resources (Friedman and Friedman, 1980; Lazonick and O'Sullivan, 2000). Opposing this view are scholars who theoretically and empirically demonstrate the importance of state intervention (albeit of different degrees and types) to economic and wider social development (Chang, 1996; Dore, 2000).

Within this broader political economy context, the question of which countries pay attention to the women on boards debate and how they approach this from a policy perspective is an intriguing one. Grosvold and Brammer (2011) showed national institutional factors, including the political economy regime, to be explanatory variables for the extent to which women are represented on boards. The question is whether such national characteristics also explain policy-making towards gender diversity on boards. Following the political economy logic, we would expect to see liberal market economies eschew direct forms of legislative intervention, and instead show a greater reliance on market mechanisms to redress gender gaps. On the other hand, coordinated and mixed market economies might be expected to favor legislative devices such as quota regimes rather than advocating business self-regulation. In order to examine these propositions, we use data from Catalyst (2012) which created an index of current formal approaches to gender diversity on boards. Catalyst (2012) identifies three formal approaches: (1) quota legislation which mandates a minimum percentage for certain groups of companies with associated legal sanctions for non-compliance; (2) regulation, which includes corporate governance codes and disclosure regulations which typically have no formal sanction but are used on a 'comply or explain' basis; and (3) voluntary efforts where companies sign up to voluntary pledges or targets. We plot the Catalyst (2012) data against the Hall and Gingerich (2009) 'varieties of capitalism' country classification in Table 24.1.

Table 24.1 shows that very few Organisation for Economic Co-operation and Development (OECD) countries to date have adopted legislative devices: six of the OECD countries have passed legislation, with a further three countries having proposed doing so. None of the liberal market economies have legislated for gender diversity, as opposed

Table 24.1   *Formal approaches to board gender diversity based on 'varieties of capitalism' in OECD countries (year of passage in brackets)*

	Legislation (quota laws)** *and proposed*	Regulation (corporate governance codes or disclosure regulation)	Voluntary efforts**	No formal approach
Liberal market economies*	*Australia* *Canada*	Australia (2011) Ireland (2010) United Kingdom (2010, 2012) United States (2010)	Canada (2012) United Kingdom (2010, 2011) United States (2010)	New Zealand
Co-ordinated market economies*	Belgium (2011) Finland (2005) Norway (2003) *Netherlands*	Austria (2009, 2011) Belgium (2009, 2011) Denmark (2008, 2010) Finland (2010) Germany (2010) Netherlands (2008) Sweden (2007, 2010)	Denmark (2010) Netherlands (2008)	Japan Switzerland
Mixed market economies*	France (2011) Italy (2011) Spain (2007)	France (2010) Spain (2006)		Portugal Greece

Notes:

* Classification based on Hall and Gingerich (2009).
** Based on Catalyst (2012).

to six of the coordinated and mixed market economies. Further, voluntary efforts are most prevalent in liberal market economies as predicted theoretically. Thus, differences in policy approaches to women on boards broadly align with political economy models – but there are two important anomalies. First, Table 24.1 also identifies a number of OECD countries that have not yet engaged in any formal efforts to promote women on boards. This includes liberal market economies (New Zealand) as well as coordinated and mixed market economies, the most prominent of which is Japan. The question of which countries have (so far) avoided formal approaches to gender diversity (and why) is one we will return to below. Second, across the spectrum of countries, corporate governance codes, sometimes also referred to as 'soft law', are prominent (Abbott and Snidal, 2000). Shaffer and Pollack (2010) argue that such soft law may not always complement legislation (hard law); rather, it may act antagonistically by, for example, softening hard laws or vice versa. The experience from both liberal market and coordinated market economies suggests that corporate governance codes may be used by governments that seek to avoid the 'heavy hand of the state', combined with a clear message that such a regime will be hardened if companies fail to make significant efforts (Weber-Rey in Chapter 26, Schulz-Strelow in Chapter 25, and Sealy and Vinnicombe in Chapter 28, in this volume; Davies, 2011). The sequencing of soft versus hard laws appears to support this view, with hard laws frequently following corporate governance codes. Regardless of their political economy orientation, it appears that (some) governments strategically use the threat to harden laws if companies' actions are incompatible with the desired outcome to achieve gender diversity on boards.

Are there then differences in countries' legal systems that may account for how to approach the promotion of gender diverse boards? La Porta et al. (1996) have long argued that legal systems are strong explanatory factors for differences in corporate governance regimes. Taking an agency-theoretic perspective on governance, their research focused mainly on differences in investor protection and found that common law countries generally offer higher levels of investor protection compared to civil law ones (La Porta et al., 1996). In similar vein, Zattoni and Cuomo (2008) found that common law countries tend to be early adopters of good corporate governance codes aligned with efficiency motives. Might therefore civil law countries be more likely to legislate on gender-diverse boards, a corporate governance issue which is not ostensibly linked to shareholder supremacy and investor protection? In Table 24.2, we use the La Porta et al. (1996) classification of legal families (English legal origin associated with common law; and French, German and Scandinavian legal origin associated with civil law) and plot the current state of formal approaches to board diversity against these legal family groups.

Table 24.2   Formal approaches to board gender diversity based on legal origin

	Legislation (quota laws)** and proposed	Regulation (corporate governance codes)**	Voluntary efforts**	No formal approach**
English legal origin*	Israel Kenya *Australia* *Canada* *Israel*	Australia Ireland Kenya Malaysia Nigeria South Africa United Kingdom	Canada United Kingdom United States	Hong Kong India New Zealand Pakistan Singapore Sri Lanka Thailand Zimbabwe
French legal origin*	Belgium France Italy Spain *Netherlands* *Philippines*	Belgium Luxembourg Netherlands Spain	Netherlands	Argentina Brazil Chile Columbia Ecuador Egypt Greece Indonesia Jordan Mexico Peru Portugal Turkey Uruguay Venezuela
German legal origin*		Austria Germany		Japan South Korea Switzerland Taiwan
Scandinavian legal origin*	Finland Iceland Norway	Denmark Finland Iceland Sweden	Denmark	

Notes:

* Based on La Porta et al.'s (1996) classification.
** Based on Catalyst (2012).

One striking pattern from the analysis in Table 24.2 is the prevalence of formal approaches to gender diversity in Scandinavian legal origin countries, where all countries have either hard or soft laws (and sometimes both).The same is not evident in the other two sets of civil law countries. For example, out of the six countries included in the La Porta et al. (1996) classification of German legal origin, only two have soft laws in place (Austria and Germany), whereas the six French legal origin countries with soft or hard law are outweighed by 15 countries that have neither. Common law countries are balanced in terms of the numbers of countries with legislative and regulatory regimes and those that have neither. Thus, rather than ascertaining differences in terms of civil versus common law countries, we find a regional salience around the Scandinavian countries in their efforts to embrace formal mechanisms to gender balance on boards.

What role does the level of economic development play in whether countries pay attention to the matter of women on boards? Ever since Boserup's ground-breaking work (Boserup, 1970), scholars and policymakers alike have been interested in understanding the interactions between gender inequality and economic development. More recent research has shown that: (1) the relative status of women is strongly associated with the level of economic development; and (2) there is a curvilinear relationship between economic development and gender inequality, with countries at intermediate levels of development showing higher levels of gender inequality (Forsyth et al., 2000). These results would suggest that countries with higher levels of economic development are more likely to have formal approaches to gender diversity on boards, since both the status of women and recognition of the deleterious effects of gender inequality are more pronounced. Mapping World Bank data on economic development measured by income bands with the Catalyst (2012) listing, this pattern is supported. Of countries that have formal approaches to gender diversity on boards, 5.6 percent are of low income (Kenya and Malawi out of 36 countries), 3.8 percent are middle-income countries (1 out of 54 lower-middle-income countries – Nigeria; and 1 out of 54 upper-middle-income countries – South Africa) and 25 percent are high-income countries. The Forsyth et al. (2000) study showed that in particular Latin American countries experienced no changes in the levels of gender inequality despite economic development and rising levels of income. This picture is echoed on the legislative front in that no Latin American country has thus far made formal approaches to increasing women's representation on boards. A worrying trend is also that some of the largest and fastest-growing economies show no efforts to address gender imbalances on boards. For example, none of the BRIC countries

(Brazil, Russia, India and China) have mooted attempts at voluntary or soft law approaches, even though there is an increasing debate about the issue in these countries (see for example Sharma and Mukherji, 2012). But there are some notable outliers in highly developed and industrialized countries as well. In Asia, neither Japan nor the Republic of South Korea have shown any inclination to address gender equality in their upper echelons despite having globally one of the poorest records regarding women's representation on boards (0.9 percent for Japan and 1 percent in South Korea; Davies, 2011). In the European Union, Portugal is a noticeable laggard combining a low percentage of women on boards (according to the Davies, 2011 figures only 0.4 percent on average) with no efforts to initiate policies or policy debates. Thus, despite there being an association between levels of economic development and formal approaches to gender diversity on boards, there are some notable outliers in both fast-growing economies and highly developed industrialized countries.

A society's culture, and within that its level of gender equality, might be a further aspect to be taken into consideration when seeking to understand differences in formal approaches to gender representation on boards. Two relevant studies on levels of gender equality are the GLOBE study (House et al., 2004), and the Global Gender Gap Report by the World Economic Forum (WEF, 2011). The GLOBE study is of interest because it provides scores on both the practice and the value of gender egalitarianism in societies. Gender egalitarianism is defined as 'The degree to which a collective minimizes gender inequality' (House et al., 2004, p. 30). This construct covers equality on two dimensions, minimizing gender discrimination and minimizing gender role differences. An example of the items used to measure the latter dimension is: 'Boys are encouraged (should be encouraged) more than girls to attain a higher education' (reverse-scored). This means that societies scoring high on gender egalitarianism would not encourage boys more than girls to attain a higher education, and not encourage men more than women to attain important positions such as on boards and board chair positions. This definition of high gender egalitarianism therefore includes societies where both genders are encouraged and supported to the same level (for example due to legal requirements). In other words, gender-equal societies are those where gender is no longer a relevant factor in business in comparison to other factors such as ethnicity, family background, elite status or expertise.

Based on the GLOBE study we find remarkable differences in the scores on gender egalitarianism (the range is from one to seven, and the global mean for gender egalitarian practice is 3.37). For example,

Denmark has a practice score of 3.93, Great Britain has a practice score of 3.67, and France has a practice score of 3.64. In contrast, the German-speaking part of Switzerland has a practice score of 2.97 and Spain has a score of 3.01. Interestingly, Great Britain, Sweden and Denmark as high-ranking countries on the practice dimension show even higher scores on the value dimension. Unfortunately, Norway has not been covered yet by the original GLOBE study. However, recently Warner-Soderholm (2012) used the GLOBE instrument to identify a Norwegian practice score of 4.03, which tentatively could be used for comparison. Hypotheses could be developed and tested connected to the position of the respective society on the value and/or the practice level of gender egalitarianism, and policy approaches to gender diversity on boards. It may also be of interest to further analyze the gap between value and practice in each country.

Another helpful way of understanding the attainments in gender equality of societies could be the Global Gender Gap Index developed by the World Economic Forum (WEF) which is based on research collaboration between Harvard University and the University of California, Berkeley. This complex indicator covers economic, political, educational and health factors. The Scandinavian countries have been top of this list for many years, while Ireland is hard on the heels of Sweden. Austria and Portugal were ranked 34 and 35 in 2011 respectively, with Portugal having a relatively stable position whereas Austria has a history of ups and downs (see WEF, 2011). Altogether, it is perhaps not surprising to find that countries scoring high on gender egalitarianism are also at the forefront of developing formal approaches to gender equality on boards.

The reflection on the wider macro context within which formal approaches to women's representation on boards emerged shows that the phenomenon is associated with Scandinavian legal origin countries, coordinated and mixed market economies, levels of prevailing economic development and gender egalitarianism. This finding is similar to studies on the evolution of corporate governance codes which highlighted national institutional characteristics as determinants of code adoption practices (Aguilera and Cuervo-Cazurro, 2004; Zattoni and Cuomo, 2008). However, contrary to general corporate governance codes, early adopters of formal approaches to gender diversity show almost diametrically opposite institutional characteristics compared to early adopters of codes (Zattoni and Cuomo, 2008). However, as code researchers remind us (Aguilera and Cuervo-Cazurra, 2009; Zattoni and Cuomo, 2008), it is not only a question of whether governance legislation is adopted but also what these policies encompass. The next section will turn to a reflection on the nature of the policies and their associated sanctions, in order to shed light on their relative efficacy.

As outlined above, formal approaches to gender diversity fall into three broad camps: legislative approaches (quota laws), regulatory measures and corporate governance codes (soft law), and voluntary approaches. It is only the first type of approach which is, in theory, associated with legal sanctions in case of non-compliance. Yet the nature of these legal sanctions and their scope vary greatly between countries, as Table 24.3 illustrates.

Table 24.3   Scope of existing gender quota laws on boards and level of sanctions

	State-owned enterprises	Public-listed companies	Other companies
Individual directors	Belgium (33%)	Belgium (33%) France (40%)	Belgium (33%) France (40%)
Directors and company		Italy (33%)	
Company	Norway (40%)	Norway (40%) Spain (40%)	
None articulated	Finland (40%) Israel (50%) Kenya (33%)	Iceland (40%) Israel (1 woman director)	Iceland (40%)

Source: adapted from Catalyst (2012).

Quota laws are most frequently enacted for publicly listed and state-owned companies, a pattern that is similar to the evolution of corporate governance regulation in general (Aguilera and Cuervo-Cazurra, 2004). What is particularly interesting is the level at which legal sanctions are applied. Very rarely do legal sanctions target the company directly, and only in the case of Norway can non-compliance result in the dissolution of the company. This stands in strong contrast to Spain where no specific penalties are applied in the case of non-compliance; rather companies' compliance is taken into account when state subsidies or contracts are awarded (Catalyst, 2012). The other approach to sanctions is at the individual director level and this can be via fines levelled at the board (Italy), suspension of pay and benefits of directors (Belgium, France) or voidance of appointments (Belgium). Finally, many of the quota laws do not articulate sanctions directly but are tied in with other pieces of hard and soft legislation. The diversity of approaches, and leniency of sanctions, may therefore substantially undermine the efficacy of such legislative routes, resulting in a softening of hard law legislation (Shaffer and Pollack, 2010).

Given the prominence of soft law in the formal approaches to gender diversity, the question of why companies would pay attention and comply becomes an important one. One explanation, as already discussed, could arise from their actual or potential connection to hard laws. A second explanation may lie in the observation that companies voluntarily choose to comply with codes if it suits their circumstances and perceived efficiency needs (Aguilera and Cuervo-Cazurra, 2009). For example, as Sealy and Vinnicombe in Chapter 28 in the volume, and elsewhere (Sealy and Vinnicombe, 2012) show, FTSE 100 companies generally perform better than other listed companies in improving gender balance on their boards, and are more inclined to follow voluntary guidelines compared to other listed companies. The increasing interest shown by investors, especially socially responsible investors, serves to act as a further stimulus, with rating agencies such as Bloomberg and Governance Metrics now routinely compiling board gender statistics. Thus, the combination of market and legislative sanctions creates a particularly powerful driver for changes in gender representation on boards (Grosvold and Brammer, 2011). Finally, an explanation that has received relatively little attention to date may be found in demands for democratization and procedural fairness by stakeholders. Gomez and Korine (2005), in examining the historical development of corporate governance, argued that it has evolved in line with democratic procedures of enfranchisement, separation of powers and representation. Congruent with such political philosophy arguments, companies may face increasing demands for procedural fairness by their stakeholders, including fair procedures for board appointments. The arguments surrounding whether and how affirmative action relates to procedural fairness have been explored by Seierstad in Chapter 20 in this volume.

To summarize, the last few years have witnessed an increasing momentum internationally in formal approaches to gender diversity on boards, accompanied by intense debates on the merits of such approaches. The contributors to Part V have been at the leading edge of advocating policies on board gender diversity albeit from different perspectives and championing different approaches. We open with two contributions from Germany. Monika Schulz-Strelow is the President of FiDAR (Women on German boards) and in Chapter 25 and elsewhere outlines the rationale for campaigning for quota laws in Germany. Whilst not disagreeing with the need for greater women representation, Daniela

Weber-Rey as a member of the German Corporate Governance Commission in Chapter 26 argues that soft laws are more appropriate in advancing this agenda. Only if companies continue to disregard women on boards as a governance issue, should more coercive measures be considered. Having examined two different but complementary perspectives from Germany, we turn towards Italy with Brogi's Chapter 27. As an academic, board member and leading Italian lobbyist for gender equality on boards, Brogi provides some unique insight into how Italy came to pass a quota law. Chapter 28 on UK developments comes from Sealy and Vinnicombe, two scholars whose long-standing research has been extremely influential in informing UK policy-making on gender diversity in boards. After detailing the changes in the UK board gender landscape, Sealy and Vinnicombe proceed to identify the formal and informal drivers that have led to these changes. The capstone to Part V is Chapter 29 authored by Viviane Reding, the EU Vice-President and Commissioner for Justice, Fundamental Rights and Citizenship. As a prominent campaigner for equality, Reding in her chapter outlines the various initiatives taken by member states in relation to women on boards, and reflects on the need to explore policy options at European level. Unlike corporate governance codes, where many international codes exist to complement national ones, the European Commission's initiative represents the first step in exploring formal approaches to gender diversity internationally.

REFERENCES

Abbott, K.W. and Snidal, D. (2000) Hard and soft law in international governance, *International Organization*, 54(3): 421–456.

Aguilera, R. and Cuervo-Cazurra, A. (2004) Codes of good governance worldwide: What is the trigger? *Organization Studies*, 25(3): 417–446.

Aguilera, R. and Cuervo-Cazurra, A. (2009) Codes of good governance, *Corporate Governance: An International Review*, 17(3): 376–387.

Boserup, E. (1970) *Women's Role in Economic Development*, New York: St Martin's Press.

Catalyst (2012) Increasing gender diversity on boards: Current index of formal approaches, available at http://www.catalyst.org/publication/514/increasing-gender-diversity-on-boards-current-index-of-formal-approaches (accessed July 2012)

Chang, H-Y. (1996) *The Political Economy of Industrial Policy*, Basingstoke: Macmillan.

Davies, E.M. (2011) *Women on Boards*, Independent review into women on boards in the UK, available at http://www.bis.gov.uk/assets/biscore/business-law/docs/w/11-745-women-on-boards.pdf (accessed July 2012)

Dore, R. (2000) *Stock Market Capitalism: Welfare Capitalism*, Oxford: Oxford University Press.

Forsyth, N., Korzeniewicz, R.P. and Durrant, V. (2000) Gender inequalities and economic growth: A longitudinal evaluation, *Economic Development and Cultural Change*, 48(3): 573–617.

Friedman, M. and Friedman, R. (1980) *Free to Choose*, Harmondsworth: Penguin Books.

Gomez, P.Y. and Korine, H. (2005) Democracy and the evolution of corporate governance, *Corporate Governance: An International Review*, 13(6): 739–752.

Grosvold, J. and Brammer, S. (2011) National institutional systems as antecedents of female board representation: An empirical study, *Corporate Governance: An International Review*, 19(2): 116–135.

Hall, P.A. and Gingerich, D.W. (2009) Varieties of capitalism and institutional complementarities in the political economy: An empirical analysis, *British Journal of Political Science*, 39(3): 449–482.

Hall, P.A. and Soskice, D.W. (2001) *Varieties of Capitalism: The Institutional Foundations of Comparative Advantage*, Oxford: Oxford University Press.

House, R.J., Hanges, P.M., Javidan, M., Dorfman, P.W. and Gupta, V. (eds) (2004) *Culture, Leadership, and Organizations. The GLOBE Study of 62 Societies*, Thousand Oaks CA: Sage.

La Porta, R., Lopez-de-Silanes, F., Shleifer, A. and Vishny, R.W. (1996) Law and finance, NBER Working Paper 5661, Cambridge MA: National Bureau of Economic Research.

Lazonick, W. and O'Sullivan, M. (2000) Maximizing shareholder value: A new ideology for corporate governance, *Economy and Society*, 29(1): 13–35.

Sealy, R. and Vinnicombe, R. (2012) The female FTSE board report 2012: Milestone or millstone, Cranfield University, UK, available at http://www.som.cranfield.ac.uk/som/dinamic-content/research/documents/2012femalftse.pdf. (accessed July 2012)

Shaffer, G. and Pollack, M.A. (2010) Hard vs. soft law: Alternatives, complements and antagonists in international governance, *Minnesota Law Review*, 94: 706–799.

Sharma, R.R. and Mukherji, S. (2012) Women in India: Their odyssey towards equality, in Groeschl, S. and Takagi, J. (eds), *Diversity Quotas, Diverse Perspectives: The Case of Gender*, Farnham: Gower.

World Economic Forum (WEF) (2011) The Global Gender Gap Report 2011, available at http://www.weforum.org/issues/global-gender-gap (accessed 17 August 2012)

Zattoni, A. and Cuomo, F. (2008) Why adopt codes of good governance: A comparison of institutional and efficiency perspectives. *Corporate Governance: An International Review*, 16(1): 1–15.

25. Women on boards: lessons learnt from Norway

Monika Schulz-Strelow

We all agree that to increase the number of women in leadership positions of companies is an essential requirement to achieve equal opportunities and to improve management. This was revealed most recently by the financial and economic crisis that started in 2008. However, the European countries have taken different developments paths. Concerning the topic of women on boards, Germans can learn a lot from the Norwegians.

Looking at it from a management and business, national economy and politics point of view and comparing it internationally, it is totally unacceptable that in Germany women and men are educated and qualified in the same manner but there are only 4 percent women on boards of directors representing shareholders, and approximately 12 percent women if we include female employee representatives. Germany is ranked in the middle when comparing European countries' positions in respect of women on boards of directors of listed corporations. And this position is only attained because of the German feature of employee representation on boards. Germany would be found in the last third if we discounted the female employee representatives.

One question that has existed for a long while is how this situation can be changed. For this reason, a group of high-ranking women from areas such as economics, politics and science came together to form the initiative FidAR – Frauen in die Aufsichtsräte e.V. (Women onto Boards). This group works nationwide, above party lines and voluntarily with the aim to bring factual discussion on this topic into the public domain, and to get more qualified women into jobs serving on boards of directors. During the past years, more and more women's associations formed and appealed together with FidAR for an increased share of women on boards of German listed companies. In March 2011, FidAR was supported by over 250 female and male members, and is nowadays demanded as the favored partner for media and for federal and national hearings on the topic of women on boards, based on our professional knowledge. Also, FidAR is in demand as interlocutor for parliamentary groups for their internal opinion forming.

FidAR advocates emphatically an improvement of management control and increased diversity on boards. After the failure of an equality law for the German economy in 2001, a non-binding agreement between the federal government and the leading associations for the advancement of equal opportunities for women and men in the private sector was not taken seriously by companies, and it did not lead to an advancement of chances for women in the private sector. It is considered a failure. Therefore, FidAR thinks that a binding requirement for a minimum share of women on German boards of directors is necessary, and demands a realistic women's quota of 25 percent or more, which is stipulated by law and which can be reached in the foreseeable future. The aim is to provide equal representation on the boards on the shareholders' side.

The expectations of the federal government, which has in the coalition agreement of 2009 established a plan to increase the share of women on the boards of directors of private and public corporations in stages, have not been realized yet. At the moment there is no evidence that the staged plan can be achieved, and additionally the responsible ministry is distant towards demands for a quota regime. Discussions in the Federal Minstry of Family, Seniors, Women and Youth center around the possibility of a so-called flexi-quota, but a detailed outline of this proposal has not been published yet. However, not much is expected from the proposal of a flexible quota.

Recommendations made by the German Corporate Governance Code Commission in 2010 caused concern among listed companies, and resulted in intensified debate and even more concrete planning. According to the recommendation, the board of directors shall identify concrete targets related to its composition, which will include targets to reasonably increase the participation of women. These aims and targets, as well as progress in achieving these, shall be published in each company's Corporate Governance Report. We must wait and see about whether these recommendations lead to actual and extensive changes in the composition of boards and associated changes in corporate culture.

FidAR, together with the Women on Board Index, takes an active role to realize the request of the German government, the European Commission as well as the government commission of the German Corporate Governance Code to have more transparency concerning the women's quota in board positions. All 160 corporations listed on the DAX, MDAX, SDAX and TecDAX were asked by FidAR in December 2010, and again in January 2011, about the share of women on their management and supervisory boards. Based on these purely quantitative data, FidAR has built the Women on Board Index.

The project was supported by the Ministry of Family, the Elderly, the Youth and Women, and the results were published in cooperation with the *Manager Magazine* as the WoB Index in February 2011, and it irritated the DAX companies. Until recently, only percentages had been published, whereas the WoB Index now clearly showed with its ranking the positions of the 160 listed companies within the index. Such data were understood by the businesses, but it was often pointed out to me, as President of FidAR, that the timing for the data collection was inappropriate since they are addressing this topic in their planning, but cannot yet show precise numbers and achievements. To this I just answered that we are happy about any improvement to the position in the ranking, and that we would report immediately on these changes. The WoB Index is updated twice a year. We have intentionally collected the data at the beginning of this year (2011), and we will now continuously keep a record of the changes on the board of directors until 2013, in order to give the companies enough advance notice. This is because in 2013, due to the change-over cycle, most of replacements on the boards of directors will have taken place and until then companies can prove that they are serious in their effort to bring more women onto boards. Men understand numbers and rankings very well, so there is no need for elaborate explanations and interpretations.

The WoB Index shows clearly that many of the listed companies are still light years away from achieving an appropriate representation of women on boards: 74 out of 160 companies, or 46 percent, have neither a woman on the executive board nor on the supervisory board representing shareholders. This is a confession of failure; the zeros have to go.

On the other hand there are businessmen who stepped up as role models for the equality of women in management and thus improved their companies' positions in the ranking. These businessmen also told us that due to the higher number of women on the boards, the board work became more factual, efficient and transparent.

Our research shows that the reform of the German Corporate Governance Code has some positive effect on some corporations. More and more companies become engaged in the topic of diversity. This is documented in annual reports and code compliance statements. Fifty-eight percent say they are following the regulations of the German Corporate Governance Code, even though there are as yet no women present on the management or supervisory boards. At least 43 percent of the companies that completed the code compliance statement responded to the topic diversity, but of those 25 percent explain explicitly that they digress from the recommendations. And only 12 percent point out that in this year they want to put in place a plan concerned with an appropriate gender representation, with only a small handful having announced concrete targets.

In order to avoid a stand-still or even a worsening of progress regarding women's representation on boards when it comes to the next extensive replacement round of board positions, continuing activities that are public and effective are required. Among these are the FidAR fora, which with around 300 participants reflect the current state of discussion in economics, politics and research.

A range of complementary activities involving different actors are necessary to show that there is a demand in Germany for fundamental changes, to break through existing barriers, and to give women the space so that they can add to the success of companies with their abilities and in collaboration with men. For this, it is important to keep up the connection to relevant networks and to be capable of positioning oneself adequately. However, stronger support for women also requires a rethinking from women, and this is not yet self-evidential practice. More women on boards gain a different public perception and therefore have to be role models. Besides functioning as role models, a critical mass of women can also change culture. This is unlikely to be achieved by filling just one vacancy with a woman; instead a critical mass of at least three women is required to trigger a lasting change.

It is clear that we still have a lot to do, not least in combining efforts to keep the topic in public and policy debates. We can already notice a tendency for corporations to recruit international female directors to boards in order to simultaneously serve two diversity goals: gender and international diversity. In this context it is made clear to us that now that female appointments have been made, we should quieten down with our demands. This attitude shows that we are not dealing with fundamental changes in companies' or boards' culture, rather that they have yielded to public pressure. Indeed, we accomplished that we are now taken seriously. However, this is not enough. Our hopes now belong to the decisions by the European Commission that will hopefully keep up the necessary pressure and lead to a quota regulation. Without the pressure of a quota there will not be a change. The level of the quota is not our point; instead we want to use the quota to accelerate the opening of doors to the male-dominated German company elites. It goes without saying that everyone has to prove herself or himself on their own. But for that to happen, women and men should have the same opportunities. In Germany we are certainly far away from this condition – but we are working on it!

26. Professionalization on the supervisory board, diversity and women

Daniela Weber-Rey

The extension of the candidate pool of potential members of the supervisory board of stock market-listed companies, and the concomitant increase of the representation of women in the economy and especially in supervisory boards, is a major socio-political challenge, and one that particularly includes legal aspects. The top priority for both the management and supervisory boards has to be to act in the company's best interest and to pursue value creation.

COMPOSITION OF SUPERVISORY BOARD

In accordance with the 2005 recommendation of the European Union (EU) Commission which deals with the independence of supervisory board members of listed companies, the German Corporate Governance Code states that there should be members on a supervisory board who have the essential knowledge, abilities and technical experience to execute their tasks effectively. This means that not every single member of the supervisory board has to have all necessary competences, but that the members of the supervisory board as a team should have the essential diversity of knowledge, faculty of judgment and experience to perform their tasks properly. Additionally, related to the composition of the supervisory board, the Code recommends paying attention to the international activities of the company, avoiding potential conflicts of interest, to determine an age limit for board members, and to bear in mind gender diversity. The call for a more heterogeneous composition of the supervisory board and the associated mix of different skills and competences will necessarily lead to an increased demand for diversity on German supervisory boards, always bearing in mind the goal of furthering the company's interest.

In 2010, the governmental commission on the German Corporate Governance Code emphasized especially the need for enhanced representation of women within the remit of increasing board diversity. As several studies have shown, women are still severely underrepresented in the top management and controlling bodies of companies in Europe, especially in Germany. This also applies to German supervisory boards.

EXTENSION OF THE CANDIDATE POOL

The emphasis on diversity within the Code arose on the one hand from the recognition that the skills and experience of women were underutilized. One the other hand, increasing attention has been paid to requirements for the 'right' composition of the supervisory boards. These include restrictions on the number of seats, the protection of a cooling-off period, demands for higher time commitment, professionalization and appropriate qualifications of the members of the supervisory board. As a consequence, there are increased liability risks. These criteria require that the candidate pool from which members of the German supervisory boards are recruited needs to be extended. The supervisory board has to think outside its existing networks when establishing job and competence specifications for future members of supervisory boards. Usually, this is done through the nomination committee, which only consists of shareholder representatives, but any such recommendations for the election of new board members need to be voted on at the annual general meeting. Here again, they have to strive for a more diverse composition of the supervisory board, taking into account the increased requirements for the profiles of its members.

SOFT LAWS VERSUS WOMEN'S OR FEMALE QUOTAS

I am convinced that it is better to use recommendations of the Code, so-called soft laws, to create an environment that enables a change in attitudes towards the representation of women rather than introducing a fixed legal quota. Such an environment enables women to position themselves for leading jobs within the company, and especially for supervisory board seats. However, if this approach towards using the potential of women does not succeed in the medium term – despite all efforts and good intentions – other ways for increasing the representation of women have to be found. In Norway, for example, a very significant increase in the representation of women has been achieved by introducing a law mandating a female quota of 40 percent on boards. Even in France, the Netherlands and other member states of the EU, measures more drastic than the ones which are discussed in Germany are either planned or already implemented. This is being done either by legal regulations or at a minimum within the framework of a corporate governance code, but one which incorporates specific women's quotas for the supervisory board.

Not using the full potential of women is akin to mismanagement and means a waste of existing resources. Not promoting the potential of women and not demanding this potential is certainly not good corporate governance. The introduction of a legally binding women's quota would necessarily be a rigid rule, which would not exclusively orient itself towards the company's interest.

Therefore, it is up to companies to make a concerted effort take up the offered and recommended initiatives, and to show a willingness to change – not only for the companies' interests, but also in the interest of women. If the opportunity offered by the Code's recommendations is not used to increase the representation of women voluntarily as is appropriate for the particular company, taking coercive action by introducing a legal women's quota is expected by the legislator in the foreseeable future.

27. Italy's lessons learnt from Norway

Marina Brogi

Italy's lessons learnt from Norway can be seen from three different and yet complementary viewpoints. The first is academic: how can the introduction of a quota law influence corporate governance and boards in theory? The second is based on experience as a board member: how can a greater number of women influence board dynamics in practice? Lastly, and perhaps most importantly, how is it possible to promote a quota law with such a potentially far-reaching impact in a country like Italy?

Three aspects appear to be particularly important in the lesson (almost) learnt from Norway: (1) some background information on Italy; (2) why a quota law is necessary and how it is progressing through the Italian Parliament; and (3) some concluding but not conclusive thoughts about serving on boards.

Italy is one of the major industrialized countries in the world. Depending on the ranking it is in 7th or 8th position globally in terms of gross domestic product (GDP), even though it is among the slowest-growing countries. Italy is bottom in terms of growth but has done well in the past, and that is why it is still big. Italy has 60 million people, a large GDP, but is suffering from an insufficient growth rate. This leads straight into the second point. The Bank of Italy recently estimated that if Italy achieved the target of the Lisbon treaty – that is, a 60 percent participation of women in the workforce – GDP would grow by up to 7 percent. This testifies to a considerable source of untapped potential, and begs the question of why Italy is missing out on it, and how best to react in order to reverse the negative trend registered by GDP in the past. It is a particularly challenging task since Italy has a high national debt and thus cannot afford to catalyze change with public money.

When Lella Golfo, the chairwoman of Fondazione Bellisario, one of the first women leadership organizations in Italy, was appointed to Parliament in 2008, she gathered a few members of Fondazione Bellisario and asked for suggestions on what she could propose to change things for women in Italy. Being an economist I suggested that any measure to have any chance of being passed would need to have a zero cost for the national budget. A quota law seemed to meet the zero cost requirement and at the same time be an effective measure as it could contribute to change stereotypes and at the same time provide role models for future generations. Norway was the obvious example to study, as it had already introduced the quota law, and I suggested that Lella Golfo meet Morten Huse. In drafting the bill Lella Golfo considered that whilst other countries passed a 40 percent quota, for Italian companies it would have been an overly challenging target considering that listed companies were starting from a 6 percent level. Based on the critical mass theory that you find in Morten Huse's research, you need three women on a board to make a difference. Considering that the average board in Italian listed companies is made up of 10 members the bill sets a more realistic quota for Italy, that is, a one-third quota. The economic rationale and the business case which provides support for the bill are clear and can be synthesized by just one number: in 2010 there were 190 000 cum laude graduates in Italy, and 60 percent were women. So there are many talented Italian women who just do not get to leading positions, which by the way is also a terrible waste of public money, because Italian universities are mainly public. In order to stimulate growth Italy must tap its female talent pool. A quota law could promote change from the top in two ways: first, by changing gender stereotypes; and second, by providing examples and role models and creating a more women-friendly environment in Italy. Recent estimates show that one-third of working women leave their jobs after having two children (as the combined impact of women who leave their jobs after their first child and those who leave their job after their second child). Minor changes to office practices could contribute to help women achieve a more sustainable work–life balance. For example, holding meetings in the morning, as opposed to 6 pm, is a concrete way of contributing to a more women-friendly environment. Women in Italy often need to go back home at six o'clock because the public childcare system is not sufficiently developed. Many mothers rely on grandparents, but cannot stretch their work day till 8 pm. Planning late-night meetings in advance is another way of enabling young talented women professionals to continue working. Even an extraordinary effort can probably be achieved if scheduled in advance. This is the sort of innovation needed in Italian companies and part of the rationale for a quota law in Italy.

The milestones of the Italian quota bill are: on 7 May 2009 Lella Golfo, a right-wing member of Parliament (MP), proposed the first quota law. It provided for a minimum threshold for the less-represented gender on the boards of Italian listed and state-controlled companies, therefore a third of board members would need to be women; and that the rule be applied from the first board renewal after publication of the law in the *Official Gazette* of the Italian Republic. The bill went through the Lower House and was approved unanimously (nobody took it seriously) on 2 December 2010 after examination by the Finance Committee, which merged the original Golfo bill with the quota bill proposed by Alessia Mosca, a left-wing MP, on 18 November 2009, some six months later. On 6 December 2010 it was sent as a bipartisan measure to the Upper House and when it reached to the Senate, it started to fuel a very negative reaction. In a joint press release the Italian Trade Association, the Italian Bankers Association and the Italian Insurance Companies Association declared that the quota law would greatly harm Italian business. However, a lot of work had been done through the media and this had already created great awareness and even considerable support for the law. Many Italian journalists contributed significantly, including Cinzia Sasso who attended the workshop in Oslo. She is a very influential journalist, writing for *Repubblica*, one of Italy's most read newspapers, which sells 800 000 copies a day and has 1 million readers. She and her newspaper have done a lot in support of the law.

The bill was amended and 'toned down' by the Senate and must return to the Lower House for definitive approval. Perhaps the new version will be passed. It provides for a more gradual application: a one-fifth quota for the first term in office and a one-third quota for the subsequent two terms. The 'toned-down' version of the law will therefore be temporary and will be applicable for three terms of office: a little over a decade in which Italian women will need to prove their worth if the law is to have lasting effects. It would be important for the bill to be definitively passed now (March 2011) because Italian companies mostly hold their general shareholders' meetings in April, and a 20 percent quota of women appointed to boards starting in April would be a very strong step in the right direction.

Just a few concluding but not conclusive thoughts on the third and final point: concrete experience on serving on boards. I chair the board of statutory auditors of a spirits company that sells its products all over the world. Statutory auditors in Italy are responsible for controls and must attend board of directors meetings. As I am the chairwoman I also have the opportunity of discussing important issues with the owner. The company used to have advertisements with scantily clad women. In one of our meetings I pointed out to the owner that I doubted that those ads were effective. The new ad, on air in Italy in March 2011 as well as in Copenhagen in Denmark, and due to be broadcast in other countries, shows a man explaining that our leading product is wholly natural and made with herbs – no women. Even though they do involve some power, boards are about serving and contributing to the right decisions. Italy can greatly improve its track record on gender issues; stereotypes presented daily on television are bad for both girls and boys. Though it is anecdotal and has no statistical relevance, in an infinitesimally small way, changing an advertisement may contribute to modifying stereotypes. This could be the sort of difference that women on boards can make. It could turn out to be a small step in the right direction. And every long journey starts with the first step.

To conclude, a quote from Seneca, a Roman philosopher from the first century, who said: 'There's no such a thing as luck, luck is what happens when preparation meets opportunity.' Quota laws all over the world may be the way in which many talented women meet their opportunity.

POSTSCRIPT

The Golfo–Mosca bill for Italian listed and state-controlled companies was definitively approved by the Lower House on 28 June 2011 and published in the *Official Gazette* of the Italian Republic as Law 120 of 12 July 2011. It required compliance by companies as of July 2012.

28. Women on boards in the UK: accelerating the pace of change?*

Ruth Sealy and Susan Vinnicombe

THE GLACIAL YEARS

Since 1999, Cranfield School of Management's International Centre for Women Leaders (CICWL) has produced an annual census of women on corporate boards in the UK, called the Female FTSE Report. From an initial 1999 figure of 6.9 per cent of top 100 listed board seats held by women (including executive, insider and non-executive, outsider directorships), the figures increased incrementally year on year. But by the end of the first decade, it appeared that the growth in numbers of women on boards had faltered. The 2010 Female FTSE Report described stalling figures of 12.5 per cent (Vinnicombe et al., 2010). Interestingly, a similar two- to three-year plateau could be seen in figures from the USA and Canada (at between 14 and 15 per cent respectively), the other two Western economies monitoring this issue for the previous decade.

But 2010 signalled change in the UK. The CICWL team have always worked closely with both government and big business, keeping both informed of the status quo in other countries and on various initiatives implemented at organizational and governmental policy level. The 2010 Female FTSE Report received increasing media coverage as the topic of women on boards started to hot up across Europe. The topic of quotas was on the table with many European governments, but this was never going to sit comfortably in the UK. We watched with interest in 2010 how business in Australia responded to the government's blatant quota threat. Business countered by taking action for change introducing, in the Governance Code, a requirement for reporting on diversity policies and actions and gender metrics at all levels of the organization. Australia and the UK are similar both in their corporate structures and in their dismissive attitudes to legislative intervention. The behaviour of businesses is regulated through a Corporate Governance Code, which operates on a 'comply or explain' basis, or in Australia the rather more pithy 'If not, why not?'

In the UK in May 2010, the Financial Reporting Council (the body monitoring listed companies' governance) announced an amendment to the Governance Code, introducing a new principle on board appointments (Financial Reporting Council, 2010). Chairmen were required to 'pay due regard for the benefits of diversity on the board, including gender'. Whilst many were disappointed by the lack of boldness of this change, this was the first time gender had been put on the agenda.

In the summer of 2010, a new Conservative–Liberal Democrat coalition government was elected in the UK. They were aware of other countries starting to act on women on boards as well as the discussions led by Vivian Reding, Justice Commissioner for the European Union (EU). The UK government did not want to be left behind. So they set up a review into women on boards, led by Lord Mervyn Davies, a male, ex-Trade Minister from the previous government and ex-Chairman of Standard Chartered Bank. The review included extensive consultation with many different stakeholder groups. This was a very clear signal that from the UK's perspective this was not an equality issue, it was a business issue.

That December, the 2010 Female FTSE Report focused on the fact that the figures of women's representation at the top had plateaued. What had only ever been glacial progress had stalled. In addition, we had conducted a number of interviews with FTSE 100 Chairmen, discussing what their role is or should be in increasing women's representation at board level – if indeed they saw it as necessary – and their take on the new Governance Code. They were all, without exception, adamantly against quotas, but interestingly a number of them (particularly the big players) were keen to introduce what they described as 'soft targets': individual organizations setting their own targets and being held responsible for them.

In January 2011 the Confederation of British Industry – a body representing the interests of all UK industry, not just the large corporates – published a report. Their recommendations followed the Australian example: make further changes to the Governance Code; bring in gender metric reporting on a 'comply or explain' basis; and get the chairmen to pledge a target and stick to it. They also pointed to more work needing to be done around the appointment process, which was becoming recognized as one of the big sticking points for women wanting board positions in the UK.

At the end of February 2011, Lord Davies published the outcome of his review (Davies Report, 2011). His report focused on the main issues that affect women at the most senior levels of corporate life and, very importantly, addressed issues for other stakeholders within the process of getting women to board positions, as opposed to giving a list of activities or behaviours for women themselves to address. The recommendations were aimed at UK PLC voluntarily addressing the issue of women on boards so as to avoid any need for further government intervention, although Lord Davies specifically did not rule that out. Box 28.1 outlines the main recommendations of the Davies Report.

BOX 28.1   SUMMARY OF THE MAIN RECOMMENDATIONS OF THE DAVIES REPORT (FEBRUARY 2011)

All FTSE 350 Chairmen should set aspirational targets for the percentage of women they aim to have on their corporate boards by 2013 and 2015. FTSE 100 companies should aim for a minimum of 25%.

- Quoted companies should disclose proportions of women in their workforce and in Senior Executive positions. Chief Executives should review the percentage of women they aim to have on their Executive Committee.
- The Financial Reporting Council (FRC) should amend the UK Corporate Governance Code to require companies to establish a policy on boardroom diversity, including measurable objectives and disclose annually their progress.
- Chairmen will be encouraged to sign a charter supporting the recommendations.
- Chairmen should disclose meaningful information about board appointment process.
- Investors should pay close attention to recommendations when considering companies.
- Companies are encouraged to advertise NED positions.
- Executive Search Firms (ESFs) should draw up a voluntary Code of Conduct addressing best practice for gender diversity on boards.
- The pool from which potential female directors are drawn should be widened. As well as the current corporate

---

> mainstream, female academics, entrepreneurs, civil serv-
> ants and those with professional services backgrounds
> should also be considered.
> ● The Steering Board should meet every six months to
> review and report progress.
>
> *Source:* Davies Report (2011).

The Report garnered a positive response from the UK's mainstream media. That level of support would have been unimaginable just a couple of years earlier. But the tone of the media's reporting had changed. The public debate had become vociferous and various stakeholders had become engaged. The media had been leading the debate in a positive way, focusing discussion on what was the best way to change the status quo, as opposed to whether we need to change it. In a majority positive response, the criticism from those who did not support the Report was that it did not go far enough.

ACCELERATING CHANGE

Between 1999 and 2010 the percentage of women on the UK top 100 boards increased incrementally from 7 per cent to 12 per cent. At that pace of change it was going to take several decades before we could ever reach any degree of parity. Following the Davies Report there have been some substantive changes.

Based on the turnover figures from previous Female FTSE Reports (an average of 14 per cent over six years), the Davies Report had speculated that if one-third of all new FTSE 100 board appointments were given to women from 2011 onwards, then from a starting point of 12.5 per cent female directors, a figure of 23.5 per cent could be achieved across the FTSE 100 companies by 2015. However, ensuring that only two-thirds of all new appointments go to men would signify quite a change in behaviour, as the yearly percentage of new appointments going to women over the decade 2001–2010 was on average 14.2 per cent, hence the very incremental changes made over that period. Therefore, the first point of interest was that in the 12 months following the Davies Report, the percentage of new appointments going to women was almost 25 per cent.

This took the headline figure of women on the top FTSE 100 boards from 12.5 per cent to 15.6 per cent by March 2012 (170 out of 1089 directorships held by women). In addition, the turnover figure also rose to 17.5 per cent (however, this is not unprecedented and may have been due to the economic climate). Of the FTSE 100 companies, at the start of 2012, 89 had at least one woman on their board (an increase of ten since 2010) and half of the companies had multiple female directors (an increase of 11). The percentage of female executive directors, however, had increased from just 5.5 per cent to 6.6 per cent. This figure is clearly still very low and yet needs to be addressed.

Trajectories are hard to predict, but useful in order to see the levels of activity required to reach particular goals. In Figure 28.1, the lower line shows the outcome of maintaining the current pace and rate of change, that is, 25 per cent female appointees of a 17.5 per cent annual turnover. This predicts a total percentage of women on boards of 22.2 per cent by 2015 and 27.5 per cent by 2020.

However, there is a noticeable momentum in the UK and thanks to the Davies Report there are multiple stakeholders engaged in and motivated to solve this problem. Many of those involved believe that in fact there will be an increasing percentage of new appointments going to women, which will create a 'wave effect'. This has started to occur in the past year (2011). In 2010, the percentage of new appointments going to women was 13.3 per cent. The Six Month Monitoring Report of October 2011 recorded women taking 22.5 per cent of new appointments (Sealy et al., 2011). By January 2012, this had risen to 24.7 per cent and by 1 March 2012 had reached 26.7 per cent. Therefore, in the higher trajectory, this gathering of momentum is demonstrated with an increased percentage of appointments going to women, increasing at a rate of 2.5 per cent every six months until it reaches 35 per cent at the end of 2014 and is then held constant until 2020. The 'wave effect' is clear. In both lines the annual turnover going forward has been held constant at the current 17.5 per cent. This predicts a total percentage of women on boards of 26.7 per cent by 2015 and 36.9 per cent by 2020. After a decade of incremental increases, these trajectories feel pleasantly optimistic.

TARGETS AND PIPELINE MEASUREMENTS

The majority of public limited companies (PLCs) in the UK are not in favour of any quota legislation and have said that this should be an issue for business to sort out itself. The Davies Report set out how it believed business and other stakeholders could act to ensure a sufficient, timely and sustainable increase in the proportion of women in leadership positions. The Davies Report asked chairmen to announce aspirational

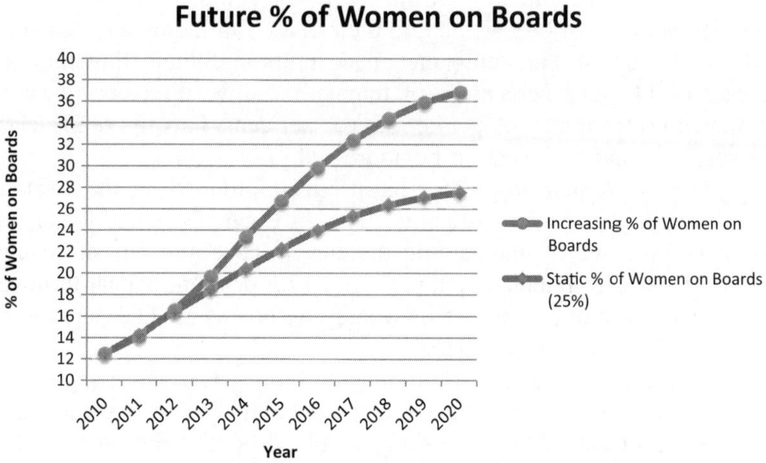

Future % of Women on Boards

Figure 28.1   Trajectories of future women on UK FTSE 100 boards

targets for their percentage of women on boards, but by February 2012 just 38 of the FTSE 100 companies had done so.

For the 2012 Female FTSE Report, CICWL requested information about the percentage of women at all levels of each FTSE 100 organization. Of the 68 responses to this request, 33 provided information on their female pipeline. It was interesting to note that whilst some companies could easily pull these data off various reporting tools, most organizations clearly did not routinely track this information. In addition to those companies who did provide information, a few stated that the requested information would be reported in their annual report later in the year. Companies need to be encouraged to monitor this information going forward. It is critical in optimizing talent management that these organizations are aware of diversity at all levels.

FINANCIAL REPORTING COUNCIL CHANGE OF CODE

Following public consultation after the Davies Report, the Financial Reporting Council (FRC) conducted a consultation and subsequently amended the UK Corporate Governance Code to require companies to report on the board's policy on boardroom diversity, including gender, on any measurable objectives that the board has set for implementing the policy, and on the progress it had made in achieving the objectives (FRC, 2012, Supporting Principle B.2.4). In addition, the FRC amended the Code to identify the diversity of the board as one of the factors to be considered when evaluating its effectiveness (FRC, 2012, Supporting Principle B.6). These amendments formally applied to financial years beginning on or after 1 October 2012.

CHARTER

In March 2011 EU Justice Commissioner Reding launched a 'Women on the Board Pledge for Europe', calling for EU listed companies to sign up before March 2012 (Europa Press Release, 2011). The Davies Steering Board decided that a separate UK pledge would be counterproductive, so this was not pursued.

DISCLOSURE ON APPOINTMENTS PROCESS

In accordance with the Code of Governance, the Davies Report recommended that companies give detailed information about the work of their Nomination Committee, including the process used to search and appoint directors. The Six Month Monitoring Report revealed that almost all of the FTSE 100 companies had a section in their Annual Reports giving details on the work of the Nominations Committee. Almost three-quarters gave reasonable detail regarding the transparency of their process. In line with best practice recommended since 2003 (Higgs, 2003), 73 per cent stated that they engaged an external executive search firm in the appointment process. Given that the amendment to the Code mentioning diversity was made in 2010, it was disappointing that only 43 per cent addressed diversity and only 20 per cent specifically mentioned gender diversity in regard to their appointment process. Following the further amendment to the Code in October 2011, it is expected that many more companies will report in more detail and refer to gender diversity in their Annual Reports.

INVESTOR INVOLVEMENT

Historically, it has been challenging to engage investors on diversity issues. However, since the Davies Report the investor community has been very proactive in its response. Recommendation 6 of that report stated that investors 'should pay close attention' to the behaviours of companies in terms of the Davies recommendations, including company transparency around targets, reporting on proportions of women at various levels, the appointment process, boardroom diversity policies and measurable objectives. There has been a very positive response from some of the UK's largest institutional investors – with a total of over £1.7 trillion worth of investment – setting out their own policies on how they will engage with companies on the diversity issue. Investors need companies to report diversity information, and increasingly the sense from them is that those companies that do not are at best ignorant (and therefore inactive) or at worse obstructive.

ADVERTISING NON-EXECUTIVE DIRECTORS

This recommendation was included as part of the aim to increase transparency in the recruitment process. There has been little evidence that business has taken up this recommendation and there appears little appetite for this to be the case.

EXECUTIVE SEARCH FIRMS NEW CODE OF CONDUCT

As a result of the Davies recommendations, in an unprecedented move in July 2011, leading executive search firms (ESFs) came together and developed a Voluntary Code of Conduct (PR Newswire, 2011). To date, there have been 22 signatories of the major firms. A number of FTSE companies have stated they will only use ESFs who are signatories to the Code. The Equality and Human Rights Commission have commissioned research into the role of ESFs in the board appointment process following their new Code. Whilst the board appointment process remains opaque and typically driven by a small group of elite chairmen, there is much opportunity for subjectivity around the notion of 'fit'. Prior research has reported collusion between chairmen and ESFs that resulted in a lack of diverse candidates (Vinnicombe et al., 2010). However, in 2011, ESFs reported a heightened awareness of the need to address the issue at board level, both within their firms and among their clients. A number of good practices were found, although the extent to which they are embraced varied from search firm to search firm. Whilst some ESFs appeared to be paying lip-service, a number were proactively engaged with the need to rapidly diversify the largest boards.

EXPANDING THE TALENT POOL

In the 12 months to January 2012, 47 women took up new roles on FTSE 100 boards (25 per cent of all new appointments). Of these, 29 women (62 per cent) had no prior FTSE 350 board experience. However, most of these new women did have experience on a range of other boards, including public and charitable sector boards. This is encouraging and shows a change from past trends, when previous Female FTSE Reports have reported a relative recycling of female directors (Sealy et al., 2008). This represents a good addition to the talent pool, suggesting that the appointment process is beginning to open up to new women, and chairmen and ESFs are being a little more creative with their directorship brief.

OVERALL IMPACT

From the autumn of 2010 onwards, the issue in the UK of women on boards has really gained momentum. The previous cycle of a decade of incremental annual changes appears to have been broken with a new 'wave effect' clearly demonstrated from 2011 to 2012. The government, investors, ESFs, the FRC and a significant tranche of the corporate business community appear to be behind the initiative to increase gender balance. The time appears to be right for significant change. Recent Female FTSE Reports (Sealy et al., 2009; Sealy and Vinnicombe, 2012) had demonstrated a substantial talent pool of senior executive women, and the catastrophic failure of the corporate sector in the global financial crisis meant that minds were open to change and different ways of doing business. On the other hand, the voluntary measures instigated since 2011 have no strict compulsion and some would argue that in the current economic climate, business should be focused on other priorities. However, peer pressure from the larger listed PLCs and fear of legislative intervention, at either a governmental or a European level, may well just be enough to tip women's representation to the critical mass.

NOTE

* Sections of this chapter have previously appeared in the 2012 Female FTSE Board Report (Sealy and Vinnicombe, 2012).

REFERENCES

Davies Report (2011) *Women on Boards*, February, available at http://www.bis. gov.uk/assets/biscore/business-law/docs/w/11-745-women-on-boards.pdf.

Europa Press Release (2011) EU Justice Commissioner Reding challenges business leaders to increase women's presence on corporate boards with 'Women on the Board Pledge for Europe', Brussels, available at http://europa. eu/rapid/pressReleasesAction.do?reference=MEMO/11/124.

Financial Reporting Council (2010), *The UK Corporate Governance Code*, London: FRC, available at http://www.frc.org.uk/documents/pagemanager/ Corporate_Governance/UK%20Corp%20Gov%20Code%20June%202010.pdf.

Financial Reporting Council (FRC) (2011), Feedback Statement: Gender diversity on boards, London: FRC, available at http://www.frc.org.uk/images/ up loaded/documents/Feedback%20Statement%20on%20Boardroom%20Diver sity%20October%202011.pdf.

Financial Reporting Council (FRC) (2012) *The UK Corporate Governance Code*, London: FRC, available from http://www.frc.org.uk/Our-Work/ Publications/Corporate-Governance/UK-Corporate-Governance-Code-Septem ber-2012. aspx.

Higgs, D. (2003) Review of the role and effectiveness of non-executive directors, London: Department of Trade and Industry.

PR Newswire (2011) Executive search firms launch voluntary code of conduct in response to the Davies Review of Women on Boards, available at http:// www.prnewswire.co.uk/cgi/news/release?id=328122.

Sealy, R., Doldor, E., Singh, V. and Vinnicombe, S. (2011), Women on Boards: 6 month monitoring report, Cranfield School of Management, UK, http://www.bis.gov.uk/assets/biscore/business-law/docs/w/11-p124-women-on- boards-6-month-monitoring-october-2011.pdf.

Sealy, R. and Vinnicombe, S. (2012), *The Female FTSE Board Report 2012: Milestone or Millstone?* Cranfield: Cranfield School of Management.

Sealy, R., Vinnicombe, S. and Doldor, E. (2009), *The Female FTSE Report 2009: Norway and Spain Join Our Census to Benchmark Corporate Boards*, Cranfield: Cranfield School of Management.

Sealy, R., Vinnicombe, S. and Singh, V. (2008), *The Female FTSE Report 2008: A Decade of Delay*, Cranfield: Cranfield School of Management.

Vinnicombe, S., Sealy, R., Graham, J. and Doldor, E. (2010), *The Female FTSE Board Report 2010: Opening up the Appointment Process*, Cranfield: Cranfield School of Management.

29. Winning the board game: Europe's economy needs more women in business

Viviane Reding

GENERAL CONTEXT

In the past few decades, Europe has made significant progress in getting more women into the workforce. The female employment rate is now 62 per cent, up from 55 per cent in 1997. Moreover, women are also making great strides in education, representing 60 per cent of new university graduates. European Union (EU) legislation and EU funding have contributed to these advances.

Despite this progress there has been one significant shortfall: the lack of women at the top levels in companies. Many qualified women cannot break through the glass ceiling when climbing the corporate ladder. The facts are bleak: just one in seven board members (13.7 per cent) at Europe's top publicly listed companies and one in 30 boardroom chairs (3.2 per cent) is a woman.

The European Commission is committed to increasing the percentage of women in economic decision-making positions; equality in decision-making is one of the five priority areas in both the Women's Charter and the European Commission's Strategy for Equality between Women and Men (2010–2015).

Against the backdrop of the economic crisis, an ageing population, low birth rates and an anticipated skills shortage, it is increasingly important to take advantage of everyone's skills. As said previously, women represent 60 per cent of new university graduates and generally leave university with better qualifications than men. Despite this academic prowess, women struggle to climb the corporate ladder, with their professional careers failing to properly reflect their knowledge and skills. Human capital is key to competitiveness in the global economy. Women are underrepresented in economic decision-making positions; consequently we are losing out on essential skills and talent.

THE BUSINESS CASE

Empowering women to take leadership positions is important for economic growth and a competitive internal market. It can help us kick-start Europe's economic engine. There is a clear business case for greater gender diversity in corporate boards both from the microeconomic perspective, in terms of individual companies' performance; as well as from a macroeconomic perspective, in terms of higher, sustainable rates of economic growth.

THE MICROECONOMIC PERSPECTIVE

Many business leaders have realized that gender diversity is a driving force for performance. Here are some economic arguments in favour of more gender diversity on company boards:

- Improved company performance. Studies from various countries show that companies with a higher share of women at top levels deliver strong organizational and financial performance (for example Smith et al., 2004; McKinsey, 2007, 2009, 2010; Catalyst, 2007; Finnish Business and Policy Forum, 2007; Ernst & Young, 2010; Davies Report, 2011). Amongst these studies, research from McKinsey & Company shows that companies with the most gender-diverse management teams had 17 percentage-point higher stock price growth between 2005 and 2007 compared to the industry average, and their average operating profit was almost double the industry average between 2003 and 2005 (McKinsey, 2007). Catalyst (2007) research found that companies with more women on their boards were found to outperform their rivals with a 42 per cent higher return in sales, 66 per cent higher return on invested capital and 53 per cent higher return on equity. Studies have also shown that where governance is weak, female directors can exercise strong oversight and have a 'positive, value-relevant impact' on the company. A gender-balanced board is more likely to pay attention to managing and controlling risk (TCAM, 2009).
- Mirroring the market. According to recent estimates (Bloomberg, 2011), women control about 70 per cent of global consumer

spending. More women in management positions can therefore provide a broader insight in economic behaviour and consumer choices, leading to market share gains through the creation of products and services that take better account of consumers' needs and preferences.

- Enhanced quality of decision-making. Diversity among employees and board members boosts creativity and innovation by adding complementary knowledge, skills and experience. A more diverse board of directors contributes to better performance because decisions are based on evaluating more alternatives compared to homogenous boards.
- Improved corporate governance and ethics. Studies have shown that the quality of corporate governance and ethical behaviour is high in companies with high shares of women on boards (Franke et al., 1997; Conference Board of Canada, 2002).
- Better use of the talent pool. More than half of the students graduating from Europe's universities are women. By excluding them from decision-making positions, female talent would be underutilized and the quality of appointments may be compromised. Systematically including suitable candidates of both genders ensures that board members are selected from amongst the best distribution of both men and women.

THE MACROECONOMIC PERSPECTIVE

Drawing on women's talent and professional skills for leadership positions is likely to become increasingly necessary as ageing populations and the resulting shortages of skilled labour put an increasing brake on economic growth. The glass ceiling that keeps women out of decision-making roles is likely to discourage women from fulfilling their full professional potential. Poor career prospects could dissuade women from continuing in paid employment; this could therefore reduce the labour supply and ultimately hamper economic growth. The absence of women in senior positions may trigger vicious cycles that further widen both the gender employment gap and the gender pay gap.

Strong economies and sustainable pension systems in the future will depend on higher female employment rates and high wage returns on paid jobs (OECD, 2008). This is why the Europe 2020 Strategy sets a target of raising the employment rate for women and men aged 20 to 64 to 75 per cent. Achieving this target requires greater participation of women in the labour market. Therefore, incentives for women to stay in the workforce, including credible prospects of career progress, are essential; one such incentive consists in opening the door to top management positions.

Diverging national rules on gender equality in some member states, and the lack thereof in others, should be taken into consideration as this may have a bearing on the functioning of the internal market. There may be an impact on the cross-border establishment of companies or on the prospects for successful participation in public procurement abroad (for example, an international company may be operating in several EU member states that either have no quota law, or have different quota rules). Companies need legal certainty and not conflicting rules.

THE FIGURES

A year ago the European Commission challenged publicly listed companies in the EU to voluntarily improve the gender balance in corporate boards. Chief executives were asked to sign the 'Women on Board Pledge for Europe' (http://ec.europa.eu/commission_2010-2014/reding/womenpledge/index_en.htm) to voluntarily increase women's presence on corporate boards to 30 per cent in 2015 and 40 per cent in 2020.

On 5 March 2012, the Commission presented a progress report on women in economic decision-making (http://ec.europa.eu/justice/gender-equality/files/women-on-boards_en.pdf) to see if there is sufficient progress and enough commitment to achieve a faster and more meaningful change.

The key indicator of gender representation on corporate boards in the EU shows that the proportion of women involved in top-level business decision-making remains very low, although there are small signs of progress. In January 2012, women occupied on average just 13.7 per cent of board seats of the largest publicly listed companies in EU member states – up from 11.8 per cent in October 2010 (European Commission, 2012).

In Germany, the situation is somewhat better, with women making up 15.6 per cent of supervisory board members, up from 12.6 per cent. Across the EU, the proportion of women on corporate boards increased by 1.9 percentage points between October 2010 and January 2012. This equates to around 1.5 percentage points per year, which is above the long-term average of 0.6 percentage points per year. However, progress remains slow and at this rate it would take decades to achieve real gender equality on boards. Furthermore, the performance of individual countries varied.

Women occupy a quarter of the seats on boards in large listed companies in Finland, Latvia and Sweden, and just over a fifth in France. Yet there are less than one in ten in Ireland, Greece, Estonia, Italy, Portugal, Luxembourg and Hungary; less than one in 20 in Cyprus; and around one in 30 in Malta.

France saw the most notable improvement, having adopted a legal quota in January 2011. France's quota is 40 per cent by 2017 with an intermediate target of 20 per cent by 2014. In fact, the proportion of women on the boards of French companies in the CAC 40 index[1] in January 2012 had increased by 10 percentage points to 22.3 per cent, up from 12.3 per cent in October 2010. This change, prompted by the binding quota, makes up more than 40 per cent of the total change EU-wide. Quotas are clearly controversial. And I personally am not a fan of quotas. But I very much like the results that quotas bring.

People in Europe clearly agree that the situation in Europe should be changed. According to a new Eurobarometer survey published in March 2012, 88 per cent of Europeans believe that given equal competences women should be equally represented in the top jobs in business. Moreover, 75 per cent of those asked are in favour of quota legislation in case progress cannot be achieved otherwise (Eurobarometer, 2012).

EXAMPLES OF INITIATIVES IN THE MEMBER STATES

To increase gender diversity in boardrooms an increasing number of member states have resorted to legislative measures establishing quotas or targets for gender representation on company boards. This is a very recent development as practically all the member states concerned adopted the relevant laws only in 2011.

Quota Measures

France, Italy and Belgium have enacted quota legislation for company boards that includes sanctions. These countries followed the example of Norway, which has seen rapid progress and widespread compliance with a 40 per cent quota passed in 2003. The three EU member states' legislation is considerably diverse concerning the targeted quota, the deadlines and other modalities, the scope of companies covered and the sanctions to be applied in case of non-compliance.

The Netherlands and Spain have also passed quota laws; however these rules are more lenient as they are not binding or tied to any significant sanctions. In the Netherlands, the requirement of achieving a 30 per cent representation of each gender among board members in big companies is combined with a 'comply or explain' mechanism rather than with concrete sanctions that apply in case of failure to reach the target. The Spanish legislation adopted in 2007 encourages large companies to alter the membership of their boards gradually until each gender makes up at least 40 per cent of board membership by 2015. The relevant provision is a recommendation.

Rules Concerning State-Owned Companies

In addition to member states which have enacted rules covering the boards of all listed companies or companies of a certain size, several others have prescribed gender requirements specifically for the composition of boards of state-controlled companies. In Denmark, Finland and Greece such requirements are set out in the gender equality legislation. In Austria and Slovenia, they have been established by means of administrative regulations. Across many EU member states, a wide range of voluntary initiatives and tools have been developed to address the underrepresentation of women in senior leadership positions.

Setting of Voluntary Targets

In the United Kingdom, the government appointed Lord Davies to lead a review to examine the way in which obstacles can be removed for the participation of women on boards. In his report, he recommended that UK listed companies in the FTSE 100 should aim for a minimum of 25 per cent female board member representation by 2015 (Davies Report, 2011). The report said that companies should set targets for 2013 and 2015 to ensure that more talented women can get into the top jobs in UK companies. On the basis of these recommendations the government is encouraging all FTSE 350 companies to specify the percentage of women they aim to have on their boards in 2013 and 2015. The six-month monitoring report showed some progress was made (Sealy et al., 2011): women now make up 14.2 per cent of FTSE 100 directors, up from 12.5 per cent in 2010. Thirty-three FTSE 100 companies have set targets for the percentage of women they aim to have on their boards.

Corporate Governance Codes

In Austria, Belgium, Denmark, Finland, France, Germany, Luxembourg, the Netherlands, Poland, Spain, Sweden and the UK, the national corporate governance codes encourage, to a different extent, gender diversity on company boards (www.ecgi.org). Latest developments include the revision of the recommendations of the corporate governance code of Denmark in 2011. It stresses the need to strive for more women in management by setting up targets for achieving progress. In 2012, a revised corporate governance code should be issued in Austria. Under the current draft proposals, more efforts will be made to increase the proportion of women on executive and supervisory boards.

Charters That Companies Can Sign

In the Netherlands, the charter 'Talent to the Top' (http://www.talent naardetop.nl/Home_NL/Charter/Ondertekenaars/) requires companies to establish quantitative goals for the representation of women in senior management, measure their achievement and report annually. Feedback is given by the Talent to the Top Monitoring Committee. In 2010, the share of women in senior positions in companies having signed the charter in 2008 and 2009 grew by 7.5 per cent. Overall, the vast majority of the signatories (72 per cent) have recorded an increase.

In Denmark, the 'Charter for more women in management' (http://www.kvinderiledelse.dk/charter_paa_engelsk.asp) encourages companies to inspire more women to take up management positions and to evaluate their initiatives every second year. Moreover, since 2010, Denmark has implemented the 'Recommendation for More Women on Supervisory Boards' (Operation Chain Reaction) according to which the companies undertake, *inter alia*, to work to recruit more female managers to the supervisory boards of Danish limited liability companies.

Business Initiatives

In Germany, companies in the DAX30 have announced their individual targets for increasing the presence of women in management positions (Reuters, 2011). These range from 12 per cent to 35 per cent of women in management positions with various deadlines for achieving these targets. However, they do not target specifically supervisory or executive boards.

Some countries are asking state-owned companies to promote gender equality. In November 2011 the Finnish government adopted a resolution outlining the objectives and principles for a state ownership policy. This policy plays a dual role: to pay attention to the formation of companies' boards, and to emphasize the need to promote gender equality. Moreover, in some member states, there are databases promoting female candidates for board functions, prizes and/or awards for businesses aiming to promote women in senior management and government measures to support women's entrepreneurship.

State of Play and Next Steps

The Commission's Legislative Work Programme for 2012 includes an initiative to address this situation. The Commission will now explore policy options for targeted measures at European level to enhance female participation in decision-making.

In parallel to the publication of the progress report, the Commission launched a public consultation that will contribute to assessing the impact of possible EU measures to redress the situation. The Commission is seeking views from all stakeholders on possible action at EU level, including legislative measures. The public consultation ran until 28 May 2012. Following the input from the public consultation, the Commission will take a decision on possible measures.

Breaking the glass ceiling for women on company boards is a common challenge facing Europe's economy. We can no longer afford to waste female talent. The talent is there. Just have a look at the rich list of 3500 'boardable' women that business schools and prominent senior women executives have gathered (http://www.edhec.com/html/Communication/womenonboard.html). These are women who have all necessary qualifications to go on the boards – as of now. All of them fulfil stringent criteria for corporate governance as defined by publicly listed companies. So the pool is there. Companies should now make use of it.

Persistent failure to encourage and enable women to make full use of their potential has cost us dearly. In these challenging times, the stakes are too high to keep the status quo. Across Europe, from politicians to academics to business leaders, people are aware that women mean business. This is a big step forward. It is time to act now in order to speed up progress and achieve more concrete results.

NOTE

1. The methodology for the collection of data on large companies in each country covers nationally registered members of the main blue-chip index (according to the ISIN code). When the sample was taken the CAC-40 index for France included three companies registered outside France which were therefore excluded from the data: Arcelor Mittal (Luxembourg), EADS (Netherlands) and STMicroelectronics (Netherlands).

REFERENCES

Bloomberg (2011) Women controlling consumer spending, available on http://www.bloomberg.com/news/2011-07-24/women-controlling-70-of-consumer-spending-sparse-in-central-bankers-club.html (accessed December 2012).

Catalyst (2007), *The Bottom Line: Connecting Corporate Performance and Gender Diversity*, New York: Catalyst.

Conference Board of Canada (2002), Women on boards: Not just the right thing ... but the 'bright' thing, available on http://www.europeanpwn.net/files/women_on_boards_canada.pdf (accessed December 2012).

Davies Report (2011) Women on boards, February, available at: http://www.bis.gov.uk/assets/biscore/business-law/docs/w/11-745-women-on-boards.pdf.

Eurobarometer (2012) Women in decision-making positions, Special Eurobarometer 376, available on http://ec.europa.eu/public_opinion/archives/ebs/ebs_376_en.pdf (accessed December 2012)

European Commission (2012) Database – Women and Men in Decision-making, available from http://ec.europa.eu/justice/gender-equality/gender-decision-making/database/index_en.htm (accessed December 2012).

Finnish Business and Policy Forum EVA (2007), *Female Leadership and Firm Profitability*, available at http://www.frauen.bka.gv.at/DocView.axd?CobId=37906 (accessed December 2012).

Franke, G.R., Crown, D.F. and Spake, D.F. (1997), Gender differences in ethical perception of business practices: a social role theory perspective, *Journal of Applied Psychology*, 82(6): 920–934.

McKinsey & Company (2007, 2009, 2010), *Women Matter*, available at http://www.mckinsey.com/features/women_matter (accessed December 2012).

OECD (2008) *Employment Outlook*, Chapter 3, available from www.oecd.org/dataoecd/36/17/43244511.pdf (accessed December 2012).

Reuters (2011) German firms set goals for more women in management, available on http://www.reuters.com/article/2011/10/17/us-germany-women-idUSTRE79G4L920111017, (accessed December 2012).

Sealy, R., Doldor, E., Singh, V. and Vinnicombe, S. (2011), Women on Boards: 6 month monitoring report, Cranfield School of Management, Cranfield. Available at: http://www.bis.gov.uk/assets/biscore/business-law/docs/w/11-p124-women-on-boards-6-month-monitoring-october-2011.pdf.

Smith, N., Smith, V. and Verner, M. (2004) Do women in top management affect performance? A panel study of 2500 Danish firms, *International Journal of Productivity and Performance Management*, 55(7): 569–593.

TCAM (2009), *Diversity and Gender Balance in Britain PLC*, TCAM in conjunction with *The Observer* and as part of the Good Companies Guide, London: TCAM.

30. Concluding remarks to Part V

Katrin Hansen and Silke Machold

We started Part V by discussing three formal approaches to gender diversity on boards: (1) quota legislation which mandates a minimum percentage for certain groups of companies with associated legal sanctions for non-compliance; (2) regulation which include corporate governance codes and disclosure regulations which typically has no formal sanction but is used on a 'comply or explain' basis; and (3) voluntary efforts where companies sign up to voluntary pledges or targets. We learnt that different countries prefer different approaches and connected this to national characteristics, including political, economic, legal and gender equality dimensions.

This discussion leads directly to the question whether a European solution should be found and realized, as Vivian Reding's arguments in Chapter 29 suggest, or whether it is more appropriate for countries to develop their own policies and strategies. As we learnt from the political 'parents' of the gender quota law in Norway (see Chapter 1 of this book), a legal step of such magnitude had a long history of political and social activities, even in country renowned for its gender egalitarianism. Therefore, country-specific social, economic and political conditions may well be an important factor in shaping policies and strategies for increasing women in leadership positions.

Possibly strategic patterns and paths of movement in respect of formal approaches to women on boards could be identified by analyzing in further detail characteristics of the societies in question. An even deeper insight could be provided by discourse analyses (see Bührmann's Chapter 22 in Part IV) analyzing the political debates in core publications, the media and government reports, and comparing the results from different countries over time. Such a rather dynamic approach should further look for inversely u-shaped curves, meaning that 'hard laws' might more easily be develop and accepted in societies with a reduced gender gap and medium to high gender egalitarianism, meanwhile in societies with further increasing high gender egalitarianism and a low gender gap those hard measures might be seen as superfluous and soft or voluntary efforts be preferred.

Nevertheless, we should be careful and not underrate the necessity of strong interventions. Bleijenbergh et al. (2012) showed that the progress of the share of women in organizations was systematically under-estimated. In their research experiment, two-thirds of the participants severely underestimated the percentage of women that needs to be hired to reach an equal gender balance at a given point in time. Moreover, 34 percent of the participants recommended a hiring percentage of women by which an equal gender balance would never be reached at all. The researchers found cognitive bias and stereotypes as relevant factors to explain their results (Bleijenbergh et al., 2012). Qualitative approaches to understanding culture-specific stereotypes should be used to complement the insights from quantitative research, to generate knowledge on barriers to national and international policies. Further, our analysis at the outset of Part V suggests that there are clusters of countries that due to shared economic, political, legal and social characteristics may also act in tandem when it comes to formal approaches to women on boards. The spread of such clusters may well provide further impetus and acceleration for change internationally.

There is also the question of whether one type of policy approach fits all companies in every country. Combining different types of formal approaches, from legislative interventions to voluntary efforts, could be a strategy to overcome the limits of each individual approach and possibly create synergies. Sealy and Vinnicombe conclude in Chapter 28: 'However, peer pressure from the larger listed PLCs and fear of legislative intervention, at either a governmental or a European level, may well just be enough to tip women's representation to the critical mass.' Weber-Rey, being herself a member of the Germany Corporate Governance Code Commission, which has primarily stood for soft laws, states in Chapter 26 that: 'If the opportunity offered by the Code's recommendations is not used to increase the representation of women voluntarily as is appropriate for the particular company, taking coercive action by introducing a legal women's quota is expected by the legislator.'

In Germany, the Federal Minister of Family, Seniors, Women and Youth, Kristina Schroeder, opted for a combined strategy of a 'hard quota law' (forcing the discussion and decision on quotas on the companies affected) with flexible quotas which are to be developed as firm-specific targets by the companies themselves. The overall goal of this strategy is a share of women on boards and in top positions in Germany's largest firms to reach 30 percent on average by 2020. FidAR has developed the

WOB Index to publicly rank listed companies in order to assert additional pressure for compliance with the German Corporate Governance Code, and to advance FidAR's agenda for a hard quota law (see Chapter 25 by Schulz-Strelow). Companies themselves answered this challenge by setting firm-specific and even department-specific goals, which were connected to managers' performance-related pay. Others, such as Telecom, voluntarily decided to follow a general quota; in this instance the company pledged to have 30 percent for all leading positions filled by women by 2015.

From a systems perspective it would be very interesting to analyze how the political, social and legal systems and the embedded organizational system are coupled in this process of promoting women in leadership, and which factors help or hinder this process. Further research is especially needed on the recruitment process of and onto the boards themselves. As Sealy and Vinnicombe in Chapter 28 point out, few UK companies to date report on strategies for addressing gender diversity in their board appointment processes. Important issues here are the interplay between internal and external actors, and the dynamic of the process when regulation, legislation and voluntary efforts become part of the context. For example, what impacts do quota regimes have on board recruitment practices? Are there national differences based on the nature of the quota? Has the recruitment of women to boards also affected other board diversity indicators (internationalization, ethnicity, social status)? This is a good time to study these dynamics in Europe given the heightened political discourse nationally, and the announcement of Vivian Reding in Chapter 29 to find a European solution.

Further research should finally be dedicated to analyze and understand the outcomes of each of the three different formal approaches to gender on boards. As discussed in Chapter 24, even within legislative approaches the scope and the nature of legal sanctions vary. Will lower threshold quotas, or quotas with minimal legal sanctions, trigger a substantial culture change in boards? And do formal approaches to gender diversity genuinely tap into the talent pool of qualified women, or will we see the emergence of a new female corporate elite? By assessing and discussing the effects of political interventions, the societal and the business case must be clearly differentiated. Identifying and discussing conflicts among those fields as well as synergies is a still underresearched field, and has the potential to shed light on the efficacy of different approaches.

REFERENCE

Bleijenbergh, I., Van Engen, M., Vennix, J. and Jacobs, E. (2012) *Setting Targets Is Not Reaching Goals: The Dynamics Behind Gender Target Figures*. Paper presented at EURAM Annual Meeting in Rotterdam.

Conclusions

Katrin Hansen and Silke Machold

In this book we have documented and reflected on contributions from practitioners, policy-makers, principle-setters, advocacy groups and researchers about the state of play on gender balance in the boardroom, the outcomes of the Norwegian quota law and its snowball effects in other countries. The core of the book was developed by the Think Tank organized in Oslo in March 2011, complemented by further contributions from important actors in the field of gender balance on boards. Oslo was chosen as the Think Tank location since it was home to the original legislative proposals on gender balance on boards, the effects of which have since reverberated in Europe and around the world. The Norwegian quota law demanded a minimum share of either gender of around 40 percent on boards of public listed companies, and it directly affected approximately 1500 corporations at January 2008. Norway was the first country to bring into force such a radical law, but others are following the trail blazed by the Norwegians. It is therefore apposite to reflect on the achievements to date. Our main questions for the Think Tank and later for this book were: Can we now conclude whether the Norwegian law about gender balance in the boardroom has been positive for society, for women and corporations? What more do we need to know before we can arrive at firm conclusions? And what are the implications for other countries?

We reflected on these overall questions in five parts dedicated to perspectives from particular stakeholder groups. Part I introduced the history of the Norwegian quota law through the stories of politicians who were involved in its conception and implementation. We learned that even with Norway's proud history of gender equality, the profile of its boards was woefully gender-imbalanced and voluntary initiatives had little effect in changing this. It took the extraordinary action of a minister in the form of an unauthorized press announcement to initiate a profound change to the composition of Norwegian public company boards. Whilst Gabrielsen achieved a high international profile as the champion of the law, we also hear about political initiatives prior to Gabrielsen, as well as

the ceaseless work by other politicians, administrators and public serv-
ants that accompanied the eventual passage of the law. Finally, the
contributions in the chapter outline the rationales behind the quota law,
and the law's strong roots in Norwegian political efforts for gender
egalitarianism. The quota law legislated for approximately 40 percent of
either gender to be represented on boards, and is thus part of a broader
societal effort to create opportunities for both men and women, and break
down gender stereotypes. In considering the achievements of the law to
date, the contributors conclude that it has been successful in attaining its
objectives.

In Part II, actors in the Norwegian and international advocacy movement that promote the case for women on boards were introduced. The
advocacy movement spans a wide spectrum of actors in companies,
universities, the voluntary sector and membership-based organizations
who either directly or indirectly influence policies and processes of
getting women on to corporate boards. We argued that through the
normative and mimetic influence of education, networks and networking,
research and information, and the increased visibility of role models,
women on boards become institutionalized. From the evidence it can be
shown that the advocacy movement supports the case for women on
corporate boards at the individual, board and societal level. At the
individual and board levels, it contributes to human and social capital
formation by developing competences of actual and potential board
members. At the societal level, the advocacy movement serves an
important role shaping the discourse on women on boards, and legitimiz-
ing the practice.

Part III documents authentic experiences of women on Norwegian
boards. By exploring their background, their motivations for becoming
board members, and the contributions they make to the boards on which
they serve, the heterogeneity of women board members is highlighted.
The term 'Golden Skirts' that has been so widely proliferated by the
media is not only derogatory but also misleading as it assumes a
similarity in characteristics and motivations of female board members
that is not evident. Analyses also showed that the patterns of multiple
board appointments held by women in Norway is different from that of
men, suggesting that we do not see the emergence of an 'old girl's
network'. We concluded that there is neither a single nor a static type of
woman director in Norway, and that consequently there are differential
effects on board dynamics and performance arising from their presence.

In Part IV we presented different research approaches to understanding
the situation and the effects of women on boards in Norway and
elsewhere in the world. One of the key results is that there is no evidence

of a negative impact from the Norwegian quota law on society, corporations and individuals involved. To the contrary, we find that women on boards play an important role in shaping board processes and their outcomes. Taken together, these findings make a compelling argument for increasing the number and overall proportion (or critical mass) of women on corporate boards. This is very much encouraging for actors on all three levels and makes Norway a benchmark for other countries. Nevertheless, future research is needed. We concluded that the existing research focused on either qualitative or quantitative methodological approaches, and concentrated on a particular level of analysis regarding the phenomenon. Therefore, future research should be developed in a more integrative setting, take advantage of mixed methods, and utilize multi-level modelling. Such a holistic approach will not only enrich our current knowledge but will also provide more robust implications for policy and practice.

Part V presented different strategies internationally to increase the share of women on boards. We categorized these into three formal approaches: (1) quota legislation which mandates a minimum percentage for certain groups of companies with associated legal sanctions for non-compliance; (2) regulation which include corporate governance codes and disclosure regulations which typically have no formal sanction but are used on a 'comply or explain' basis; and (3) voluntary efforts where companies sign up to voluntary pledges or targets. To explain why countries pursue different formal approaches (or simply do nothing), we investigated patterns related to national characteristics including countries' political economy, legal origin and gender egalitarianism. The discussion leads directly to the question of whether a European solution can or should be found, as suggested by Vivian Reding in Chapter 29. Another possibility is to develop different tiered approaches internationally, tailored in pace and scale to clusters of countries based on shared characteristics. Another important result of Part V is that the different formal approaches are not exclusive. In order to achieve greater women representation on boards a combination of actions and incentives may be utilized, such as the fear of legislative intervention, soft-law recommendations ('Comply or explain!'), peer group pressure and the desire to use voluntary efforts as an image factor. This could create an environment that enables and sustains a change in attitudes towards the representation of women on boards and in leading positions more generally, thus strengthening the 'snowball' effect.

WHAT CAN BE LEARNED FROM THIS BOOK ...

This book addresses three main audiences. One group is corporate governance practitioners such as board members, board chairs, actors involved in the decision process of whom to recruit to a corporate board, and actors in charge of supporting processes related to women on boards such as human resource professionals. A second target group is formed by politicians, principle-setters and activists who develop strategies and policies to increase the share and the impact of women on corporate boards based of experiences from Norway and other countries. The third audience comprises scholars and students with an interest specifically in the study of women on boards, or more generally in the field of corporate governance and/or gender and diversity. To guide these audiences in using insights from the different chapters of this book, we highlight the most important outcomes from their respective domains of interest.

... BY PRACTITIONERS ON BOARDS?

Central to this book were the experiences of and outcomes from Norway as the pioneer of legislative action to increase the share of women on corporate boards. We learned that there is no reason to be afraid of a quota law. Instead, studies from Norway have demonstrated how some of the key criticisms of using radical affirmative action strategies have been unjustified. The companies are taking advantage of a wider pool of candidates. The women themselves feel that they are being listened to; their opinions are taken seriously and are included in information-sharing, in decisions and in social interaction with other board members. Women role models were emerging in an area that women historically have been excluded from. We presented such role models and typologies of different types of women on boards holding multiple positions, and showed their distinct impact as independent board members.

And we found that being a 'quota woman' is not a flaw: 'The women now coming onto boards are much more conscious than the men in that they are there due to their qualifications, and not because they are quota'd in' (Thorhild Widvey in Chapter 13 by Nergaard et al.). This experiential evidence is backed by statistical survey studies that show female board members have similar or higher qualifications than their male counterparts (Heidenreich in Chapter 17). Women being elected to board positions should view it as a long-overdue recognition of their competences and skills.

Each of the women board members who contributed to this book recounts her own particular lessons, and within these we find some striking similarities. Working on boards is not a glamorous job, it invariably involves hard work and a strong moral compass. Growing a thicker skin also helps – the ability to speak out, ask the awkward question and challenge the status quo are important albeit sometimes uncomfortable requirements of being an effective board member. The women are also unanimous in that there are rewards to the role: for the boards that they contribute to and for themselves in meeting different aspirations. In order to realize these benefits, however, an important lesson is to not to give in to pride and vanity when being asked to serve on a board, but to do your homework on the company and board first.

Even if radical affirmative actions have demonstrably had the greatest impact on changing the gender balance on boards, firms are urged not to wait for or rely on quota legislation, and instead look into developing firm-specific approaches for recruitment and development of board members. Even the impressive European Union database of 'boardable' women initiated by Viviane Reding may not be able to satisfy the needs of all European firms when it comes to recruiting high-potential women to more than a critical mass for their boards. Companies and boards themselves need to be proactive in their recruitment strategies and talent management programs. The 'war for women's talents' has seen the opening moves by the most active and high-profile firms, and those waiting in the wings risk being left behind. To further broaden the pool of women board members, potential candidates must given the chance to gain needed experience and to further develop their competencies. Talent management was among the top three board activities identified in a global McKinsey survey of directors as the highest priority for their boards (McKinsey, 2011). Human resource (HR) management is already widely embedded in European corporations, and programs focusing on the development of women and men as future top managers and board members must be given sustainable momentum.

Recruitment is a crucial process here. Compilation rather than composition seems to be the better mode of recruiting, looking for the optimization of the whole board's profile and competences instead of substituting an outgoing director with a new one that is similar. The recruitment process itself deserves more scrutiny and firms should not stop short in their efforts to further shaping this process. Making the most of women's potential for corporate boards means that all board processes in their complex interplay can and should be further improved. As Torchia's Chapter 18 shows, and Bolsø et al.'s arguments in Chapter 19 support, it is not gender per se that enhances the level of innovation, the quality of decision-making and the value creation of the board. Instead, we have to look out for other interrelated factors such as board task performance, board dynamics and climate, gender (competence) of the chair, to name but a few.

Women on boards have become a signal for a progressive culture of a corporation and its board, a signal that is read and interpreted by various actors and stakeholders and ultimately informs how they shape their relationships with the firm. Initiatives such as the FidAR WoB Index with its public ranking can be useful for improving a corporation's image as progressive firm, as a women-friendly employer, and as a social responsible organization. This is expected to show positive effects in labor, goods and capital markets. Regarding the latter, agencies such as Bloomberg and Reuters now routinely compile indices for socially responsible investors which include women representation on boards as one of the governance metrics. To build a sustainable reputation, companies' top-ranking must be secured by a well-founded governance and HR strategy over a long-term horizon.

... BY POLITICIANS, PRINCIPLE-SETTERS AND ACTIVISTS?

As Viviane Reding points out in Chapter 29, 'people are aware that women mean business' but their potential is still under-used. She concludes: 'In these challenging times, the stakes are too high to keep the status quo ... It is time to act now in order to speed up progress and achieve more concrete results.' What can politicians learn from this book to accelerate progress?

The Norwegian example shows that legislative actions have been successful in changing gender imbalances and improving equality in the labor market, both from a justice and a utility point of view. In particular, benefits were identified on different levels and studies found strong support for the use of radical strategies to challenge vertical sex segregation in the private sector. Nevertheless, one size does not necessarily fit all (see Chapter 27 by Brogi, and Chapter 28 by Sealy and Vinnicombe), and there may be scope for combining legislative and voluntary actions creatively and effectively (see Schulz-Strelow's Chapter 25). Politicians from different countries should work with the business community and scholars to analyze and evaluate the approaches and their effects in other countries and societies, in order to develop suitable combinations in their own context.

For policy-makers in countries that are considering legislative interventions, three insights from the contributions may be especially pertinent. First, in almost all countries, Norway included, the first attempts are rarely successful – it requires perseverance and sometimes there is a need to make compromises in the short term to achieve longer-term goals (see Brogi, Chapter 27; and Davøy, Chapter 2). Second, although the initial impetus often comes from ministries of Equality, Justice or similar, it requires collaboration and broad coalitions between and across different ministries to make a difference. For example, in Norway the momentum generated by the unconventional intervention of the Minister for Trade and Industry proved instrumental in finally passing the law. Third, politicians need to consider carefully the sanctions for non-compliance with the law. As we have shown in Part V, there is substantial variance internationally in the scale, level and scope of sanctions associated with quota legislation, which may ultimately affect how companies behave and respond.

We have also explored the pivotal role played by advocacy groups and principle-setters in creating the conditions under which formal approaches to gender diversity on boards can come to fruition. Universities play an important role here in that they generate new knowledge on the phenomenon of women on boards as well as educating and training future generations of male and female leaders. Other important actors include private and not-for-profit organizations that inform, train and facilitate networking for women that are on or want to get onto boards. A key lesson is that the efforts of such diverse groups can be exponentially enhanced through collaboration. A prime example is the previously mentioned database of Global Board Ready Women, a collaborative venture between the European Union, business schools, advocacy group, and conventional and social media (EU, 2012) that has grown within one year (2011–2012) from approximately 3500 to 8000 entries.

A very interesting and currently much-discussed question is whether there should be a European-wide strategy or whether specific country-level strategies are more recommendable. Alternatively, is the way forward to have a combination of both? To find an adequate answer, further investigation of the following questions in a dialogue between politics and research is required: Which differences and similarities of societies relevant to women on boards can be identified? What patterns of strategy development in the respective societies can be identified? Is it possible to distinguish certain clusters of societies? Does this imply the need for society-specific or cluster-specific approaches or are generic strategies recommendable? What implications derive from these insights for future political measures?

... BY RESEARCHERS?

As researchers we learned about the content and methodologies deployed in the field of women on boards. Research is increasingly conducted in countries all over the world triggered by the snowball effect that was started in Norway. We find qualitative and quantitative approaches but these are seldom combined. Mixed-method studies, meta-analyses and discourse analysis could in future derive even more interesting results.

Content-wise, we showed that the field of women on boards is a very heterogeneous one with contributions from different disciplinary origins (e.g. sociology, philosophy and psychology) and from different subject perspectives (e.g. corporate governance, entrepreneurship, gender studies). In relation to the business case for women on boards, research is moving beyond simplistic models linking gender diversity with firm performance, and instead scholars are opening the 'black box' to go beyond the readily visible and obvious demographics. We discovered some interesting fields of further research.

Country Comparisons

These should be conducted to better understand macro-determinants and consequences of formal approaches to gender diversity on boards. This may also focus on country clusters related to common cultural, economic and legal characteristics that can inform sharing of policy approaches. The Norwegian results should be continually analyzed and ongoing comparisons conducted.

Comparison and Combination of Formal Approaches to Gender Diversity

Which approach shows what impact in which context? What patterns of strategy development can be identified? To what extent should legislative, regulative and voluntary actions be separated? Through what mechanisms do soft law approaches work? The answers to questions like these can help inform the tailoring of policy approaches.

Processes and Behaviors

There is now a substantial body of evidence showing that the presence of women on boards per se cannot be linked simplistically to firms' performance. Their impact depends on the context (and women are part of the context); is influenced by board processes and behaviors including the building and reshaping of routines; and is moderated by micro-foundations such as expectations, attitudes and beliefs. Taken together, these factors determine the presence and emergence of more or less inclusive board climates, and understanding their complex interplay opens new fields of research.

Dynamics

The research field is a very dynamic one, not least because we see very rapid developments on the policy front. Therefore, longitudinal studies should chart these developments but also allow for comparisons of results and outcomes at different stages, for example before and after quota laws come into force. The more women become board members in Norway and in other countries and the longer this process is unfolding, the more possible it is to address questions such as: Do the recruitment processes to boards change under the pressure of hard laws? How does the board climate develop in the long run? Are there first-mover advantages in board diversity practices? What intersectional patterns can be identified and which effects do they have on the performance of boards?

Discourse

The discourse on women on boards in itself is a highly interesting research topic. Who are the participants? What trends, stages and milestones can be identified? Are there connections to other topics? Who has been influencing whom and using which media? Conducting such research we can map the field, compare the dynamics in different countries and learn more about the emergence of social norms.

To find answers to these and other questions, scholars should conduct multidisciplinary and interdisciplinary research using venturesome yet rigorous research designs. And to create relevant and impactful research, there needs to be greater collaborative effort between scholars, practitioners and policy-makers at all stages of research from inception, execution to dissemination. The Oslo Think Tank and this book have hopefully started the snowball rolling.

REFERENCES

McKinsey (2011) Governance since the economic crisis, available from https://www.mckinseyquarterly.com/Governance_since_the_economic_crisis_McKinsey_Global_Survey_results_2814, last accessed December 2012.

European Union (EU) (2012) Shattering myths and glass ceilings: Launch of database 'Global Board Ready Women', available from http://europa.eu/rapid/press-release_IP-12-1358_en.htm, last accessed December 2012.

Index

2020 Women on Board Campaign
  aims of 203–4
  creation of 117

Accenture 32, 45
advocacy groups 64
  examples of 31–2
  promotion of female role models by
    32
Affirmative Action (AA) 140, 142–3
  criticisms of 139–41
  influence of 115
  liberal strategies of 139
  radical strategies of 139, 142, 144,
    219
age
  role in demographic categorization
    148
Anglo-American plc 45
atmosphere 42, 89, 128
  competitive 44
Audit committee
Australia 3, 138, 144, 192
  Equal Opportunity for Women in the
    Workplace Agency 114
  government of 114
  use of gender-equality quota
    legislation in 114, 191
Australian Stock Exchange
  'comply or explain' system 60
Austria 172
  corporate governance code 206
  ranking in Global Gender Gap Index
    174

Bedogni, Carla Rabitti 57
Bekkemellom, Karita
  Norwegian Minister of Equality
    14–15

Belgium 52, 144
  corporate governance code 206
  gender quota legislation in 53, 138,
    205
  growth of female entrepreneurship in
    116
  percentage of female corporate board
    members 155
Bergstø, Kirsti
  Norwegian State Secretary in
    Ministry of Equality 9, 15
BoardEx 45
board identity 71–2
  independent 71, 73
  insiders/quasi-insiders 71–2
  stakeholder related directors 71–2
board-ready women
  necessity of proactive behaviour 42–3
Bond, Sir John 44
Bondevik, Kjell Magne
  administration of 17
  Norwegian Prime Minister 9, 12, 24
Bråthen, Prof Tore 38
Brazil
  lack of soft law approach use in 173
Brogi, Prof Marina 57
Bundesversamlung 47
business case 3, 85, 97, 102–3, 106, 113,
  140, 142, 188
  as support for increased gender
    diversity 13, 61, 140, 202, 212,
    222
business initiatives 207–8

Calvosa, Lucia 57
Canada 138, 144, 191
Cancellieri, Annamaria
  Italian Interior Minister 56
career 11, 13, 34, 54, 75, 92, 155–6, 203

habitus 162
progression 2, 14, 29–30, 33, 61,
    83–4, 124, 143, 204
Carr, Sir Roger 44
Catalyst 62, 102–3, 105, 168, 202
    formation of (1962) 31–2, 60
    personnel of 34
    view of quota system 60–1
Chair 80
    demands of role 79, 86–7, 90, 93
challenging
    of stereotypes 33–4
Charles, Gay 27
charters 193
    examples of 197, 201, 207
childcare
    coverage provided for 22
    systems 188
China
    lack of soft law approach use in 173
Christian Democratic Party 17
civil law 172
    example systems of 3, 11, 170
Cmi 45
co-determination
    corporate 11
coercive isomorphism
    concept of 28
common law
    example systems of 170
competence 18–20, 23, 29, 81, 84,
    89–93, 107, 123, 130, 142–3,
    148–9, 152, 156, 162, 184–5, 205,
    218–20
    board-level 37–9, 65, 86
    development of 20, 22, 30, 33, 216
    incompetence 19
composition 180, 185, 206, 215, 219
    board 28, 69, 71, 85–6, 94, 104–6,
        120, 141, 152, 156, 161
    gender 124
    of supervisory board 105, 184–6
Confederation of British Industry 192
Confederation of Norwegian Enterprise
    (NHO) 14, 38
    Female Future Programme 38
    'Women to the Top' 14
Conservative Party 17–18

members of 24
contribution 2, 33, 44, 102, 126, 128–9,
    140, 148–9, 161–2
    to board decision-making 107, 147
    to value creation 18, 84–5
control 80
    aspect of board work 84
    management 180
convention
    social 158
Cooper, Lisa 45
corporate governance codes 10–11, 29,
    155, 177, 191–2, 196, 203, 206
    as example of coercive mechanism 28
    as example of soft law 175
corporate social responsibility (CSR)
    141
Cranfield School of Management
    Female FTSE Report (2010) 191,
        196, 199
    International Centre for Women
        Leaders (CICWL) 191, 196
critical mass theory 126–7, 199
    concept of 126
    use in observation of women in
        corporate director positions
        127–33
cumulative abnormal returns (CAR)
    147
Cyprus
    percentage of female corporate board
        members in 205
Czech Republic 52

Davies, Lord Mervyn
    Davies Report 192–8, 206
Dåvøy, Laila
    Norwegian Labor and Administration
        Minister 14
    Norwegian Minister of Equality 9,
        15, 17–18, 24
DAX
    companies listed on 102, 106 180–1,
        207
Denmark
    'Charter for more women in
        management' 207
    Copenhagen 189

corporate governance code 206–7
GLOBE study score 174
'Recommendation for More Women
    on Supervisory Boards' 207
use of gender-equality quota
    legislation in 113
Deutsche Bank 45
disclosure 197
    regulations 168, 210, 217
discrimination
    social 108
diversity 86, 107
    gender 182
    international 182

education 30, 64
    admission of women into higher
        education institutions 64
    business schools 29–30, 37–9
employee-elected board members 11,
    141
    variation of 107
empowering
    economic influence of 202
Enron Scandal (2001)
    impact of 85
environment, social, governance (ESG)
    investment
    development of 32
Estonia
    percentage of female corporate board
        members in 205
ethical 82, 86, 101–2, 203
    dilemmas 101
    individualism 139
    unethical behaviour 56
European Central Bank
    managing committee of 54
European Commission 182, 184, 204
    Legislative Work Programme (2012)
        208
    personnel of 48
    Strategy for Equality between
        Women and Men (2010–15) 201
European Economic Area
    legislative influence of 13

European Professional Women's
    Network 155, 159
European Union (EU) 34, 138, 173,
    186, 197, 201, 204–5, 208, 219
    'Global Board Ready Women'
        initiative 30–1, 221
    Lisbon Treaty 187
    personnel of 6, 177, 192
executive search firms (ESFs) 193,
    198–9
    Voluntary Code of Conduct 198
experience 38, 40, 45, 75, 79, 124,
    149, 185, 187, 189, 199, 203,
    219
    CEO 41, 94–5
    corporate 116
    management 147
    necessary levels of 29, 41, 70, 86,
        147, 184

family-owned
    companies 86, 116
Female Board Pool (FBP) 31, 49
    founding of 46, 48
    objectives of 48–9
female leadership
    influence on female authority 54
feminism 9, 24, 143
    corporate 136
FidAR (Women on German boards) 31,
    182
    formation of 179
    objectives of 180
    personnel of 176, 181
    support for 179–80
    Woman on Board (WoB) Index
        180–1, 211–12, 220
finance 54
    growing presence of women in
        banking sector 56
Finland 144
    corporate governance code 206
    government of 207
    percentage of female corporate board
        members in 113, 205
    use of gender-equality quota
        legislation in 113, 138

Fondazione Bellisario
  personnel of 187
Fornero, Elsa
  Italian Labor Minister 56–7
Fortune 100
  women in chief executive positions in
  115
Fortune 1000
  women in chief executive positions in
  115
Fortune 500 115–16
  companies listed on 102
  women in chief executive positions in
  52, 60
Four Seasons Venture 41
France 22–3, 52, 144
  corporate governance code 206
  gender quota legislation in 53, 138,
  205
  GLOBE study score 174
  Parliament 113
  percentage of female corporate board
  members in 52–3, 113, 155
FTSE 100 176, 192–4, 196, 199, 206
  companies listed on 102
  presence of Professional Boards
  Forum personnel in 64
FTSE 350 193, 199, 206

Gabrielsen, Ansgar 12–13, 18, 24
  Norwegian Minister of Trade and
  Industry 1, 3, 9, 11, 15, 17–18
GEM
  Report (2006) 116
gender balance law 1–2, 15, 27, 69, 75,
  78, 94, 97
  enactment of 18–19
  social impact of 85
gender diversity
  positive impact of 202–3
  use of legislation in implementing
  205
gender equality 21–2, 82, 89, 101, 119,
  138, 174, 210–11, 215–16
  discrimination 53–5
  impact of media entertainment on 55
  parental leave 21–2

social changes in 13
gender hierarchy 121
gender parity 21, 28, 40, 44
German Corporate Governance Code
  Commission
  members of 176–7
  Report (2010) 180
German Institute for Economics (DIW)
  105
Germany 5–6, 31, 52, 105, 172, 176,
  179, 182–3, 186, 204
  Corporate Governance Code 180–1,
  184–6, 206, 211
  economy of 180
  government of 180
  Ministry of Family, the Elderly, the
  Youth and Women 181
  percentage of female corporate board
  members in 52, 155
Giroud, Francoise 20
glass ceiling 2–3, 13, 32, 65, 137, 156,
  201
  concept of 10, 203, 208
glass cliff 156
glass wall 156
Global Financial Crisis (2008–9) 101
GLOBE study
  findings of 173–4
  score data 174
Gold Sacks 94
  concept of 73
Golden Skirts 69–70, 75–6, 94–5
  concept of 73–4
  media image of 69, 78, 82, 136, 216
  origin of term 136
  as replacement for old boys' network
  72–3
Golfo, Lella 188
  Chairwoman of Fondazione
  Bellisario 187
Greece
  percentage of female corporate board
  members 155, 205
Grieg Group 44

habitus
  career 162

concept of 155
Hampton, Sir Philip 44
hard law 175–6, 223
Haugland, Valgerd Svarstad 17
  Norwegian Minister of Equality 14,
    24
Hoel, Marit 20
Hogan Lovells 45
Hole, Arni
  Director General of Ministry of
    Children and Family Affairs 17
homosocial reproduction 142–3
human capital 21, 140, 143, 161–2, 201
  formation of 30
  unit-level 161
human resource (HR) management 219
human rights 13
Hungary
  percentage of female corporate board
    members in 205
Hurvenes, Elin 83
  founder of Professional Boards
    Forum 31
Huse, Prof Morten 37–8, 188
Hytta, Olav
  former Chairman of DnBNOR Bank
    41

Iceland
  use of gender-equality quota
    legislation in 113, 138
IFPM Centre for Corporate Governance
  34
  Direction and Control of Small and
    Medium-sized Enterprises 49
  founding of FBP 46
  personnel of 48
independent director 72–3
India
  lack of soft law approach use in 173
Industrial University
  venue for Leadership from a Female
    Perspective by 37
information 55, 64, 81, 86–8, 103,
    105, 107–8, 149–50, 193, 196–8,
    216
  asymmetry 147

informal 148
  publicizing 31–2
  role of 28
Innovasjon Norge (Innovation
  Norway)
  'Female Future' 20
  formerly SND 37
  personnel of 37–8
innovation 21, 105, 188, 203, 219
  firm 108, 114, 126, 128–9
  influence on economies 116
  organizational 128–30, 133
Institute for Social Research 106
institutionalized 27, 139, 216
  responsibility 157
interlocking directorates 70
International Monetary Fund (IMF)
  personnel of 54
intersectionality 158–9
inter-discourse
  concept of 156
investor 31–2, 40–4, 71, 73, 94, 122,
    170, 176, 193
  activism 10, 176, 197–9, 220
Italian Bankers Association 189
Italian Insurance Companies
  Association 189
Italian Stock Exchange
  companies listed on 56
Italian Trade Association 189
Italy 5–6, 34, 187–9
  Finance Committee 189
  GDP per capita 187
  gender quota legislation in 53, 188–9,
    205
  percentage of female corporate
    board members in 56–7, 113,
    155, 205
  Senate 113, 189

Japan
  as example of MME 170
  percentage of female corporate board
    members in 173
justice 13, 101, 141–2, 163, 220
  individual 139, 143–4
  social 140

Kenya
  use of formal approach to gender
    diversity on corporate boards in
    172
Kittelsen, Anne Marie 38
knowledge 29–30, 37, 45, 65, 74, 81,
    84, 88–90, 93, 107, 120, 128, 130,
    148–9, 155, 157, 161–3, 184, 201,
    203, 211, 217
  common 38
  intensity 116
  professional 180

Lagarde, Christine
  Managing Director of IMF 54
Latvia
  percentage of female corporate board
    members in 205
Leadership Foundation 45
Leadership from a Female Perspective
  creation of program 37
legislation 168
  equality 113
  governance
  quota 205
  use in increasing gender diversity
    205
Leuthard, Doris 49
Leveraging Diversity Conference
    (2010)
  participants in 44
Lewis, Mark 136
Liberal Party 17
Likestillingsrådet
  funding provided for Leadership
    from a Female Perspective by
    37
Lütken, Merete 78, 95
  background of 83–4, 87–8
Luxembourg
  corporate governance code 206
  percentage of female corporate board
    members in 205
Lysbakken, Audun
  Norwegian Minister of Equality
    15

Malawi
  use of formal approach to gender
    diversity on corporate boards in
    172
Malta
  percentage of female corporate board
    members in 205
Margetts, Sir Rob 44
market economies
  coordinated (CMEs) 167–8
  liberal (LMEs) 167–70
  mixed (MMEs) 167–8, 170
McKinsey & Co. 44, 54, 85, 202,
    219
  Women Matter 32
Merkel, Angela
  media image of 33
mimetic isomorphism
  concept of 28, 32–3
mindset
  collective 54
  conservative 53
Mosca, Alessia 189
multi-board member 70
  increase in number of 124
Myhre, Ingvild 78, 95
  background of 90–3

Nergaard, Nini Høegh 95
  background of 78–81
Netherlands 45, 52
  corporate governance code 206
  percentage of female corporate board
    members in 52–3
  'Talent to the Top' 207
  use of gender-equality quota
    legislation in 205–6
network/networking 155
  gender-based 14, 40–1, 64, 92
  global 30–1
  role in development of social capital
    30, 56
  social 149, 156
New Zealand 3
  as example of LME 170

Nigeria
  use of formal approach to gender
    diversity on corporate boards in
    172
Nixon, Richard 55
Nominations Committee 197
non-executive 191, 198
  directorship 162
  roles 41, 43, 45, 83, 94
normative isomorphism
  concept of 28
Norsk rikskringkasting (NRK)
  personnel of 83
Norway 1–5, 9, 24, 28, 31, 33, 40, 45–6,
    69, 87–8, 94, 105–6, 109, 114,
    124, 126–7, 129, 147, 149–50,
    185, 187, 216–18, 221–3
  Basic Agreement 11
  Bergen 42
  Company Law Act 85, 87, 119–20
  economy of 114
  Gender Equality Act (1988) 13,
    18–19
  gender quota legislation in 53, 75,
    141–2, 155, 161, 175, 205, 215
  Ministry for Foreign Affairs 44, 88
  Ministry of Children and Family
    Affairs 17, 19, 44
  Ministry of Fishery 88
  Ministry of Equality 9, 15, 221
  Ministry of Trade and Industry 41, 44
  Moss 42
  Oslo 42, 78–9, 83, 106, 189, 215
  Parental Leave Scheme (1993) 21–2
  Parliament 18–19, 88, 136
  Public Limited Companies Act 9–10
  Stavanger 42
  Trondheim 42, 90
Norwegian Business School
    (Norwegian School of
    Management) (BI)
  courses at 37–8, 79, 88
  faculty of 37–8
  Value Creating Board 38, 79, 88
  Women on Board Conference (2011)
    113
Norwegian Confederation of Sports 14
Norwegian Pension Fund 90

Norwegian Research Council 90
  personnel of 91
  research funded by 136–7

Odgers, Berndtson
  personnel of 27
old boys' network 72
  concept of 70
  Golden Skirts as replacement of 72–3
Organisation for Economic
    Co-operation and Development
    (OECD) 168–9
Oslo Stock Exchange
  companies listed on 11, 15, 41, 90
  impact of gender quota legislation on
    147, 150
ownership 17
  concentration of 11
  groups of 71
  interests 122
  positions of 80
  private 114, 116
  state 207

Pelosi, Nancy
  media image of 33
Poland
  corporate governance code 206
policy-makers 4, 138, 168, 215, 221,
    223
Pomodor, Livia 57
Portugal
  percentage of female corporate board
    members 155, 173, 205
  ranking in Global Gender Gap Index
    174
power 23, 102, 125, 137, 142, 158, 162,
    189–90
  access to 124
  dynamics 18, 86–7
  positions of 138, 140, 148
  techniques 75
PricewaterhouseCoopers (PwC) 32,
    44–5
private limited company (AS) 11, 80
Professional Boards Forum 34, 42
  expansion of 44–5

founding of (2003) 40–1
Oslo meeting (2004) 42
personnel of 31, 64
public limited companies (PLCs) 119,
    125, 142, 193, 199, 211
  decline in 123
  female directorships in 147–51
  gender quotas implemented for
      119–20, 124, 195
  shift to private limited companies 123
  stock value of 152
publicly tradable company (ASA) 11,
    64, 72, 76, 78, 80–1, 84, 86
  Annual General Meeting (AGM) 82
  examples of 41–2
  multi-board memberships of 70
  proposals for gender ratio in boards
      of 14–15

qualifications
  Master of Management 38
  MBAs 29, 40
quality 44, 61, 80, 136, 143, 162
  of decision-making 203, 220
  of education 30
quota legislation 56, 124–5, 141–2, 161,
    175, 182, 205, 210, 212, 215
  introduction of 53, 113, 188–9
  opposition to 195
quotas 47–8, 60–1, 138, 195
  constraints of 152
  recruitment methods 122–3

race
  role in demographic categorization
      148
Radiotelevisione Italian S.p.A. (RAI)
  personnel of 56–7
recruitment 219
  use of headhunters 122–3
Reding, Viviane 210, 217, 220
  Justice Commissioner for EU 192
  Vice-President of European
      Commission 48, 177
  Women on the Board Pledge (2011)
      197
Reichilin, Lucrezia 57

Repubblica
  circulation of 189
Republic of Ireland
  percentage of female corporate board
      members in 205
  use of gender-equality quota
      legislation in 113
Rossello, Cristina 58
Royal Bank of Scotland (RBS) Group
    44–5
Russian Federation
  lack of soft law approach use
      in 173

S&P GovernanceMetrics 114
sanction 18–19, 168, 175–6, 205–6,
    210, 212, 217, 221
  application for legislative breach 120
Sanner, Aud 37
Sasso, Cinzia 189
Schei, Bitten
  leader of Women in Business 37
Schroeder, Kristina
  General Federal Minister of Family,
      Seniors, Women and Youth 211
Schulz-Strelow, Monika
  President of FidAR 176, 181
Scott, Jane 44
Severino, Paola
  Italian Justice Minister 56
shareholder 85, 137, 155–6, 179–81,
    185, 189
  major 122–3
  supremacy 170
Six Month Monitoring Report of
      October (2011)
  findings of 195, 197
Slovenia
  gender administrative regulations 206
soft law 170, 173, 175–6, 222
  corporate governance codes as
      examples of 175
  support for use of 185
South Africa
  use of formal approach to gender
      diversity on corporate boards in
      172

South Korea
    percentage of female corporate board
        members in 173
Spagnoli, Luisa 58
Spain 144
    corporate governance code 206
    percentage of female corporate board
        members in 113
    use of gender-equality quota
        legislation in 138, 175, 205–6
stakeholder 71, 195, 215
    external 107
    internal 107
Standal, Kjell 38
Stautberg, Susan
    co-founder of WCD 57
stereotype 53–4, 133, 156, 211
    challenging of 34, 65, 144, 188, 190,
        216
    gender 55, 188, 216
    self-reinforcing nature of 33
Stoltenberg, Jens
    administration of 19
student 37–9, 203, 218
    percentage of female graduates 18
    politics 79–80
supervisory board 3, 106, 108, 181, 204,
    207
    composition of 105, 184–6
Sweden 52, 138, 144
    corporate governance code 206
    GLOBE study score 174
    lack of gender quota legislation in 53,
        138
    percentage of female corporate board
        members in 205
    ranking in Global Gender Gap Index
        174
Switzerland 31, 34, 46
    company law in 47–8
    GLOBE study score 174
    government of 47
    growth of female entrepreneurship in
        116

Talent Tuning 31

Tarantola, Anna Maria
    President of RAI 57
Thatcher, Margaret
    media image of 33
Think Tank 15, 215, 223
    participants in 9, 78, 101
top-management teams (TMTs) 161
training 15, 30, 48, 64–5, 221
    formal 39
    providers 29, 34
trans-disciplinarity 157, 159
Treu, Donatella 58

underrepresentation 47, 206
    social impact of 55
United Kingdom (UK) 3, 6, 43, 52, 136,
    138, 144, 177, 191, 198
    corporate governance code 196, 206
    Financial Reporting Council (FRC)
        192–3, 196–7, 199
    GLOBE study score 174
    government of 113, 192
    London 88
    percentage of female corporate board
        members in 52
    use of gender-equality quota
        legislation in 113–14, 138
United Nations (UN)
    Convention on the Elimination of
        Discrimination against Women
        64
    legislative influence of 13
United States of America (USA) 3, 5,
    60, 114, 191
    government of 114
    growth of female entrepreneurship in
        116
    population of 115
    Securities and Exchange
        Commission (SEC) 114–15
    Supreme Court 55

value creation
    process of 129
Verdane Capital
    formerly Four Seasons Venture 41

voluntary 2, 24, 61, 168–9, 173, 175–6, 199, 206, 210–12, 215, 217, 220, 222
  gender balance 21
  sector 65, 216

Weber-Ray, Daniela 176–7
Widvey, Thorhild 78, 95
  background of 88, 91
  Minister of Oil and Energy 88–9
Women Corporate Directors (WCD) 34
  Global Nominating Commission 57
  personnel of 57–8
Women in Business
  members of 37

women in society
  changing role of 10
Women's University
  venue for Leadership from a Female Perspective by 37
women-friendly
  employers 220
  environments 188
World Bank 172
World Economic Forum (WEF)
  Global Gender Gap Index 174
  Global Gender Gap Report 173

Yssen, Ingunn
  Norwegian Director of Equality 14